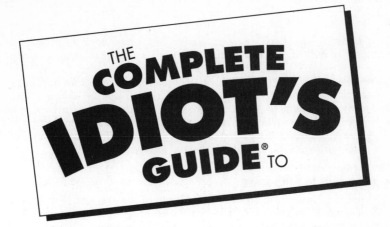

THE
COMPLETE
IDIOT'S
GUIDE® TO

Cold Calling

Keith Rosen, MCC

D1113471

ALPHA

A member of Penguin Group (USA) Inc.

To my loving wife, Lori, my eternal partner in life who, while pregnant with twins and on bed rest, was still a living testament to the true meaning of strength, integrity, compassion, and resilience.
To my four-year-old daughter, Jessica (the greatest salesperson in the world), who continually reminds me that at any age, "dreams really can come true."
And to my twins, Jett and Nicole, who recently joined the family. You keep my eyes focused on my priorities and the daily miracles in life that really matter.
You are all the center of my universe and will forever be my greatest source of inspiration. I am forever grateful to have you in my life.

Copyright © 2004 by Keith Rosen

All rights reserved. No part of this book shall be reproduced, stored in a retrieval system, or transmitted by any means, electronic, mechanical, photocopying, recording, or otherwise, without written permission from the publisher. No patent liability is assumed with respect to the use of the information contained herein. Although every precaution has been taken in the preparation of this book, the publisher and author assume no responsibility for errors or omissions. Neither is any liability assumed for damages resulting from the use of information contained herein. For information, address Alpha Books, 800 East 96th Street, Indianapolis, IN 46240.

THE COMPLETE IDIOT'S GUIDE TO and Design are registered trademarks of Penguin Group (USA) Inc.

International Standard Book Number: 1-59257-227-8
Library of Congress Catalog Card Number: 2004105319

09   08   8   7

Interpretation of the printing code: The rightmost number of the first series of numbers is the year of the book's printing; the rightmost number of the second series of numbers is the number of the book's printing. For example, a printing code of 04-1 shows that the first printing occurred in 2004.

Printed in the United States of America

Note: This publication contains the opinions and ideas of its author. It is intended to provide helpful and informative material on the subject matter covered. It is sold with the understanding that the author and publisher are not engaged in rendering professional services in the book. If the reader requires personal assistance or advice, a competent professional should be consulted.

The author and publisher specifically disclaim any responsibility for any liability, loss, or risk, personal or otherwise, which is incurred as a consequence, directly or indirectly, of the use and application of any of the contents of this book.

Most Alpha books are available at special quantity discounts for bulk purchases for sales promotions, premiums, fund-raising, or educational use. Special books, or book excerpts, can also be created to fit specific needs.

For details, write: Special Markets, Alpha Books, 375 Hudson Street, New York, NY 10014.

Publisher: *Marie Butler-Knight*
Product Manager: *Phil Kitchel*
Senior Managing Editor: *Jennifer Chisholm*
Senior Acquisitions Editor: *Mike Sanders*
Development Editor: *Nancy D. Lewis*
Production Editor: *Janette Lynn*
Copy Editor: *Sara Fink*
Cover/Book Designer: *Trina Wurst*
Indexer: *Angie Bess*
Layout/Proofreading: *Ayanna Lacey, John Etchison*

Contents at a Glance

Contents

Foreword

Your ability to get appointments and to spend more time with qualified prospects is the key to success in your sales career.

Now there is a single source—this book—that gives you the step-by-step, word-by-word instructions you need to get in front of more people and make more sales than ever before.

In my 30 years of selling, for 22 businesses, in 25 countries, the number-one challenge has always been to prospect, and especially *cold call*, effectively.

In every market, I started off knowing no one, with no prospect lists or leads of any kind. I got the traditional three part sales training program: (1) "Here's your cards;" (2) "Here's your brochures;" (3) "*There's* the door!"

Over the course of my career, I have trained more than 1,000,000 salespeople on the do's and don'ts of successful selling. In almost every case, the ability to prospect, cold call, and get in front of customers is the biggest obstacle they face.

In the pages ahead, you will learn proven, practical strategies and techniques that you can use to overcome these obstacles forever.

Keith Rosen has brought together, in one book, the very best techniques for getting more and better appointments ever written in the field of sales.

Put up your mental tray tables. Buckle your seat belts and prepare for an exciting journey into realizing your full potential as a sales professional. Get ready to make more sales and more money than ever before. The sky's the limit!

Brian Tracy, author—*Advanced Selling Strategies*

Introduction

Used by top-selling professionals worldwide, *The Complete Idiot's Guide to Cold Calling* is the most innovative and comprehensive prospecting system that takes the elusive art of cold calling and prospecting and delivers to you step-by-step, the skills, tools, techniques, and strategies that produce sales champions.

The selling community is evolving. Conventional "one size fits all" selling programs never fully consider the personal abilities and values of each salesperson. Instead, they tell you "what to say and how to say it."

However, reorienting your selling approach around your strengths, goals, integrity, and passions makes the selling process more natural, enjoyable, and attractive to your clients.

This provides you with the edge over your competitors, enabling you to align your prospecting approach with the prospect's preferred buying process and communication style. Now, you no longer have to push, manipulate, or rely on generic selling techniques and memorizing gimmicky closing tactics that have lost their effectiveness in today's rapidly changing marketplace.

How This Book Is Organized to Generate Unprecedented Results

This book is divided into five distinct parts. Starting with Chapter 1, each chapter builds on the previous one, providing you with the opportunity to continually reinforce what you have learned. I will walk you through the natural progression of what it takes to become a master at cold calling and prospecting. It's like having your own personal sales coach in your corner to support you through this entire process.

Part 1, "The Inner Game of Prospecting," explores the hidden secret and most often overlooked element to cold calling success. Before you can effectively launch your prospecting efforts and actually get excited to cold call, it's critical to ensure that you are managing a healthy, positive mind-set in order to eliminate the anxiety, tension, or stress when it comes to prospecting that makes the phone weigh 1,000 pounds. This is the path to becoming a fearless, resilient prospector and removing any negative thinking or misconceptions that contribute to cold call reluctance which act as a barrier to maximizing your potential. You'll learn what it takes to uncover your fuel source that will ignite your passion and drive your prospecting efforts and why it's critical to "get comfortable with being uncomfortable." Hey, if you want to become a top producer, this section will teach you how to get out of your own way so you can start thinking like one.

In **Part 2, "Building Your Expressway to New Business,"** you will discover a step-by-step process that you can put on autopilot. You will be introduced to proven techniques that capture a prospect's attention in less than thirty seconds and actually get them excited to speak with you. Worried about saying the wrong thing or sounding like every other salesperson? Not anymore, once you uncover what distinguishes you from your competition. Finally, you will be able to utilize a highly effective template to create your own prospecting system that will make your cold calls warm. Beginning with your pre-call planning strategy, you will identify the activities that prepare you for prospecting, the avenues you can travel down (other than cold calling) to find more selling opportunities than ever before, who your ideal prospect is, and a variety of vehicles you can use to deliver your message to them. Once you develop your game plan and become process driven, you will be able to begin and end your days with a smile on your face, rather than feeling discouraged or disappointed that results aren't showing up fast enough. Eliminate your diversions throughout your day so you can always get your prospecting done.

Now that you've laid the groundwork, in **Part 3, "Transforming Cold Calls into Warm Calls,"** it's time to master and embrace the five objectives during a cold call so that you can start calling on your prospects. Here is your chance to identify the type of prospector you are and develop a prospecting style that best fits you so that you can avoid the most common communication pitfalls when cold calling that destroy a sale, including the ineffective use of collateral material. Instead of "pitching" a prospect, you will be able to have a conversation with them by following my seven-step process to defuse a prospect's resistance and generate more sales in less time. And just in case you feel those pesky objections will get in the way of accomplishing your objective, you will learn to love them and understand why you will never have to "close" another prospect again. You can kiss your sales slumps and the objections that foster them good-bye forever.

Have you ever watched a selling opportunity that you've been working on fall apart right in front of your eyes? Ironically, it's most often the result of poor follow-up by the salesperson. **Part 4, "Cultivating Your Selling Opportunities to Close More Sales,"** introduces you to the inner workings of your prospecting system that maintains your competitive edge so you don't drop the ball in the middle of the game and give your sales away to your competitors. Now that you have a viable prospect, what are you going to do to keep the selling process moving forward so that you can eventually earn their business? You will be introduced to a foolproof formula to craft compelling voice mails that get more callbacks than ever before. This section of the book is packed with easy-to-use techniques that will make the gatekeeper a raving fan and your internal advocate. You will be shown how to design a "follow-through" system that will protect your potential sale, prevent your warm prospects from turning cold, and maintain your prospect's interest up until the point they become a client.

Finally, if you've ever wondered how to determine if you are investing your prospecting time wisely, by establishing the lifetime value of each client, you now have a new barometer to help answer this question.

Part 5, "The Winner's Circle—Securing Your Position at the Top," is the final section of this book that will separate the average producer from the superstar. This section stretches you to reach your fullest potential by having you do the things that the average producers are not doing. I will show you how to become a networking guru and craft an attractive "laser introduction" when meeting new people so that you can open up the floodgates and have the prospects come pouring in. Don't worry if you've never networked before. You will find out exactly what you need to do to build your own referral engine and keep it running on a consistent basis. Not sure how much prospecting is enough? You will be, after taking the time to establish your measurable goals that will make prospecting a "numbers art" rather than a "numbers game." This way, you can enjoy the benefit of having the numbers drive your prospecting efforts to ensure that your actions are aligned with your intentions.

If this isn't enough to secure your success at prospecting, I'll provide you with a process to fine-tune your prospecting system for maximum impact, uncover the best place to mine for prospects, eliminate the weight of rejection, and continually bounce back from adversity by becoming tougher than nails (teflon, in fact). After reading this section, you will actually look forward to hearing the word "no" from your prospects and understand why this word is music to your ears (really)!

Tips from Your Sales Coach

To make the learning and implementation process easier for you, I've included some tips, techniques, insights, inspiration, definitions, and red flags to watch out for that will support and complement your prospecting efforts. The following sidebars will guide you through this journey and help you navigate your path to developing your own personal prospecting approach.

Warm Wisdom

This sidebar is chock-full of suggestions, innovative ideas, and observations that are sure to inspire you and accelerate your success. These words of encouragement will squash disappointment and frustration at its core. At the very least, they are sure to make you think and say, "Hmmmm."

 ### Cold Calling Conundrum

We all make mistakes. However, the smart ones learn from other people's mistakes in order to flatten their learning curve and prevent these mistakes from reappearing. Here, you'll find warnings, pitfalls, and minefields to avoid that will act as a barrier to realizing your potential and achieving bigger goals so that you can dramatically reduce the mistakes that can cost you many selling opportunities.

Cold Medicine

In these sidebars, you will find quotes and tips that complement and expand on the concepts you are learning while positioning you to become a sales superstar.

Cold Callingo

These are definitions of words and concepts to expand your knowledge base as it relates to prospecting. These definitions add clarity to the process, providing you with a deeper understanding of what it takes to excel at prospecting.

Before you jump into this book with both feet, keep the following points in mind. In my effort to prevent any potential confusion, there are some words that I use interchangeably throughout this book.

1. **Product and Service:** Whether you sell a tangible product or an intangible service, I've used these words synonymously throughout the book. So if you see me use the word "product" more than the word "service" when discussing your deliverable, please note that it's not because I'm biased toward selling tangible products. I am simply using "product" generically to refer to both products and services.

2. **Clients and Customers:** As just mentioned, the same rule applies. I'm using these two words synonymously.

3. **Warm Calling and Cold Calling:** My commitment is to hand deliver a prospecting system to you that is so effective you will never have to "cold" call again. The objective of your prospecting system is to make all of your cold calls warm. As such, I have introduced the phrase "warm calling" to change your mind-set and thinking around cold calling. I still use the phrase "cold calling" throughout this book, because people are most familiar with this phrase when referring to this activity. Besides, referring to "cold calling" as "warm calling" certainly makes it more palatable.

4. **Prospecting and Cold Calling:** In Chapter 1, I've drawn a clear distinction between these two activities.

5. **Concierge and Gatekeeper:** I've never been thrilled with the word "gatekeeper" when talking about the administrative assistant, secretary, or receptionist who answers the phone when calling on a prospect. That's why I've introduced a new name for this person, "concierge," in order to change your thinking about them. However, just like the phrase "warm calling," I still use "gatekeeper" in normal conversation so that you can easily identify with the most common phrase associated with this position.

If you are interested in working with a sales coach to become a top producer and boost your productivity and income, would like to have Keith deliver a keynote presentation or an interactive workshop at your next meeting or sales conference, or want to receive Keith's free e-mail newsletter, "The Winners Path," contact Keith at 1-888-262-2450, e-mail info@ProfitBuilders.com, or visit his website www.ProfitBuilders.com. Keith offers personalized one-on-one and team sales coaching and training in person or by phone.

Acknowledgments

Taking a dream and bringing it to fruition could not have been possible without certain people in my life. I feel deeply fortunate to have the unconditional support and generosity of my family and friends, my wife, and especially my mom and dad, who will forever be greatly appreciated. I only wish to be able to do the same for my children as they have done for me.

A sincere thank you to my clients who have provided me with a unique and valuable opportunity to continually learn and evolve. I am always in awe of what they achieve. I appreciate each client and the opportunity I've had to work with every one.

I want to especially thank Eric Slife, who made this a viable opportunity. A heartfelt thank you to my agent, Marilyn Allen, and the entire team at Alpha Books who were so incredibly supportive, helpful, understanding, and an absolute joy to work with. Thank you for the opportunity to work with so many great people and for making this experience so rewarding and pleasurable.

I'd like to send a special thank you to you, my dear reader. Your voice has been heard. This book is my response to your request to find a solution for the timeless struggle that salespeople have with cold calling and to eliminate the anxiety, resistance, and frustration associated with this elusive activity. This book is your answer to making cold calling fun, profitable, and effortless. After implementing the strategies outlined in this book, please feel free to share your successes with me. I'd love to hear about all of them.

Finally, I would like to deeply thank a mentor of mine, Dr. Marvin Jolson, and my grandfather, Max Gelman—two very important people in my life who recently passed and always told me, "You will do great things."

Trademarks

All terms mentioned in this book that are known to be or are suspected of being trademarks or service marks have been appropriately capitalized. Alpha Books and Penguin Group (USA) Inc., cannot attest to the accuracy of this information. Use of a term in this book should not be regarded as affecting the validity of any trademark or service mark.

Part 1

The Inner Game of Prospecting

Why is it that the thought of cold calling immobilizes and terrifies some salespeople while others seem to do it almost effortlessly? Developing a healthy prospecting attitude and mind-set and actually learning how to think like a top producer is the distinguishing factor as to whether or not you become only half the salesperson you could be or truly evolve into a well-rounded sales professional. This part of the book begins your journey toward becoming the superstar you know you can be by introducing you to some fundamental guiding principles that build sales champions from the inside out. Mastering the inner game of prospecting will make this process much easier, enabling you to build a solid foundation for prospecting success.

Preparing for Cold Calling Success

In This Chapter

- The difference between prospecting and cold calling
- Discover why you'll never have to cold call again
- Determine whether you really need to prospect
- Embrace the new normal
- Get comfortable with being uncomfortable

Well, here we are at the start of your journey into prospecting. Are you strapped in for the ride? At this point, you probably have a list of questions that you are hoping this book will answer. You may also be experiencing some apprehension or resistance to prospecting. This could be one of the reasons why you purchased this book in the first place, to learn how to overcome your reluctance to prospecting. Finally, you probably have your own interpretation and opinion about prospecting: what prospecting is, what it isn't, what it takes to be successful at it, and how you go about doing it.

This chapter will provide you with a clear definition of prospecting and explain why you have already been doing this your entire life. By the end of this chapter, you will discover why prospecting is a critical ingredient in your formula for selling success. You will also be introduced to the mantra of this book.

What Exactly Is Prospecting?

I distinctly remember one of the first workshops on effective selling techniques that I delivered. After a short break midway through the program, I introduced the next topic of discussion: prospecting.

I can visualize the reaction of my audience. The mere mention of the word *prospecting* had people squirming in their seats. I could actually see their mood change as I glanced out at a sea of sour-looking faces. I felt this overwhelming feeling that seemed to grip them. It was fear, reluctance, and skepticism. Some people even got up out of their seats and walked out!

> **Cold Callingo**
>
> A **prospect** is any person you perceive to be a qualified candidate who you target as a potential customer who could benefit from your product or service, or who can act as a conduit to connect you with someone who could benefit from your product or service and who has the power to make a purchasing decision.

It was as if Godzilla had entered the room. At least that's how they reacted to prospecting, the Godzilla of sales activities. To them, prospecting was overwhelmingly big, scary, intimidating, and way too difficult to control!

This was a typical reaction from salespeople, regardless of industry or sales experience. A "necessary evil" was what I often heard when salespeople described prospecting.

To develop a deeper and healthier understanding about prospecting, let's begin chipping away at the negativity surrounding prospecting that salespeople encounter by defining what prospecting truly is so that you can establish a baseline for this elusive activity.

Prospecting is defined as ...

1. Any activity or conversation you engage in to position yourself in front of a prospect with the intention to ...

2. Inquire, assess, discover, and educate so that you can ...

3. Determine whether there's a fit and a relationship that's worth pursuing, which can then lead to presenting your product or service in order to earn your prospect's business.

If this sounds slightly different from your personal definition of prospecting, that's perfectly fine. We will be dissecting and analyzing this definition throughout this book.

A Lifetime of Prospecting

Here's something ironic that may be outside of your line of vision. You've actually been prospecting your entire life! You probably do it every day.

The word "prospecting" is synonymous with "searching, mining, seeking, and hunting." If you've ever looked for a job, purchased a home, gone shopping at the mall, or searched for your ideal soul mate or relationship, then you in fact have prospected. For example, if we were to break down the prospecting process you have used when shopping for holiday gifts, it may look something like this:

First, you identified what you wanted. You were clear about your objective. Then, you uncovered where you could find what you were looking for. Next, you found the resources or people who could provide the information you needed to make an educated buying decision. Chances are, you then asked some questions to determine if what you found was, in fact, a good fit for you. Finally, if all of your criteria were satisfied, you made the decision to buy.

The only thing that's different between this example and prospecting for new clients is this: At the end of the process it would be your *prospect* that would be making the purchasing decision rather than you. Other than that, the entire process is the same!

Prospecting vs. Cold Calling

I often hear salespeople use the word "prospecting" and the phrase "cold calling" synonymously. To eliminate any further confusion as you move deeper into this book, let's draw a distinction between the two.

When you hear the term cold calling, you may formulate a picture in your mind of a salesperson sitting at their desk with a phone book in one hand and a phone in the other hand. Or, you may have the visual of a salesperson finding a neighborhood and going door-to-door and business-to-business or standing around at trade shows or in hotel lobbies trying to track down potential unsuspecting prospects, hoping that someone somewhere will want to purchase his product or service.

Based on this depiction, cold calling would be defined as the act of calling on or approaching someone with the intention of converting him or her into a prospect and who …

◆ Does not know you.

◆ You do not know.

◆ Is not expecting your call or contact.

◆ You have never called on before.

◆ You know very little if anything about, especially as it relates to their needs, situation, challenges, decision-making process, goals, company, or career.

◆ May or may not be a fit with what you are offering.

Let's look at cold calling as one strategy or component of an entire prospecting system. It's one of several methods to generate new prospects that could lead to more sales.

Never Cold Call Again!

If this definition of cold calling doesn't have you running for the phone or out the door excited to begin, do not despair!

This may sound a bit strange, especially because it's included in the title of this book, but I'm going to suggest that you never have to cold call again.

After the feeling of relief subsides you may wonder, "Keith, if I don't cold call, then exactly how am I supposed to generate more new business?" The answer is simple: by using a prospecting system that makes your cold calls warm. Interestingly, some of the prospecting you engage in may not involve a telephone or door-to-door canvassing. In this book, you will learn how to create your own prospecting system.

Those salespeople who actually enjoy cold calling do so because they are, in fact, warm calling. They have created a process that they can follow and actually have fun doing it! They derive pleasure from the prospecting process because they have developed the right attitude, approach, and prospecting system that generate consistent, long-lasting results. Mostly, they understand the critical importance of prospecting as it relates to their entire selling process.

Unfortunately, less than 5 percent of all salespeople understand this and actually do it. If you're like the majority of salespeople who fall into the 95-percentile category, it simply means that you haven't uncovered the enjoyable and rewarding ways to prospect yet. Herein lies the opportunity for you to do so.

Cold Medicine

Here's some great news for you. You'll never have to cold call again! As long as you invest the time to develop the right attitude and prospecting system, you can then make every cold call warm. Therefore, rather than having to make cold calls, you can make warm calls.

Why Prospect?

The second most common question I hear from salespeople is this: "Keith, isn't there anything else I can do to bring in more business that doesn't involve prospecting or cold calling? I mean, do I *really* have to prospect?" The answer is a resounding "Yes" and here's why. It's because you will be doing more than picking up the phone and trying to squeeze your foot into someone's door who really doesn't want to speak with you in the first place.

But why *wouldn't* anyone want to cold call? After all, why deny yourself the pleasure of hearing multiple "No's," the joy you get from continuous rejection, the warm, fuzzy, uplifting feeling and degree of fulfillment you experience from calling on people who you don't know and who aren't expecting your call? What's more motivating than interrupting someone's busy day and hearing the sweet sound of the dial tone after they hang up on you, slam the door in your face, or tell you to never call on them again?

Let's do a quick self-test to determine whether or not you need to prospect. Do you have an unlimited number of prospects knocking down your door to purchase what you are selling? Is most of your day spent filling orders that are generated as a result of no action on your part? Are you finding it challenging to keep up with all of the inquiries from people who want to buy your product?

> **Warm Wisdom**
>
> Before you go running as fast as you can away from this book, consider that this negativity surrounding cold calling is actually great news! Because you've just begun reading this book you may be a bit reluctant, even terrified, to cold call. But remember this important point; your competition is feeling the exact same way. Talk about developing a competitive edge—just by reading this book!

If you are like most salespeople, chances are you don't have this luxury. So ...

- If your phone isn't ringing as much as it should

- If your income has dropped

- If you're feeling stressed, anxious, and uncertain about when your next sale is going to come

- If you already know deep down that you could be much more successful if only you prospected consistently ...

here are your options. You can put yourself out of your misery now and get out of sales completely, accept that you've already placed a limit on your income and performance and continue doing what you are currently doing, or make some positive long-term changes, now!

Think about when you began your career in sales. Whether it was 10 years ago or 10 days ago, once you had a solid understanding of the benefits and features of your product, you were then ready to deliver your message to your audience.

Whether you are selling consumer goods or high-tech business applications, products, or services, the only way to build your business or your practice is to see enough people as frequently as possible with the intention of presenting your product to them. Once this is accomplished, the objective is to make a sale and have them become one of your valued clients. The only way to achieve this is to prospect.

Get Comfortable with Being Uncomfortable

We are all creatures of habit. We like to do things that produce a degree of certainty in the results, even when they may not serve us best. At the same time, we want better results but resist anything new, so we recoil back into what is safe and comfortable.

The paradox is, change is the only constant. To grow and evolve, we must change and stretch beyond our comfort zone.

Consider this. If you are comfortable with the activities you engage in, then you are simply doing what you've already been doing, which will produce the same results as before. However, if you are willing to do the things that make you uncomfortable—a new activity, strategy, or developing a new skill—then you will create new results.

The lesson? If it's uncomfortable, it's probably the right thing to do and the quickest path to greater success. So, get comfortable with being uncomfortable.

You may be familiar with the definition of insanity: "Doing the same thing over and over and expecting a different result." Consider my definition of futility: "Knowing the definition of insanity, and still not doing anything about it."

It's healthy to embrace and respond to change. Your career and your peace of mind depend on it.

The Least You Need to Know

◆ Instead of cold calling, develop a prospecting system; the cornerstone to more sales.

◆ If you find what you're doing to be uncomfortable, it's probably the right thing to do to achieve greater results.

◆ Because your competitors also experience reluctance to cold calling, becoming fearless provides you with a competitive edge.

◆ One of the main reasons why businesses fail is they simply aren't prospecting effectively.

Becoming Fearless

In This Chapter

- ◆ Become a fearless prospector
- ◆ Uncover your passion for prospecting
- ◆ Get yourself out of your own way
- ◆ Discover what fear can teach you
- ◆ Boost your confidence

At this point, it's a safe bet that you've recognized that some things have got to change. Whether it's your attitude surrounding prospecting, your prospecting activities, or both—to experience greater selling success, change is inevitable.

Chapter 1 discussed how uncomfortable change can be, and introduced one mantra for generating desired, worthwhile results. That is, *get comfortable with being uncomfortable*.

The question is: What exactly makes change so uncomfortable? Why are we so resistant to change? Quite often, the root of apprehension that surrounds change and the gatekeeper to realizing our true potential is fear.

The Fear Factor

Although we may want to better our lives and accelerate our productivity, many of our decisions are governed by fear. We want more, but avoid risks, so we continually produce similar results over again. We fear change, for we may lose some degree of control over the outcome. We fear expressing how we feel or what matters most to us, in fear that it would make us vulnerable. We fear leaving what's predictable and comfortable, although it may not be best for us. We fear not having and not getting, having what we want and losing it, even getting what we want and no longer wanting it!

We fear success ("What if I actually achieve my goal? Do I deserve it? Then what do I do?") and failure, because of the negative perception society has placed around it.

Warm Wisdom

Here's one way to reframe how you perceive mistakes and failure. Realize that you cannot fail. You can only produce unexpected results. The only true mistake or failure is not recognizing the opportunity to grow from these unexpected results in order to create new possibilities and greater success. Ben Franklin is a testament to this. Ben Franklin was the man who discovered that lightning was an electrical current in nature, which led to his invention of the lightning rod. Ben was told he failed hundreds of times before his successful discovery. Ben countered with a comment that resembled the following statement, "I didn't fail hundreds of times. Rather, I've learned hundreds of different ways to produce different results."

We resist what we don't understand, preventing growth by staying with what's familiar and safe. We even do things or don't engage in certain activities in the hope of avoiding fear. Resisting the fear of the unknown paralyzes our efforts to create greater opportunities for ourselves.

Imagine what would be possible if you embraced fear and considered it to be one of your greatest teachers. If you resist fear or react when you feel fear, then you can't learn from it or even recognize any lessons that would contribute to your continued evolution. And if you aren't learning from it, then you can't look at the fear as something that can be reframed into a positive opportunity to grow and change.

Is Fear Real?

Ironically, most of our fears are not based on logic or reality. They are not real. Granted, the *feeling* of fear is very real and I'm certainly not disputing that. Fear is just another feeling, like happy, angry, frustrated, excited, or sad. These feelings often trigger a physiological reaction. Like these other feelings, our body's reaction to the feeling of fear manifests in a variety of ways such as an elevated pulse or heartbeat, temporary paralysis, a knot in our stomach, neck, or back, even perspiration.

There are actually two parts that make up the experience of fear. However, we often collapse these two parts together. If one component of fear is the feeling of fear, the other part of fear is that which we actually fear or the trigger that sends us into fear.

Because most of us collapse what we fear and the feeling of fear together without distinguishing between these two parts, we have a tendency to resist fear and make it our adversary rather than embracing fear as an ally.

> **Warm Wisdom**
>
> Consider the definition of the acronym for F.E.A.R., False Evidence Appearing Real.

We're all familiar with the three points in time: the past, the present, and the future. That which we fear is only the negative expectation or assumption of what *may* happen in the future (what we don't want to happen) and what is *never* happening in the present.

To illustrate this point, here's an extreme example. If someone held a gun to your head, chances are you'd react and go right into fear. However, think about the two parts of fear. Sure, you are certainly experiencing the feeling of fear. There's no question about that. However, think about what you are actually afraid of. Is it the gun to your head or is it the fear that the person may pull the trigger, which would lead to an unfortunate demise? Chances are, it's the latter. It's the possible negative outcome that's terrifying. That's the feeling part. However, the trigger has not been pulled yet. Therefore, while the feeling of fear is real, what you fear is never real because it hasn't happened yet!

Focus on the Positive Outcome

If we are pushed to avoid consequences or what we don't want to happen, conversely we are pulled toward what we *do* want—pleasure. Because fear is the negative assumption of the outcome, try shifting your focus to the positive outcome or what you do want to manifest, instead of what you are looking to avoid.

The key point here is this: Our fears are just as "real" as our dreams! But as long as we give more power to our fears rather than our dreams, our fears will always seem as if they are more of a reality and in turn will get the better of us. If you stop and think about it for a moment, they are both visions and pictures of a future that we have constructed or visualized in our mind's eye. Both our fears and dreams are created using the same tool … our imagination!

The quandary is that most of us spend more time focusing on that which we fear rather than the goals or dreams we want to create. Let's face it: We're all pretty good at articulating what we don't want to happen in our lives, yet fall short when trying to come up with a vivid picture of what we do want or our goals and dreams.

If you know what you don't want and don't know what you do want, then where do you think you are going to continually wind up directing your thoughts and energy? Your goals and dreams don't even stand a chance! Instead, empower your dreams and goals rather than your fears to be the driving force that moves you forward. Once you do so, you will then be able to achieve them.

The Past Doesn't Equal the Future

Consider all the fears you may be experiencing around cold calling. Whether it's the fear of failure, the fear that the prospect will not want to talk to you, the fear of looking bad, saying or doing the wrong thing, or the fear of rejection, are any of these fears actually occurring in the present moment? No they are not! The only thing that is real in the moment is the feeling of fear.

To compound how powerful fear can be, we often look at past experiences and project them into the future. For example, a client once told me, "The last time I cold called it was a waste of time and all I got was a headache from people telling me not to call them. I don't want that to happen again." This client is focusing on the pain or possible negative outcome she will experience when cold calling.

Isn't it possible that they have learned the wrong lesson? Instead of equating the past with the future (it happened once so it will happen again), maybe there's another lesson here. How about, "Gee, the last time I tried to prospect, I didn't have any training, support, tools, or templates to guide me. Maybe the real lesson here is that I need to develop a prospecting system in order to generate the results and income I really want!" Notice how the focus is now on the positive outcome that this client wants to realize.

After all, if you went out and tried to dig a 10-foot hole with a spoon, is the lesson "Gee, I guess I can't dig a hole very well" or is it "Hey, I need the right tools the next time!"? If we apply this to prospecting, most salespeople are attempting to achieve greater results by using the wrong tools, which then leads to learning the wrong lesson: "I'm not good at prospecting and I don't like doing it because it doesn't work for me."

 **Cold Calling Conundrum**

If your past cold calling efforts fell short of your expectations, instead of quickly formulating the belief that you're not good at it or it doesn't work for you, consider the alternative. You may have been working with the wrong tools.

Make Fear Your Ally

To become a fearless prospector, make fear your ally. Consider fear to be your emotional feedback loop or internal barometer for learning. In other words, when we are in physical pain, our bodies react and let us know. It's a sign of danger or that we may be sick or injured. That's our body's physical feedback loop. Quite often if we ignore the pain, it gets even worse. Instead, by acknowledging the pain we can choose to do something about it.

Embrace the belief that if and when you experience fear it is trying to teach you something. Allow yourself to experience the feeling of fear so that you can grow past it. Responding to fear in a healthier way will provide you with an opportunity to grow and learn, which leads to greater wisdom and unprecedented results. Not only that, but you will become more powerful, more confident, and more focused on achieving your goals.

Nine Steps to Managing Fear

How much of your life and your decisions are governed by fear? To start determining if the fear is actually a realistic threat or just your active imagination, the next time you experience the reaction of fear, follow these nine steps to eliminate fear from your life. This way you can upgrade your relationship with fear and learn to respond to it in a healthier way rather than continually reacting to it the way you have.

1. When you feel the sensation of fear overwhelming you, allow yourself to experience the feeling of fear, rather than freezing. Instead of looking at fear as a "stop sign," give yourself permission to acknowledge the fear as a source of valuable information by saying to yourself, "Okay, I am afraid." You'll notice that fear is simply a feeling and will begin to dissipate once you declare and experience it fully. This way, you can get complete with it rather than having it linger eternally.

2. Breathe! When we feel fear, stress, worry, angst, or excitement, it affects our breathing pattern. We begin to breathe irregularly. To avoid this, take a few deep, slow breaths. In through your nose, and out through your mouth. This exercise alone will calm you down, diminish the fear, stop your hands from shaking, slow down your heart rate, and quickly bring you back to the present situation.

3. Recognize this as an opportunity to grow and learn. ("Is the fear telling me that there may be additional information, tools, resources, and training I need?")

4. Give the fear a name by labeling it. Ask yourself, "What exactly is it that I am afraid of right now?" Example: "Will I get the appointment?" "Am I going to be able to hit my quota?" "Is my boss going to like the work I'm doing?" "Will this relationship fail because this person doesn't really want to work with me?"

"There's no way I'm going to be able to do this." "What if I don't get the result I need?" "What if I ask and don't get what I want?" "Will I look stupid?" "Am I going to be able to help this person?"

5. Embrace this feeling by saying, "Here's me feeling a fear that isn't happening in the moment. While the *feeling* of fear is real, what I am actually fearing isn't real because it's based on a *possible* negative future outcome that hasn't even happened!"

6. Shift your focus to the outcome that you do want to create or manifest instead of what you don't want or what you want to avoid. Create that vivid picture in your mind. Envision and direct your thoughts toward the positive future outcome you want to achieve. Ask yourself, "Now that I know what I don't want or what I'm trying to avoid, what *do* I want to create for myself in this situation?" (For example: happy clients, an increase in my income, more opportunities to help others, and so on.)

7. Take action. Now that you have identified the outcome you want to create, what steps can you take to achieve this outcome? If you are staring at a pile of paper, a call list, a report, or a project you need to finish that is causing your paralysis, try this. Take out a piece of paper (or on your computer) and just start listing the steps, one by one, of what you feel needs to be done to complete each task or to accomplish/overcome what it is you are afraid of in your pile of to-do's. Don't worry about whether or not your steps are perfect. Just doing this will enable you to start taking action which will remove the "overwhelm" and make the task more manageable. If you are still stuck, then ask for help in developing your action steps. Chances are, you are focusing more on getting to the end result rather than on the steps you need to take to achieve the end result. Focus on the process instead. I guarantee that after every single step you take, not only will you get closer to your goal but you will notice the fear subsiding as you take every little step. Before you know it, your task will be completed! Now you have a system to handle this fear the next time it occurs.

8. Redirect your thoughts and energy back to the present moment in time and what is actually happening in the now as opposed to a future anticipation or a past experience.

9. Finally, how can you upgrade your belief that triggers this fear? If this fear surfaces again, how can you change your thinking so that it enhances and teaches you something rather than consumes you?

That which you fear will happen is always happening in the future and, as mentioned, never in the present. The real benefit here is this. If you can stay in the present moment as opposed to worrying about the negative assumptions of the future, fear will not be able to get to you. Remember, you can't be present if you're experiencing fear and you can't experience fear if you're in the present moment! The real power is in the present moment. When you focus on the present and on your desired outcomes, you will notice that your fears will lose their powerful edge.

Choose the Fuel That Drives You

Now that you know what you can do to become a fearless prospector, what fuel are you going to use to drive you if you are no longer being driven by fear, consequence, or what you want to avoid?

It's better to find an energy source that will pull you toward something you want to create, something pleasurable, or something that you are passionate about, rather than fear, which pushes you away from what you want to avoid.

The following are some suggested fuel sources to assist you in uncovering your hidden passion that will become your driving force when prospecting and make you unstoppable:

♦ **Knowledge and Lifelong Learning.** You have a thirst for knowledge and wisdom. You are a student of life and someone who embraces their own development and evolution. You are always looking for new ways to better yourself and your situation. You enjoy the experience of adding to your knowledge base and learning how to do new things that you never did before.

♦ **Giving Value and Helping Others.** You are someone who experiences a great deal of joy when assisting other people. There's no coincidence that you are in sales. You enjoy helping people solve their problems or better their condition. You derive a great deal of satisfaction knowing that you have assisted someone by sharing your time and expertise with them. You get energized when people rely on you. You seek to serve.

◆ **Product/Service.** You possess a deep conviction about what you sell. There's no doubt in your mind that what you offer can dramatically impact your customers and accelerate their success, enhance their life or career, or simply make their life easier. As such, you're willing to talk to anyone about what you do. Your belief in your product is contagious. You feel as if you are doing your prospects a disservice if you can't share with them what you can do that would improve their current situation.

◆ **Excellence.** You simply want to be the best, not to satisfy your ego or to be in the spotlight but because you enjoy the challenge of continuous improvement. You thrive from maximizing your potential and stretching your capabilities beyond what you initially thought you were capable of doing. That's why you love to prospect! It provides you with a constant challenge. It's the journey you enjoy, knowing that each day you have the opportunity to excel even further, fully embracing the challenges and opportunities that come your way in your quest to become a master of your life and career.

◆ **Family.** At the end of the day, what's more important than family? After all, why do you go to work every day? What is the ultimate goal? To raise and support a happy, healthy family. To be a great spouse, parent, and role model. You want nothing but the best for your family. They are your number one priority which you refuse to compromise. As long as it's in your integrity to do so, you would do anything that honors the commitment you've made to them.

◆ **Relationships.** You simply love people and connecting with new customers. You enjoy being part of your community. Your career allows you the ability to interact with a broad range of people and develop relationships with them. You deeply value the relationships you've made and give each one the attention and care they deserve. Connecting with people and communicating with them on a deeper level gives you a sense of purpose, comfort, and security.

◆ **Lifestyle.** Your lifestyle is your style of living, the system or routine that you use that governs your days, which makes up your life. You enjoy maintaining balance and harmony in your life. You appreciate the richness in your days that your career offers you. The income potential and flexibility played a huge role in your decision to become a salesperson. You are able to honor the priorities in your life such as your family, health, and relationships. You feel that you own your day, which is evident in the amount of time you invest in taking care of yourself by engaging in the activities, hobbies, and sports that bring you the most joy. You are grateful for being able to create a great life and not just a living.

◆ **Creativity.** You are always on the search for something unique, new, and fun to try. You look forward to creating different strategies or tools that complement your selling and prospecting efforts. What puts a smile on your face is developing a new approach that will clearly separate you from your competition and grab your prospect's interest. You love when your prospects say, "Wow, no one's ever tried to get my attention like that before!"

◆ **Adventure.** As a thrill seeker, what greater rush is there than closing a sale and earning a prospect's business? You like the excitement and freshness that your career offers. Every day provides you with a new opportunity to create something that didn't exist before—another new and happy customer.

◆ **Money.** A high percentage of salespeople would admit that money is their primary motivator and why they got into sales in the first place. In many cases, salespeople are seduced by the thought of having a career with unlimited income potential. Before you choose money as your fuel, consider this. Is it actually the money that motivates you or is it what the money represents and what it can do for you? Does it give you security, freedom, a sense of accomplishment, peace of mind, a greater feeling of self-worth? Will money allow you to create the lifestyle you want? Does it provide you with the opportunity to buy your dream house or new car, take that family

Cold Medicine

Get out of your head. Once you get yourself out of your own way, you are then able to generate extraordinary results.

vacation, enjoy more leisurely activities? Chances are, if you explore at a deeper level why you are choosing money as your motivator, you may realize that you're better off using one of the other fuel sources that has already been mentioned.

What's the Worst That Could Happen?

It's one thing to use fear as a tool to avoid imminent danger, such as stepping back onto the sidewalk to avoid being hit by an oncoming car. But what about the fears that paralyze you and prevent you from taking action?

Here's an exercise to try the next time fear has a grip on you. Imagine the worst-case scenario. What would really happen if your fears about prospecting actually came true? How bad would that really be and what would it truly mean to you?

Most of the time, when you can envision the worst possible scenario and outcome that would result from taking the actions that are being sabotaged by the fear, you will notice that you really can handle it and keep going! Thinking about the worst possible case actually defuses the fear and takes away a large degree of its power. After all, what's the worst thing that can happen when you cold call? Someone tells you they aren't interested or not to call? Or worse, not *another* sale!

The Best-Kept Secret in Your Industry

Pssst. I have a very important secret to share with you. Come a little closer to make sure that you hear this. I'm about to let you in on the biggest and best-kept secret in your industry. Are you ready? Well here it is.

You! That's right, you are the best-kept secret in your industry. How can your prospects learn about you if you don't contact them? What's going to stop a prospect from making a bad purchasing decision if you don't communicate with them? How can they take advantage of the incredible value or opportunity you offer that would enhance the quality of their life, business, or career if you don't prospect? How can you share your incredible talents, knowledge, experience, wisdom, solutions, and support if they don't even know who you are? Finally, when will you get to hear what every salesperson loves to hear most, ("I would love to buy from you. Where do I sign?") if you aren't letting prospects know you exist?

Remember, you have something that your prospects need; they just don't know it yet. The greatest gift you bring to the table is you! Here's the chance to share your gift with others. Now that you have learned what it take to become fearless, I think it's time to let the secret out, don't you?

The Least You Need to Know

- Make fear your ally rather than your adversary so that you can learn and grow from it.

- Top producers have learned what average producers haven't: to feel their fear and do what needs to be done anyway.

- Things rarely happen the way we worry about them.

- What you fear isn't real.

- Determine your healthy and pleasurable fuel source to ignite your passion and drive your prospecting efforts.

- You are the greatest gift you can give to your prospects and the best-kept secret, so let it out!

Chapter 3

Upgrading Your Mental Operating System

In This Chapter

- ◆ Discover the hidden secret to cold calling success
- ◆ Learn the importance of a positive attitude
- ◆ Manage your mind-set for maximum productivity
- ◆ Eliminate cold calling reluctance
- ◆ Get excited to cold call

Professional development courses, self-help books, and sales trainers have discussed the importance of attitude and how your attitude affects you career as well as your life. The question is, what exactly is this thing we refer to as "attitude" and how does one improve theirs? We will be answering these two questions throughout this chapter.

This chapter of the book is more cerebral. We're actually going to work on upgrading *how you think* in order to generate extraordinary results rather than simply changing what you will be doing to achieve greater cold calling success. (The hands-on action steps and the specifics of how to create an effective prospecting campaign come later on.)

How You Think Is What You'll Get

What would it mean to you if you could develop …

1. An infallible introduction that will make the receptionist your biggest fan?

2. An initial prospecting approach that would allow you to dance right into the hearts of your prospects?

3. A surefire process to get more of your voice mails and calls returned?

4. A prospecting system that runs on autopilot so you never have to worry about the results? Instead, the results happen naturally. That's how much faith and confidence you have in yourself and in your prospecting system.

Having these components/objectives in place would certainly equate to more sales. While this may sound like an enticing agenda, the topic we're going to explore actually *precedes* what I've just shared with you and ironically, is the most overlooked and least developed component of a comprehensive prospecting system. In other words, there are certain things that must be accomplished before you even pick up the phone, visit a prospect, leave a voice mail, send a letter, or blast an e-mail.

There's a foundation for effective cold calling that must be poured *before* you attempt to communicate with each prospect.

Now, I'm not avoiding the discussion around these other essential components, nor am I mentioning them simply to entice you to read the rest of this book because the fact is, we will be covering each one of the previous four objectives later on in this book. The reason why I've alluded to these other topics is to illustrate the depth and critical importance of the topic we're about to discuss.

You see, all of the prospecting tools in the world will not help you accelerate your prospecting success unless your attitude toward cold calling or your mind-set is being managed effectively.

If you were to assign a weight to the activities that you engage in throughout your week that would be categorized as revenue-generating activities, prospecting would probably be that 1,000-pound gorilla that tips the scale and weighs you down. Although many salespeople experience reluctance when it comes to cold calling, the bigger question is, why do salespeople feel this way about cold calling but don't experience as much resistance when engaging in the other steps of their sales process?

Do You Resist What You Need to Learn Most?

Here are some interesting results from a survey I completed. I asked 254 salespeople from different industries with various levels of selling experience to rate how effective they were at five basic sales activities: cold calling, needs analysis (asking questions), presenting, follow-up, and closing. Starting with what they felt they excelled at and ending with what they deemed to be their weakest link, here's what they reported.

1. Greatest Strength—Presenting

2. Closing

3. Needs Analysis

4. Follow-Up

5. Weakest Link—Cold Calling

Salespeople have a tendency to engage in the activities that they feel they are good at and are most comfortable doing.

I then asked them to rate the importance of each activity, starting with the most important sales activity. (Of course, every sales activity is important to some degree. However, without the prospect, the other activities can't even happen.)

1. Most Important—Cold Calling

2. Follow-Up

3. Needs Analysis

4. Closing

5. Least Important—Presenting

Interestingly, this list also depicts the activities that salespeople are most resistant to doing—cold calling and follow-up.

While there may be some thoughts or fears that feed the resistance you experience when prospecting, let's spend some time exploring how you can permanently eliminate any reluctance around prospecting so that you can develop a healthy prospecting attitude and actually get excited to prospect!

Managing a Healthy Prospecting Mind-Set

According to the dictionary, attitude is defined as a state of mind or a feeling.

In the spirit of cold calling, I will define attitude as how you think or your set of beliefs, how you interpret or perceive each experience or each person in your life. (In other words, your reality.)

We all have a certain set of beliefs or rules formed through our up-bringing, education, and experiences that influences our decisions and shapes our attitude toward life and our career. The belief system we have in place may seem to work for us, because it's what we have operated from to create what we have defined as our reality and generate the results we've experienced throughout our entire life. It is a safe place for us to reside, as these rules or beliefs predict our probable reaction to various situations that create a somewhat familiar outcome.

Although some of our thinking may be considered healthy, there are also those old limiting and confining beliefs that often keep us prisoner, stall our professional growth, keep us stuck at a certain level of performance, and prevent us from creating greater selling opportunities.

When Do You Lose a Sale?

When I ask salespeople at what stage in their selling cycle they feel the sale is lost, I get a variety of responses, which include …

 ♦ Upon first contact with the prospect (during a cold call).

 ♦ During their presentation.

 ♦ While attempting to close the sale.

Here's an interesting fact to consider and where it also gets a little strange. Consider that the result of your prospecting efforts and the relationship you have with each prospect is actually established *before* you begin prospecting, make first contact, or meet with the prospect.

Cold Calling Conundrum

The sale is lost even *before* you make first contact with the prospect.

How can that be? Let's go back to the universal law I introduced to you earlier in this chapter: *How you think is what you get.* Another way of saying this is, "Beliefs precede experience," or "Your outlook determines your outcome."

The Secret to Becoming a Top Producer

In all of my years of selling as well as training and coaching thousands of salespeople, I've learned that there are only two ways to generate greater results:

Change what you do, and, more importantly, *change how you think.*

Picture the top producers in your industry. Do you think they have a different attitude, a different mind-set than those who aren't performing up to their level? The fact is, top producers in your industry or profession think differently than those who may not be as successful. In essence, they are wired differently.

There is a direct relationship between increasing your sales volume and your perception or how you think about cold calling. That is, the more you upgrade your thinking toward a healthier mind-set, the more effective and successful you will be.

Warm Wisdom

Although it's essential to manage your prospecting activities and what you do, managing how you think has been proven to dramatically increase personal productivity and become the primary conduit to achieving greater cold calling results.

If you want to generate average results, you can always try a different cold calling technique that you have read about or heard another salesperson use. While you may notice some improvement doing so, to produce unprecedented, breakthrough results requires a shift in your thinking.

How Are You Wired?

If you've ever upgraded your computer, you'll understand what I mean. Like your computer's operating system, we all operate from a certain system. The way we approach selling, how we communicate, and our attitude toward people, our experiences, our career, and our life operates from a certain system that produces a fairly consistent result.

You may have been in a position where your computer technology reached a point where it could no longer function or perform the way you wanted. If you were using an old computer with a 386 processor and an earlier version of your operating system, you would notice that it would only produce limited results very slowly.

Eventually, not upgrading your computer becomes more costly than maintaining it. You may start running into challenges or compatibility problems with new software. Having a slower processor or an older operating system may prevent you from using new software programs. Existing programs may not run or start freezing and performance slows down to the point where the computer can no longer handle the workload.

Cold Callingo

Mental operating system is the belief system we have, which encompasses our thoughts, assumptions, and expectations that determine the way we approach selling, how we communicate, and our attitude toward people, our experiences, our career, and our life that produces a fairly consistent result.

In order to produce new and better results quickly with greater functionality, you upgrade and expose yourself to new and better technology. The same philosophy holds true regarding how you think and your attitude. Therefore, to upgrade your attitude, it's important to first uncover the *mental operating system* you're currently using. This way, you can recognize what needs to change in your thinking and take the steps to begin the upgrading process.

Now, you can remove any faulty beliefs or corrupt files in your system that are inhibiting your ability to grow, learn, and achieve more.

After all, if success in selling were only dependent on what you did, then every salesperson who memorizes a presentation or follows a certain selling system should be able to theoretically perform at the exact same level. From what I see this is not true at all.

Professional selling and the ability to prospect effortlessly are a combined result of who you are, how you think, and the way you come across, not solely a function of what you do.

Imagine for a moment that each person looks at life and more specifically, cold calling, through a certain set of lenses or a set of beliefs that define our perspective about life, our career, and the events that we experience.

Warm Wisdom
To achieve greater success, managing a positive mind-set and healthy attitude toward cold calling will have more of a profound impact on your performance than what you do or the cold calling activities you engage in. Just think of the slogan the army adopted that reinforces this truth. "Be all you can be," not, "Do all you can do."

Imagine looking at a piece of art or even going to a movie. Two people exposed to the same stimuli will have two totally different experiences and different points of view.

There is a saying I heard early on in my sales career, "Selling is a transference of feeling." Although this is true, consider what happens if the feeling you are transferring to your prospects is the wrong feeling because your beliefs or thinking are coming from a negative, fear-based, limiting, or self-serving place. If you are prospecting because you need to close more sales in order to save your job or to make enough money to pay your bills, you can bet that your prospects are going to pick up on your underlying intentions and run the other way.

Consider one of the objectives of a cold call: to create a feeling within the prospect that stimulates interest and motivates them to take the next step and hear more about what you have to offer.

Therefore, it's critical that you are transferring the right feeling and attitude to your prospects.

Overcoming Cold Calling Reluctance

Are you aware of the limiting thinking you may be harboring toward cold calling and your prospects? When salespeople resist cold calling, a typical response from many sales managers is to provide additional training, role-playing, a revised presentation, or more qualified prospects to call on as the solution to improving cold calling results and productivity.

Granted, salespeople do report an increased level of confidence and a decrease in call reluctance when they have been provided with the right tools, processes, and systems. Unfortunately, these tactics don't always eliminate the anxiety or level of resistance that salespeople experience when cold calling.

Perhaps the real issue is not tapping into the source of cold calling reluctance. Fixing the symptom without understanding the true source of the problem only results in a temporary solution.

Instead of focusing on strategies that only address the symptom, explore the source of your anxiety to permanently overcome the fear and resistance to cold calling: your beliefs surrounding cold calling.

Cold Calling Isn't a Dirty Word

Let's do a quick exercise to uncover what your true feelings are toward cold calling. Read the following statements. After each statement, pay close attention to your first reaction—the initial adjectives, thoughts, or assumptions that come to mind regarding how you perceive each topic. Pause briefly after each statement to give yourself some time to recognize how you instinctively respond.

Complete the following sentences:

Cold calling is _____.

Salespeople are _____.

My prospects are _____.

Here's a key point. Notice that based on your responses, you have already made the decision in terms of how you feel about cold calling, salespeople, and your prospects. As we've discussed, how you think is what you get.

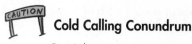

Cold Calling Conundrum

Don't let your negative assumptions sabotage your cold calling efforts.

In other words, *where* you focus your energy and thoughts is exactly *what* you're going to create or attract into your life.

When I ask salespeople about their feelings or attitude toward cold calling, I hear the following responses. Compare your list to the following common responses:

♦ I fear rejection.

♦ I don't want the prospect to say "No" or hang up on me because I take it personally.

♦ The people I call on have other things to do than speak with someone they don't even know. I'll just be interrupting them.

♦ I'm a stranger. Why should they talk to me and give me their time?

♦ I don't want to say the wrong thing.

♦ I don't want to come across the wrong way.

♦ I'm not going to come across professionally. I would rather meet with them face-to-face, because I present myself better in person.

♦ I'm not comfortable with my prospecting approach and I don't want to look bad.

♦ They're not interested.

♦ I don't want to be intrusive.

♦ They're probably happy with their current vendor. If they weren't they would call me.

♦ I hate being cold called!

♦ I don't want to have to close hard or push something on someone.

♦ I don't want to deal with shoppers.

♦ They never answer the phone and I hate leaving voice mails.

Conversely, when I ask salespeople what they love about cold calling, what I get is complete silence.

Whatever you assume or believe about cold calling, your prospects, yourself, selling, and your career is exactly what you'll manifest in your life.

I know this may challenge traditional wisdom and your current beliefs as well as stretch your perception and point of view. However, if you're looking for extreme results, then it calls for extreme thinking and not just a change in what you do and how you do it. With the business community continually evolving, change is critical. And in Einstein's words, "The level of thinking that got us here is not enough."

Don't Believe Everything You Hear (and See)

I remember an experience years ago that reinforced this lesson. One of the businesses I used to own employed about 30 salespeople. I was in the process of recruiting two more salespeople to add to our team. During the initial training program, I had each new recruit spend the day going out on appointments with a seasoned salesperson. When the time came for my new salespeople to spread their wings and go out on their own, I noticed some interesting results.

> **Warm Wisdom**
>
> We've all heard the saying, "I'll believe it when I see it." Challenge this adage and consider the alternative. "I'll see it when I believe it."

After a few weeks of being in the field, one salesperson quickly demonstrated his selling competency, reinforcing that I made the right hiring decision. However, the other salesperson's performance was questionable.

How can that be, I wondered? They both received the exact same training and support. They both passed the initial exam demonstrating their knowledge and selling ability. After many skill practice scenarios and role-playing, they both seemed capable of selling effectively.

In my quest to find the answer, I went back to the two seasoned sales-people who took them out in the field for the day to see if I missed anything.

I sat each veteran down one at a time and asked them, "When you took the new salesperson out in the field, what did you tell them?"

One salesperson responded, "I simply shared with him my personal experience here. I told him not to expect any sales activity until your third month. I also said that you're not expected to perform immedi-ately and because of the vast amount of product knowledge you need to assimilate, what needs to be learned can be very overwhelming."

The other salesperson shared, "I told him that you have an opportunity to deliver incredible value to each prospect. You'll probably wind up selling most of the prospects you speak with. Because the product prac-tically sells itself, my customers feel that it's really a 'no brainer' to make this purchasing decision. Sometimes the prospect may have one or two concerns, but for the most part, you'll always be able to design a solution that addresses and defuses their concerns. Therefore, expect to close nine out of every ten presentations you deliver."

The lesson? Even though people say, "Seeing is believing," the truth is, "Believing is seeing."

What we believe in our hearts and our attitude toward our career, other people, and more specifically cold calling affects our behavior, which then creates our experiences and results.

Here were two new salespeople with a desire to succeed who shared the same level of product knowledge and completed the same training program. Yet each of them performed very differently based on their belief around what to expect regarding their career as well as their level of productivity.

Once again, "How you think is what you get."

What Are You Thinking?

As we've discussed, what you believe is what you will manifest in your life. More specifically, what you believe to be true about cold calling is exactly what you will continue to experience in your career.

The bottom line is, if you can change your thinking to a more positive model you will then produce the results you really want with much less of an effort.

Conversely, there is a downside. If you continually focus on what you *don't* want, then what you don't want will also show up in your life.

Think about where your focus is and where you direct your thoughts and energy. In other words, do you focus on what you don't want to happen or what you want to avoid? Or, do you focus on the results that you do want to create?

The fact is, most of us focus more on what we don't want to happen rather than what we do want. When I coach people and ask them to describe their ideal life or career, most often they'll start telling me what they don't want.

For example, "I don't want a stressful job, I don't want to waste my money, I don't want to be in a toxic relationship, I don't want a boss who's going to micromanage me, I don't want problem customers, and so on."

Refer back to the responses in the section, "Cold Calling Isn't a Dirty Word," regarding salespeople's feelings or attitude toward cold calling. You'll notice that the statements in this list are either a negative assumption of what would happen or something they don't want to happen, all of which are based in fear.

Salespeople have a tendency to exploit all of the reasons why they don't like cold calling or why they won't succeed at cold calling. However, have you ever taken the time to develop the reasons why you *will* succeed? We explored this in Chapter 2 and will do so in more detail shortly.

To make this real for you, if you believe that cold calling is, "Forcing someone to accept something they don't want, intrusive, annoying, manipulative, a waste of time, intimidating, scary, something I hate being subjected to myself, and so on," that's exactly what you'll continue to experience every time you cold call.

If you believe that all prospects are a certain way (uninterested, shoppers, rude, are only concerned with price) then how do you think you are going to approach cold calling and deliver your presentation, whether you realize it or not?

Think about the type of prospect that you are going to be attracting and the kind of objections you'll be hearing. Based on your current assumptions surrounding cold calling, prospects, and selling, every new experience will now become a self-fulfilling prophecy.

The Joy of Cold Calling

To combat this, consider challenging these assumptions and replacing them with healthier ones that would better serve you. For example, I love to cold call because …

- ◆ Cold calling is informative. It lets the prospect know where they can locate the best product/service they need.

- ◆ Cold calling is beneficial. I can share all the incredible advantages of my product/service with the people who can benefit from it most.

- ◆ Cold calling is a way to genuinely deliver value, educate my prospects, serve people, and improve people's lives, regardless of whether I make the sale.

- ◆ Cold calling enables me to become a prospect's trusted expert or advisor so that they can make the best purchasing decision.

- ◆ Cold calling is a way to prevent people from making potentially costly mistakes that result from purchasing the wrong product/ service or using a company that may not effectively fill their needs.

- ◆ Cold calling makes it possible to earn the business of more prospects who I wouldn't have the opportunity to connect with otherwise. The more I cold call, the more I sell. The more I sell, the more happy customers I have.

Create a few healthy assumptions of your own!

- ◆ _____

- ◆ _____

- ◆ _____

When working with different sales teams, I always find it interesting that some salespeople attract the difficult customers. They then find themselves in a position where they have to negotiate price, have more cancellations or returns, or have to deal with prospects that want to review three separate proposals before making a purchasing decision.

Conversely, there are other salespeople who seem to effortlessly generate the best leads and get the desirable, loyal customers and repeat business.

This is not a coincidence. At some point, you need to ask yourself, "What role is my attitude playing in this? How is my thinking affecting my performance?" Once you can identify your current limiting beliefs surrounding cold calling, I'm sure you will see the answers to these questions staring you in the face.

How you think about cold calling and your prospects is a prime example of how a salesperson can actually create an objection or remain stuck at a certain level of performance.

CAUTION

Cold Calling Conundrum _____

Salespeople wear their emotions on their sleeve. As such, your prospects will sense your reluctance or fear. A prospect wants to do business with a salesperson who's excited about what they have, not someone who is struggling to promote their product or service. Rather than a sign of conviction, this can be construed as a sign of doubt or uncertainty. If you're not convinced that what you have to offer is important enough to make a call, then how can you expect your prospects to be? This will sabotage your cold calling efforts, cultivating an unhealthy relationship from the start.

What a Fabulous View!

One of Sam Walton's business commandments is, "Avoid conventional wisdom." In order to make a profound difference in your performance, you must upgrade or shift your attitude around how you perceive cold calling, your prospects, and yourself.

I'm not simply talking about putting on an inauthentic smile before you cold call or walk into a meeting with a prospect because if your thinking or your attitude is not aligned with your strategy or intention, you will come across as inauthentic. It would be the equivalent of telling a salesperson to sell a product they don't believe in.

A shift in your attitude is different from a change in your behavior. It's about changing how you think and how you approach cold calling, not simply changing what you do. The real benefit is when you change your thinking first, the byproduct is then a change in behavior and is likely to continue effortlessly. If we were to chart this progression, it would look something like this.

> Uncover Your Mental Operating System/Beliefs → Upgrade Your Attitude → Take Specific and Measurable Actions → Attract the Right Prospects → Produce the Desired, Specific, and Measurable Results → Great Lifestyle and Extraordinary Performance

Consistent, healthier thinking leads to consistent, more effective action which in turn will yield the results you want. Following this model is a surefire way for you to become fearless when it comes to prospecting.

You Look Marvelous!

Imagine that we all have a certain set of lenses we're looking through that give us what we see when it comes to cold calling, our career, and our life. Some are green, yellow, or red. Changing your thinking requires taking off your lenses and trying on a new pair.

What will limit your ability to create a more appealing view, a healthier attitude, and greater selling opportunities will be the limiting thinking you have about cold calling or the old programming and assumptions that you are still carrying around.

To become someone who is incredibly successful at cold calling, it's important to embrace that some of your beliefs or programming might not work for you anymore.

Cold Medicine

The next chapter, "Thinking Like a Top Producer," will provide you with more specific examples of how you can upgrade your thinking so that you can achieve peak performance.

Therefore, it's up to you to challenge your limiting beliefs and replace them with healthier ones that would better serve you.

In the following chapter, we're going to explore the top four critical mind-sets that all top producers share. This will provide you with the structure and foundation you can then build on to become a top producer and make your prospecting efforts become effortless.

The Least You Need to Know

◆ If you want to become a top producer, start thinking like one. You have the power to choose how you think.

◆ The relationship you have with each prospect is established *before* you begin prospecting.

◆ Prior to cold calling, focus on the reasons why you love to cold call and the benefits your prospects can realize.

◆ Direct your thoughts toward what you want to create (pleasure), rather than what you want to avoid (fear, pain, or consequence).

◆ Rather than exploit all of the reasons why you won't succeed at prospecting, develop the reasons why you *will!*

◆ Changing your perception or beliefs empowers you to tap into the greatest freedom you have: your freedom of choice.

Chapter 4

Thinking Like a Top Producer

In This Chapter

- ◆ Learn how to think like a top producer
- ◆ Connect with your prospects on a deeper level
- ◆ Remove the pressures that cause cold calling paralysis
- ◆ Uncover the primary objective of cold calling
- ◆ Harness the power of positive thinking
- ◆ Become resilient and handle rejection like a pro

When you think about laying a foundation, a house or a building may come to mind. And with any building, the taller the building, the deeper the foundation needs to be. Reason being: If the foundation of a building is weak then it won't be able to support what is built on top of it. The result? The building will crumble.

The same holds true for the line of thinking surrounding cold calling, which encompasses the structural integrity of your cold calling efforts. If you don't have the right mind-set for the cold calling process, you're setting yourself up for failure.

This chapter will identify the most common misconceptions around cold calling and how you can avoid them. This way, you can develop a strong foundation for cold calling success, providing you with the opportunity to learn how to think like a top producer.

Change Your Mind

We've all changed our mind at one point or another regarding how we feel about someone, something, or an experience we've had. Depending on the complexity of the situation, there's a good chance that you change your mind on a daily basis regarding certain preferences, such as favorite food, color, store, restaurant, leisurely pastime, TV show, hobby, sport, activities, experiences, and even certain people.

You may have changed your mind regarding a certain experience you had. For example, Mary, a client of mine, shared an experience she had regarding a sales call she went on. When Mary left the meeting with a prospect, she called me sounding very upset. After presenting her product to this prospect and following up with them a week later, the prospect decided to use another vendor. She felt frustrated, upset, and dejected. She was ready to leave her sales position, feeling as if she failed and this wasn't the career for her.

After talking with her about this sales call in more detail, it sounded as if there were some holes in Mary's selling strategy that may have cost her the sale. I suggested that she look at this experience not as a failure but as an opportunity to learn and grow. As such, she changed her outlook. Mary felt better using this experience as an opportunity for continuous improvement. Together, we identified the areas that needed refinement and changed her approach when presenting to a prospect.

As a result of what she had learned, she became the number one salesperson in her company. Now, Mary knows there is no such thing as failure, only unexpected results that you can then learn from. The only way Mary can fail is if she doesn't embrace the lesson.

I remember hearing all the hype about a new television show. The reviews sounded interesting and I was willing to give it a shot. After about ten minutes of watching this particular show (a sitcom), I decided it wasn't for me. A month later, all of my friends were hooked on this show. According to them, I had to give it another chance. "It will grow on you," they said. They were right! After watching a few episodes, I was hooked.

If you look at this experience, did the program change? Not at all. What changed was my opinion and how I perceived the show. In essence, I changed my mind.

The first question my clients ask when we discuss certain *mindshifts* is, "How do I do it? How do I change my thinking?"

When it comes to *doing* something differently, such as trying a new selling approach, strategy, tool, or even using a new piece of equipment at the gym, it's more tangible and easier to envision the steps that need to be taken.

Yet, when it comes to changing your mind, you may feel that it's hard to wrap your hands around how to do this. As such there's a tendency for

Cold Callingo

Mindshift is the action of identifying a limiting belief, thought, perception, or assumption and changing or shifting that belief and how you think in a way that would accelerate your success, support your goals, and move you forward. The benefit is when you change your thinking first, the byproduct is a change in behavior that is likely to continue effortlessly.

people to be more reluctant to do so. After all, there's no action to take, no steps to follow, nothing to physically *do*. It's more a function of how you feel. If you feel happier, less stressed, and more focused, confident, motivated, and relaxed when engaging in your prospecting campaign, think about what that would be worth to you. Imagine how much more effective you would be if you felt this way when prospecting and how many more sales this would equate to at the end of the day.

As you read these essential mindshifts for cold calling success, consider that changing your mind-set is just like changing the channel on your television. Now, get ready to change some of the channels in your mind so that you can tune in to a healthy prospecting mind-set!

Make 'Em Human

Many salespeople who call on business owners, top level executives, or CEOs share a similar perception about the person they are trying to connect with.

Salespeople who cold call via the phone have a tendency to put the person they are attempting to speak with on a pedestal. That is, by assigning so much weight and importance to their position or title, salespeople psych themselves out by making the prospect larger than life or untouchable.

This leads to a feeling of intimidation and discomfort when attempting to call on these "higher level" people. Thinking about their status, the salesperson has tendency to feel, "How can I, a salesperson, call on a CEO (CFO, business owner, exec.)?" They are too busy and have much more important things to do than speak with me. They're not going to want to waste their time talking to me."

> **Cold Medicine**
>
> Instead of making the prospect untouchable, make them human. This will even the playing field when calling on prospects you consider to be at a different level than you. Now, rather than feeling intimidated when calling on them, you can connect with them. Prospects are people too!

Let's now consider that these people hold other positions as well. They are not only a top officer. They are a PTA member, golfer, sport enthusiast, cook, friend, soccer coach, and parent. Being a top officer is just one of the roles they play in their life.

What does your internal dialogue sound like when thinking about these prospects?

- ◆ They're successful in business.
- ◆ They're older than me.
- ◆ They make much more money than I do.
- ◆ They have a huge responsibility.
- ◆ They're always in the news. (A celebrity-like status.)

- They'll only speak to people that are more senior than me.

- They won't take the time to speak with me.

- They don't need what I'm selling.

And so your prospecting efforts are thwarted even before you pick up the phone due to the list of predetermined reasons you've created and assumptions you've made. The belief then becomes, "I don't feel that I'm on the same level and therefore can't relate or connect with them." Talk about a belief that will limit your success at prospecting!

If you approach the call with the attitude, "I'm not important or what I have is not important," it will come across in your delivery. Your thinking is giving them too much power, which is based on their perceived status or title alone.

I can assure you, there's no secret society of CEOs or top officers who do entirely different things during their work or leisure time.

To overcome this reluctance around calling on the top officers, change your perception. This way of thinking isn't serving you or your cold calling efforts. Because they are human, humanize them. They have families, they do barbeques in the summertime, they go to their kids' birthday parties and baseball games, they take walks in the park, they go out to the local restaurants, and they even go to the doctor when they're sick. (Their blood is the same color as ours, too.) They are just like the rest of us mere mortals!

Instead of comparing yourself to their perceived status, even the playing field by making them human. Stop comparing yourself to them in terms of why you are different and start thinking about what you are offering, a relevant and an important product or service that would contribute to their success.

Once you embrace the belief that you and your prospects are all on the same level and running the same race (the human race), your confidence will skyrocket. You will be able to call on them without passing judgment on their status and without the feeling of intimidation. This way, you (and the phone) will feel lighter when calling on them.

It Ain't About You

On a very basic level, there are five ingredients needed to create a sale:

1. The salesperson.

2. The qualified prospect.

3. A need or want that the prospect has.

4. The product or service.

5. The selling strategy or procedure you follow that guides a prospect to the natural conclusion of the selling process, the sale.

While many salespeople would say the selling process is about the customer, they wind up making it about themselves.

How do I know this? Look at some of the limiting beliefs that contribute to cold calling reluctance that we mentioned earlier.

Think about all the fears or reluctance you may experience when it comes to cold calling or selling.

- I don't want to say the wrong thing.

- I don't want to look bad.

- I don't want to be a nuisance.

- I don't want to impose.

- I don't want to be rejected or hear "No."

- I don't want to blow it!

I, I, I, I, I!

Look at the first word that begins each preceding statement. Making the selling and cold calling process about you is the number-one roadblock to successful prospecting and the number-one cause of cold calling reluctance.

If you are experiencing any fear or resistance to prospecting, look at who you're making the selling process about. Chances are, you're making it about you!

Once you shift your focus and energy toward making it about the prospect, it will immediately relieve you of the unnecessary pressure to look good and perform.

Notice how the upgraded beliefs around cold calling that we discussed in "The Joy of Cold Calling" section in Chapter 3 make the process less about the salesperson and more about the prospect.

In other words, you're either making the selling process about you and how much you can gain (money, sales, status, and so on), your fear of rejection, looking bad, or hearing "No," or you're making it about the prospect and how much value you can deliver to them. Now, the cold calling process is no longer focused on the salesperson's negative assumptions or fears but on the prospect and the advantages that your product can provide them.

After all, if you are making the sale about you and are concerned about your performance, then how are you ever going to capture their interest when all of your energy, concentration, and attention is being directed on to you rather than focused on the prospect?

Make the selling process about the prospect and the value you can deliver rather than what you can gain if you sell. Once you do so, the sale then becomes the natural byproduct of your selfless efforts and good intentions.

And the Goal of Prospecting Is ...

Think about the intention or the end result of your prospecting efforts. It's probably not what you think. Let's refer back to the definition of prospecting that I shared with you in Chapter 1: "Prospecting is defined as any activity or conversation you engage in to position yourself in front of a prospect with the intention to inquire, assess, discover, and educate so that you can determine whether there's a fit and a relationship that's worth pursuing which can then lead to presenting your product or service in order to earn your prospect's business."

Cold Medicine

Instead of focusing on making the sale, first determine if there's a good fit that is worth pursuing between you, your prospect, and what you are selling.

Instead of feeling that the intention of prospecting is to get a sale, provide a demonstration, submit a proposal, or schedule an appointment, the initial intention of prospecting is to determine if there's a fit worth pursuing.

While this may sound a bit strange, closing the sale and earning the business of a prospect is not your initial goal. Instead, your primary objective is to determine whether you and your prospect are a good fit.

Take a moment and think about how this change in your attitude and mind-set would change your cold calling approach as well as your experience.

While your traditional approach may be to produce a measurable result, now your primary objective is to discover whether you and your prospect are a good match and if this relationship is worth moving to the next stage of your selling process. If you feel that you constantly have to push the sales process forward, you're not taking into consideration that the prospect may simply not be ready, let alone may not be a good fit for what you are selling. Pushing the sales process forward before a prospect is ready only creates pressure for the both of you, fostering an unhealthy relationship from the start. Therefore, instead of asking yourself, "How can I sell this person?" change this question to, "Do I even want this prospect as a customer?"

Notice that the second question shifts the balance of power back to you. Now, you're the one making the choice about pursuing the relationship rather than surrendering all of the decision-making power to the prospect regarding whether or not they will buy from you, let alone listen to you!

Notice how this shift in your mind-set will also change your approach. Instead of feeling as if you have to convince or push the prospect into the sale (appointment, demo, proposal) by regurgitating your pitch all over them, now you're going to want to learn and gather as much information you can about this particular prospect.

How do you determine if there's a fit worth pursuing? Typically, you would conduct a process of inquiry or an investigation. Woven into the fabric of any investigation are questions. (We will explore how to craft the right questions during a needs analysis and weave them into a cold calling conversation in the chapters that follow.) Instead of the prospect interviewing or qualifying you, this brings new meaning to the phrase, "Qualify your prospects!" Now, you're the one doing the qualifying.

Shopping for Customers

Here's an interesting comparison. Cold calling is a lot like shopping. When you go shopping, you're in complete control. You decide what you are going to purchase and when you are going to make that purchase. If you are shopping for a pair of shoes, you try them on and possibly ask the salesperson some questions about the product. That's your analysis. If you like them and they fit comfortably, you purchase them. If not, they go back on the rack. Consider cold calling to be the same. You're just shopping for the right prospects. If there's not a fit, you move on to more promising ones.

When your intention is no longer about making the sale, it takes the pressure of having to sell off your shoulders. Therefore, prospect initially to see if there's a match between what you have to offer and the unique needs of each prospect. Ask more questions to determine if you want them as a customer and whether or not you can truly help them. Otherwise you're adding to the pressure of booking an appointment with someone who may not be ready or may not be the best prospect for you to invest all of your time in. This becomes a great way to prioritize and qualify your prospects.

> **Warm Wisdom**
>
> If you are focused solely on making a pitch or are pushing for the appointment or the sale rather than conducting a process of inquiry, then consider whom you're making the sales process about. And that would be you!

To eliminate your resistance to generating new business via cold calling, the next time you prospect complete this exercise beforehand. Determine the top five or ten things that you would need to know about this prospect that would enable you to determine whether or not there's a fit worth pursuing. Once you've created this list, create a question around each determining factor. This will assist you in crafting the right questions that need to be asked when speaking with the prospect. (If you find this exercise to be a bit of a challenge, that's okay. We will be discussing how to craft the right questions in Chapter 10.)

You'll notice that this shift in your mind-set will produce the outcome you want with less effort, attracting new customers toward you without having to push. Now you can enjoy shopping for those new clients.

Create Possibilities, Not Expectations

I remember talking with one of my clients. His name was John and he was a great salesperson. After working with John for a few months, I noticed that his mood or state of mind fluctuated during each meeting I had with him.

It seemed that, like many salespeople, John was allowing himself to be a victim of circumstance. He set high goals and expected nothing but exemplary performance from himself. When he experienced success from his prospecting efforts, he was in a great mood. However, on the days that he felt he wasn't producing up to his expectations, he really took it to heart and it threw him right into a bad mood. Feelings of disappointment, anxiety, and frustration overcame him. This lasted until he had another productive day cold calling. John was allowing external situations, more specifically, his daily productivity to influence or dictate his internal condition or attitude, swinging the "mood" pendulum from one extreme to another.

 **Cold Medicine**

Instead of being hooked on one desired outcome when prospecting, continually create new possibilities in the moment that would also lead to a sale.

It's one thing to experience good days and bad days. We all have them. However, it's another thing to allow your prospecting efforts to dictate whether or not you're going to be smiling at the end of the day. After coaching him around this, we soon realized that he had some unrealistic expectations regarding his performance.

I explained to John that it was wonderful to have a very clear vision of what he was trying to achieve. After all, defining your goals is a great exercise, one that I certainly endorse. However, when your goals begin to consume you and diminish the quality of your life, it's time to re-evaluate your strategy.

I then suggested to him, instead of being hooked on the *expectation* of having to generate the result he was seeking during every cold call, what if it was only a *possibility* that he would generate the desired result? I saw the confusion in his face. I then shared with John the distinction between a possibility and an expectation.

A possibility is something that may exist or what could happen, where an expectation is a hope or an attachment to a specific outcome. A subtle, yet powerful distinction. When you are open to possibility, you are inspired to innovate and create something new while being present in a conversation or with the activity you are engaged in. You feel a sense of choice in the pursuit of your goal. In other words, you can either be gripped with a certain expectation about something, in this case having to sell, or you can simply enjoy the possibility of creating a relationship with that prospect, determining whether there's a fit and providing value to them, without being attached to whether or not you will sell.

Some people have an attachment to certain outcomes during a conversation. They are so focused on having the other person see their point of view or attached to creating a specific result that they miss out on the ability to create a new and better outcome simply by listening openly to what the other person was actually saying.

Sometimes we get so attached to having others see our point of view that we exhaust all our energy just to prove a point. We might do this with our prospects, co-workers, boss, family, or friends. The problem is, if you are so attached to your own agenda inside a conversation then how can a new or better possibility ever surface? How can you listen to your prospect's wants and needs or create solutions to their initial concerns that might get in the way of the sale? It just can't happen.

A congested mind does not allow for the space to create the best solutions for your prospects during a cold call. Consider for a moment that the person you are speaking with may have a better solution or voice an initial objection, yet you can't hear it because of your attachment to the outcome.

Think about the sales you have made in your career. Picture your state of mind at the time. Were you relaxed, centered, and connected with your prospects or were you concerned, anxious, and biting at the bit while calculating how much money you would make if you sold?

Most salespeople are more inclined to generate the desired result they seek during a cold call when they aren't concerned about whether or not they will sell. And this feeling, according to them, usually surfaces right after they had a successful cold call or reached their monthly sales quota. In other words, these salespeople weren't attached to the expectation of having to sell the client because it was no longer a "have to" for them. Because they already reached their daily or monthly goal, in their mind the rest was gravy. The pressure to produce was lifted from their shoulders and they had nothing left to lose.

Many of us suffer from unfulfilled expectations. If you are attached to the expectation of having to generate certain results when cold calling and you don't produce them, think about how you feel. Lousy, discouraged, frustrated, dejected, upset, maybe even a bit drained. Not only can this destroy your productivity for the remainder of your day, but you're also less likely to want to engage in this activity again or call on other people. Setting yourself up to have unfulfilled expectations is a formula that continually reinforces negative feelings, which creates negative experiences.

Now, imagine what would be possible if you believed that every conversation you had with a prospect provided you with the *possibility* to earn their business. This way, if you don't generate your desired result, then the possibility is still just a possibility!

When something is possible for you, the process is actually enjoyable. After all, if you're going to cold call, you might as well enjoy the process. The alternative is being let down or crushed from having unfulfilled expectations.

Consider this truth. What if a surgeon in the ER expected to save every life that he operated on? Chances are, this person wouldn't be a surgeon for long, even with the best of intentions.

> **Warm Wisdom**
>
> A possibility that goes unfulfilled is still a possibility. An expectation that goes unfulfilled is a disappointment.

You know it's a possibility when you're having fun and you can't lose. It's an expectation when you are upset if it doesn't work out. As such, there's much more flexibility with possibility, where expectations are typically rigid and one-dimensional.

Detach from the Outcome

If you were ever in a situation where you've walked away from a cold calling conversation feeling drained or exhausted, chances are there was something you were attached to in the conversation. Were you attempting to control the outcome?

When cold calling, here are some attachments to be aware of that can grip you and limit your potential:

- The need to be right or look good.

- The need to make the sale (appointment, demo, proposal).

- The need to be understood or prove your point.

- The need to have people agree with you.

- The avoidance of being wrong, looking bad, and hearing "No."

If you find that you are repeating yourself, pushing to get someone to see it your way, or creating evidence to strengthen your side, you may be caught up in the ego of the situation. The conversation then turns into a struggle for power and control. When prospecting, who do you think is going to win that battle most of the time? The prospect.

Being attached to the outcome during a prospecting conversation …

1. Limits the ability to recognize or create a new or better possibility, solution, or outcome and respond to an initial objection in a healthy way.

2. Creates a barrier in your listening that prevents others from contributing to you, which diminishes your ability to learn and grow.

3. Invalidates the other person by not respecting their feelings or point of view.

4. Prevents you from adjusting your prospecting approach or strategy so that it is more aligned with that particular prospect and the way they buy. (If you were the pitcher on a baseball team, you wouldn't throw the same type of pitch each time to every player,

especially if that particular pitch wasn't working. Depending on the player, you would alter the type of pitch you throw.)

5. Inhibits your flexibility and adaptability.

Focus on the Present

In order to let go of your expectations or attachments during the cold calling process, focus on the present.

Consider the three points in time; the past, present, and the future. Sure we live in the present, but is that where you are truly living and responding to moment-to-moment? Consider that almost 85 percent of your time is spent either living in the past or in the future. (For example, reacting from a past experience or an expectation of the future.) Where is the focus of your energy and thoughts?

If you are living in or reacting from the past, that would sound like …

- ◆ "If only I (woulda, coulda, shoulda) … I would be much happier/successful today."

- ◆ "I should have done that years ago because I would have reached my financial goal by now."

- ◆ "I remember the last time something like this occurred. I'm sure it will happen again."

These examples illustrate how you are responding to and "living in the past."

If you are living in or reacting to the expectations of the future, that would sound like:

- ◆ When I (once I, if only I) buy a house (make more money, find my spouse, lose ten pounds, discover my ideal career, become a master at cold calling) then I will be truly happy and fulfilled.

If you are hooked on the future, then you are attempting to get somewhere other than where you are now. Where you are today and what you've achieved thus far doesn't seem to be enough for you or provide you with a sense of satisfaction or accomplishment. As such, you're attached to an end result that hasn't happened yet.

We often live, listen, and react from the past or are pushing for something to happen in the future. Top producers respond to and are fully living in the present. To be fully present means you are able to focus on a single person, idea, or topic. It means not having any preoccupations with the past or future. The past is gone, and unless you have a crystal ball you have no control over the future.

Expectations are based in the point of time we refer to as the future. Possibilities are happening at any moment in the present. Look at a possibility as a choice where an expectation is a rigid need that must be met in order for you to feel fulfilled and complete.

Jim was a client of mine who believed that he did not think well on his feet. Jim felt that he wasn't able to respond quickly or intelligently to certain objections or concerns that his prospects presented to him. Interestingly, Jim informed me that this only occurred in a selling situation. During other conversations, Jim stated this was never an issue.

What was it that made Jim freeze in a cold calling conversation but act quick-witted and engaging during normal conversation? As we explored this phenomenon in more depth, the reason became evident.

I asked him, "When you engage in daily conversation, is there some specific result that you are trying to achieve in each conversation?" "Not really," Jim replied. He then added, "If anything, I certainly like to help people."

"How about when you are cold calling?" I then asked. "Most definitely! I need to sell." Jim declared.

Jim had an attachment to the outcome. His focus and intentions changed depending on the type of conversation and whom he was speaking with. When cold calling, Jim was attempting to have a conversation with his focus on a future outcome (the sale), while his prospects were speaking to him in the present moment. Jim was unable to create new solutions or respond effectively to his prospects' concerns because his mind's eye was focused more on what he wanted to happen rather than what was occurring in the moment.

Being fully present takes practice, effort, focus, and a willingness to exclude all that is not directly relevant to what you are currently engaged in, especially while speaking with someone. Living in, responding to, and thinking in the moment is both healthy and more productive. If you can practice this, the quality of your communication as well as your cold calling efforts will greatly increase.

Here's a key point. An attachment is never about what is happening in the present. If you're hooked on a future, anticipated result, you can't create any new possibilities in the moment, because creation only occurs in the present. Any attachment is based in the future or the past, with the focus on a specific expectation or result that you are trying to achieve.

Cold Calling Conundrum

What *was* and what *will* be never take precedent over what *is*.

Ask yourself, "Am I responding to and living in the present?" (During a conversation, am I focused on an anticipated future outcome or stuck in the past with regrets, beliefs, or events that are really not relevant to creating something new in the present?)

Once you open up your thinking and detach yourself from the outcome during your cold calling efforts or a conversation with a prospect ...

- ◆ You will notice your energy level will naturally increase.

- ◆ You will experience less stress.

- ◆ You will uncover new and greater possibilities, solutions, and selling opportunities naturally that you would otherwise miss without having to push for them.

Detaching from the outcome frees you to embrace the truth in any situation in order to create new opportunities in the moment rather than being hooked on what you really want, what you think you want or need, or what you expect to happen.

To drive this point home, detach from the outcome so you can continually invent new possibilities that will enable you to connect with each prospect effortlessly.

Opposites Attract

We've now discussed the essential mindshifts as well as the paradoxes of prospecting that make prospecting so challenging.

◆ You want the sale (appointment, demo) but you must detach from the outcome and have no expectation, because the sale is not the initial goal of prospecting.

◆ You want the prospect to say "Yes" to taking the next step in your sales process but you have to qualify them first to see if there's even a fit worth pursuing.

◆ You want the prospect to buy from you but must learn to give value unconditionally, whether or not they buy or meet with you.

◆ You want to deliver and push through your presentation but you must get the prospect's permission even before you present.

◆ You need to keep your eye on your objective, set your goals, and plan your strategy for the future to determine the path to travel on but you must bring yourself back into the present moment during every prospecting conversation.

◆ You want to make more money and achieve greater success in your career but you have to make the sales process about the prospect, instead of you, in order to do so.

◆ You want to sell to each prospect you speak with but need to qualify *them* to see if you even want them as a customer.

Let's face it. You and I both know that the ultimate objective of your prospecting efforts is to sell more and boost your income. However, to achieve this goal, it's just not where you are going to focus your energy and thoughts.

If you can understand and embrace these paradoxes you now have the opportunity to respond to each prospect in a healthier, more productive, and more enjoyable way.

Realize that when you cold call, one of your objectives is to open up your prospect's thinking to the possibility of working with you in order to provide them with a better solution or eliminate a recurring problem.

As such, if you are attempting to change the perception or mind-set of your prospects, whose mind-set do you think needs to be changed first? Yours, of course!

 Cold Calling Conundrum _____

> When your car doesn't start, you may need to lift the hood to iden-tify the problem and see what's going on. To become someone who is incredibly successful at cold calling, it's essential that you analyze your internal operating system or the attitude you currently have toward cold calling. Realize that you can change what you do and how you do it all day long. However, if you don't upgrade your attitude, then all of the sales tools in the world are not going to help.

Remember, your life and the successes you've experienced thus far are the result of your attitude and the choices you have made in the past. Your life and your successes tomorrow will be the result of your attitude and the choices you make today.

What you tell your brain is what it will believe to be true. Therefore, it comes down to making a conscious choice to make a change in your thinking. When you exercise your power of choice and choose to up-grade your current beliefs in a way that serves you and your prospects, you'll discover a permanent solution to eliminating any cold calling reluctance while accelerating your cold calling success. Hey, you might even enjoy it!

At this point, I hope you are feeling a bit lighter when it comes to cold calling, because you can now eliminate many of the misconceptions about prospecting that weigh you down and cause cold calling paralysis. Please realize that I'm not saying this process is going to be easy, let alone happen overnight. After all, if it were easy then everyone, includ-ing your competition, would be doing it. (What a great way to develop an immediate edge over your competitors!) So if you don't get this les-son completely that's perfectly natural. After all, you've been married to your current attitude for a while now (your whole life). Take the time to read this chapter (as well as Chapters 1, 2 and 3) over until you feel that you've gotten it to the point that this new way of thinking is now part of your anatomy and mind-set.

For now, just being aware of these mindshifts and bringing them to your conscious attention moves you toward the understanding that you can, in fact, upgrade your attitude. Doing so creates awareness. And awareness then creates choice.

When I introduce this topic in a training program I never say that top producers have a healthy attitude. What I do say is that they create a healthy attitude. "Having" a healthy attitude doesn't indicate your ability to choose, where "creating" a healthy attitude indicates that you are at choice to design your career and manage your mind-set the way you really want to.

When you detach yourself from your habitual thinking and transcend your current beliefs, only then can you realize your fullest potential.

Here's your chance to begin the process of upgrading your attitude, which is the first step toward maximizing your cold calling efforts.

The Least You Need to Know

- ◆ Challenge your current limiting perceptions regarding cold calling and replace them with a healthier belief system.

- ◆ Make the selling process about the prospect and the value you can deliver rather than what you can gain if you sell.

- ◆ The initial intention of prospecting is to determine if there's a fit worth pursuing.

- ◆ Detach from the outcome to respond effectively to each prospect and eliminate the chance of unfulfilled expectations.

- ◆ Put the power in your court by asking yourself, "Do I even want this prospect as a customer?"

- ◆ Be present, because the creation of new possibilities only occurs in the moment and not in the past or in the future.

Part 2

Building Your Expressway to New Business

The "natural" salesperson may be born, but they still have to learn how to walk first. While some people may have a natural predisposition or posses certain characteristics that would lead them to a career in sales, to achieve superstar status, these salespeople must still develop and refine their skills. After all, the training and planning for the race always takes longer than the race itself. The same holds true for attaining the level of productivity and success you are looking for.

Chapter 5

Why Should I Talk to You?

In This Chapter

- ◆ Discover what it is you are actually selling
- ◆ Determine why your prospects should listen to you
- ◆ Capture a prospect's attention in 30 seconds
- ◆ Add some pizzazz to what you are selling
- ◆ Get prospects excited to speak with you

Do you know exactly what to say to a prospect that captures their attention so succinctly and effectively that they are actually asking for more? If you are being honest with yourself, it's probably the same answer I hear from most people regardless of age, industry, or experience and that is, "No."

Then how can you expect to uncover more prospects, let alone convert these prospects into customers? How can you cold call or prospect effortlessly? How can you deliver a stimulating, thought-provoking and valuable presentation?

If you are attempting to prospect without sharing the right reasons as to why a prospect needs to listen to you, then it's no wonder you are finding prospecting to be such a challenging and frustrating experience.

What are the "right reasons"? Probably the reasons that are several layers deeper than the reasons you are currently using. That's what makes this process so challenging. Once salespeople feel they have a "good enough" reason, they stop. It's like quitting the race 20 steps before the finish line. With today's competitive climate, "good enough" is what will keep you one step behind or head-to-head with your competition, rather than using this as an opportunity to develop a clear competitive edge.

If you find that you are not even getting past the first 30 seconds of an initial prospecting conversation before the prospect cuts you off and says, "Not interested," then it's safe to say that the reasons you are currently using can withstand an upgrade. Use the techniques outlined in this chapter to do so.

Develop the Hot Button That Stimulates Interest

One of the first questions you may ask before you embark on your cold calling initiative is, "How can I get a prospect interested enough to want to listen to me, let alone do business with me?"

The answer is simple: give them a *compelling reason* to listen to you. The word compelling is synonymous with "convincing, persuasive, undeniable, and gripping." When cold calling or networking, are you providing your prospects with enough of a compelling reason during the first minute of your conversation to want to speak with you and learn more about your product or service?

> **Cold Callingo**
>
> A **compelling reason** is a unique, concise, and powerful statement that can include a measurable result a prospect can expect, a personal benefit a prospect can realize, or a problem in your prospect's experience that you can solve. The objective of a compelling reason is to stimulate the prospect's interest enough to want to hear more about what you have to offer.

The intention of a compelling reason is to stimulate interest and open a conversation. Therefore, you certainly don't want to sound like all the other salespeople who are calling on the same prospects and saying the exact same thing.

Compelling reasons are the secret ingredient that many salespeople know about but don't take the time to refine and develop. If your reasons are not powerful enough to move someone from a state of inertia to interest or action, here's your opportunity to give them an overhaul.

What Do You Think You're Selling?

What is it that you are *actually* selling? Some professionals believe that their title alone conveys an accurate portrayal of the product or service they offer. According to this philosophy, the title of account executive, attorney, CPA, programmer, web developer, graphic artist, insurance agent, or consultant would be enough to educate a prospect regarding the type of service they offer.

Other professionals feel that merely stating the type of product or service they provide is actually what they are selling. If you're selling IT solutions, insurance, advertising, marketing services, web design, training, financial or legal services, staffing, consumer goods (clothes, jewelry, make up, etc.), office supplies, furniture, remodeling, software, commercial real estate, computers, or widgets, consider that your prospect isn't interested in the actual product, but *what it will ultimately do for them.*

If you think that simply telling a prospect what it is you sell is enough to stimulate interest, think again.

Crafting Your Compelling Reasons for Selling Success

If you are trying to grab a prospect's attention, your compelling reasons will *not* include …

1. Your product or service.

2. Features of your product or service.

3. Strategies on how to achieve the desired end result (the "how").

4. Unsubstantiated or lofty claims and guarantees.

You may be asking, "Keith, what *does* it include?"

Whether you're trying to craft a laser introduction (Chapter 15) for a networking event, a follow-up call, a voice mail, a presentation, or a cold calling approach when speaking to new prospects, the next sections introduce you to some guidelines to follow as we discuss the anatomy of a compelling reason.

Include the End Result of the Benefit

Your compelling reasons should include the benefit of the benefit's benefit.

Sound extreme, maybe even a bit silly? Let's check. You know you have a great compelling reason when you are able to break it down to its core or the specific result that the prospect will be able to take advantage of and most importantly, visualize and connect with.

Consider this statistic. Based on a sample group of clients that I have surveyed over the years, 14 percent of people made a purchasing decision based on prior knowledge and experience. And 86 percent of people made a purchasing decision based on a future expectation.

Imagine that your prospects secretly want you to be able to offer them something that will make them more successful while making their life easier. Because most people buy based on a future expectation, your prospects will be more inclined to listen to what you have to say if you have an end result they want.

When making an initial cold call, you have seconds to grab the attention of the person you are calling on. Therefore, you simply don't have the time to explain how you are going to achieve the end result of the benefit, let alone the product or service that will enable you to do so. You'll have the opportunity to discuss your product or the strategy to achieve the desired result later on in your sales process *after* you've set an appointment or confirmed interest.

Pass the "So What?" Test

You know you have the end result of the benefit when the statement can pass the "so what?" test.

For example, Jill, one of my clients, sells insurance and financial services. When I asked her to list the benefits of her service, she responded with the following statement: "We have an online reporting system that automates your administrative duties." My response: "So what?"

According to old-school feature and benefit selling, this is a fit. After all, an online reporting system is a great feature that her clients would benefit from. However, in today's economic climate it's no longer enough to evoke interest, let alone action, from a prospect. Because her statement did not pass the "so what?" test, we need to go a bit deeper.

The benefit Jill shared with me was, "Automates your administrative duties." Well, we're getting closer but this still doesn't pass the "so what?" test. Let's peel away a few more layers to uncover the end result of this benefit. While we're doing so, notice the questions I ask Jill and the process she goes through to finally uncover a true compelling reason, because this is a process that you will have to walk yourself through as well.

I asked Jill to tell me what the advantage was to automating administrative duties. She told me that by doing so, her clients can streamline their operations. I challenged her again by asking her to share with me what the end result would be if her clients were able to streamline their operations and become efficient. "They would be able to save a tremendous amount of time," she said.

Finally, here's what Jill and I came up with. "We have a system that will eliminate three hours of your workload every day." Now *this* passes the "so what?" test, because it demonstrates the end result of the benefit that the prospect can realize and is compelling enough to grab their attention.

If we were to break down this example, this is what it would look like:

> **Feature:** An Online Reporting System.
>
> **Benefit:** Automates your administrative duties.
>
> **Jill's Compelling Reason and the End Result of the Benefit:** Eliminate three hours of your workload every day.

Notice that Jill's compelling reason, which is also the end result of the benefit, didn't talk about what she sells that would enable her prospects to achieve this end result. At this point, the prospect doesn't really care about your product or how you're going to produce the end result. They only care about the end result.

Here are some examples of compelling reasons that I would use if I were cold calling salespeople or sales managers, inviting them to purchase this book. Notice that each sentence begins with a powerful, descriptive word that describes either an action or a result they will realize:

◆ Improve your meeting rate with qualified prospects.

◆ Accelerate your sales cycle to generate more sales in less time.

◆ Spend more time enjoying your life and your family.

◆ Exceed your sales quota.

◆ Increase your income, dramatically.

You know you have come up with a great compelling reason when your prospects respond with a question that sounds like "How are you going to do that?"

Speak to Their Ear (Make It Personal)

It's one thing to tout the intoxicating benefits of your product that the company as a whole would want to realize. However, if you're speaking to someone in HR, they may not do cartwheels when you tell them that your product or service will save the company money or increase company profitability. As important as this may be, it may be falling on a deaf ear. Therefore, you want to have a buffet of benefits that you can use depending on the scenario and the person you are talking with.

Cold Medicine

Your compelling reasons need to speak to the prospect's ear. Make it personal. The prospect wants to know W.I.I.F.M. (What's In It For Me?)

What does your product or service do for them, specifically? It's one thing to share the benefits that the company may experience but what about the person you are speaking with face-to-face or who is on the other end of the phone? After all, it's not the entire company and each individual within the company that you want to get a response from. It's the person who's making the decision on whether or not to explore your offering in more detail.

What would capture the ear of the person you are speaking with? How does your product benefit them? Speak to their unique and personal interests. Put yourself in their shoes. Imagine what their day is like, the responsibilities they have, and the problems or pressures they face.

Think back to the compelling reason that Jill created for her specific prospect. "We have a system that will eliminate three hours of your workload every day."

Jill can then expand on this compelling reason during the conversation with her prospect, an overwhelmed manager in HR who is in a situation where he is juggling a variety of tasks and responsibilities with few resources to get it all done. Here's an example. "That's 15 additional hours that you would have available each week. Mr. Prospect, what would you do with the additional 15 hours each week?"

Notice how this example speaks directly to that prospect's specific role, responsibilities, current situation, and desired outcome.

Interview Your Customers

To help craft your compelling reasons as they relate to each prospect, research your audience. Speak with some of your past and current clients and explore the following questions with them. Knowing what captured their ear that caused them to do business with you in the first place will assist you in crafting your compelling reasons.

- ◆ What are your biggest triggers of stress? (What causes a bad day?)
- ◆ If you could eliminate one problem that would make your job/life easier, what would it be?
- ◆ What problems or headaches have been eliminated or reduced as a result of using my product/service?
- ◆ What do you want most in your job/life?

- How is your performance evaluated? Based on what set of criteria? (What would make them look great in terms of how they are evaluated on their job?)

- Why did you decide to use me/my product? (What benefits have you experienced as a result of using my product?)

Warm Wisdom

To assist you in developing your compelling reasons, think about how your clients would finish the following sentence as it relates to your product. *This product is great because* _____.

To develop your compelling reasons that have the greatest impact, you are much better off asking your clients these questions rather than formulating your own conclusions. Remember, there's a big difference between what your prospects think is important and what you think is important. Therefore, people buy based on their reasons, not yours.

Include Testimonials or Measurable Results

The more you can offer and demonstrate measurable results that other customers have realized, the more of an impact it will have. It adds to the clarity of the visual picture and experience that you are trying to paint regarding what they can expect from your service rather than the generally vague picture of "making them money or saving them money."

Quantify your results. Use statistics, percentages, numbers, or testimonials. If you can save a client money, how much might you be able to save them? When it comes to saving time, decreasing client attrition, increasing employee retention, experiencing greater levels of personal satisfaction, peace of mind, well-being, and happiness, or boosting sales, productivity, and efficiency, you will dramatically increase the impact of the statement by attaching a measurement to it.

If you don't know exactly what you can do for the prospect until you learn more about their business, then use *teaser words* or *phrases* such as, "Depending on your situation, we may be able to increase staff productivity by 15 percent." You can also weave in what have you done for other customers. Who else have you helped?

If you've done something great for a client, and you have a success story to share, now is not the time to be humble.

Here are some examples:

- ◆ We've helped ABC Company reduce costs by 20 percent.

- ◆ Depending on what you are currently doing, we can show you how you can eliminate three hours of your workload every day.

- ◆ XYZ Company increased their sales 300 percent as a result of using our system.

- ◆ Mr. Smith who lives in your neighborhood was able to afford sending his three kids to college because he followed our program.

Cold Callingo

A **teaser phrase** is any word or phrase that implies a benefit or measurable result a prospect can possibly experience from utilizing your product or service. Because you don't know enough about the prospect to make a full claim or guarantee, you are basing these statements on what your other customers have encountered.

Be careful when using testimonials. Make sure you get permission from the client before using their name in your marketing and sales efforts. In addition, it's important that you know the type of prospect you're talking to when sharing a testimonial. Some prospects may feel it's important to "keep up with the Joneses" or know what their competition and the leaders in their industry are doing and may be motivated to buy based on that alone. However, for some prospects the opposite may be true. Instead, these prospects want to position themselves distinct from their competitors based on their size, reputation, product, or service. After all, not everyone wants to be a Microsoft.

Identify Their Greatest Pain

I know this may sound a bit harsh but the fact is, pain is often a greater motivator than pleasure. Many of us are driven to avoid potential consequences or eliminate problems rather than create or take advantage of a benefit. After all, aside from scheduling a complete physical, we typically don't go to the doctor when we're feeling healthy.

Think about the greatest pain, challenge, or headache that some of your clients have experienced as a result of using another vendor. What do they want to avoid most? What is the personal pain that you will solve if they utilize your product or service? What are their main problems, personal stresses, or triggers of anxiety that they experience in their job that you can eliminate? Refer back to the questions in the previous section "Interview Your Customers," when conducting your customer audit.

If I were targeting sales managers, here are a few examples of compelling reasons that focus on some of their pains:

- Reduce your workload by 15 percent.

- Experience peace of mind by reducing your financial worries.

- Drive your cost per sale down by as much as 35 percent.

- Eliminate your sales team's reluctance to cold calling so that they can make the sales that your competition is taking from them.

> **Warm Wisdom**
>
> To assist you in developing your compelling reasons, think about how your clients would finish the following sentence as it relates to a bad experience they had with another product or service. *This product/ service didn't work out (I had a terrible experience) because* _____.

If you can pinpoint and then articulate your prospect's greatest challenges or concerns during a conversation, it demonstrates your knowledge about their specific problems and that you really get what their situation looks like through their eyes. This will foster a deeper connection with each prospect you speak with.

Once you verbalize a prospect's greatest pain or problem, they are more willing and ready to resolve it.

The Shotgun Approach

Some of my clients have asked, "Keith, why develop a minimum of five compelling reasons?" Well, think of it this way. If you are calling on someone for the first time, do you know exactly what this prospect's hot button is or what will motivate the prospect to listen to you? Not exactly.

Having five compelling reasons is more of a shotgun approach rather than a rifle approach. This way, you can tailor the compelling reasons you use around each prospect that you're calling on based on their position and what you feel is most important to them.

As we discussed, there's a difference between what *you* think is important and what your *prospect* thinks is important. You just have to work on putting yourself in their position to uncover what they want and need to hear rather than either assuming what you think they need to hear or saying the same thing that every other salesperson is saying.

There are many benefits to crafting your compelling reasons. First, you are going to weave them into your prospecting template, cover letter, presentation, e-mails, networking strategy, laser introduction, follow-up calls, and voice mails.

Second, you will be using these compelling reasons during your pre-call planning which we will be discussing in Chapter 8. Reviewing your compelling reasons before you begin to prospect will put you in the right mind-set, refocus your efforts toward the value you can deliver, and remind you why your prospects need to speak with you!

If you find that you're having difficulty creating your own compelling reasons, that's perfectly normal. The fact is, this is a challenging exercise that requires some creative thinking and the ability to peel away at the traditional benefit statements in order to get to the core compelling reason. Enroll your boss or supervisor to assist you. Hire your own sales coach. If you are part of a sales force then make this a team effort. Having an entire sales team co-create these compelling reasons can be a great exercise for your next sales meeting.

Cold Medicine

If you feel you can't develop five compelling reasons, then how well do you actually know your product, customers, industry, and your competition? And if you don't know your product, then how do you expect to sell it?

Developing your top five compelling reasons why a prospect should speak with you provides a unique opportunity for you to reconnect with your product newly, to reinvent and reposition what it is you are selling, and to discover a greater value you can offer that your prospects can connect with on a deeper level.

Take a Test Drive

At this point you may be thinking, "How will I know if my compelling reasons are, in fact, compelling enough?" Great question! Here are a few barometers you can use to gauge their effectiveness.

Share them with a co-worker, supervisor, or even one of your clients that you have a great relationship with and ask for their opinion. Most of all, try them out on yourself! After all, if these reasons motivate and excite you enough to want to share them with your prospects, then you are on the right path. You'll know if you have a great compelling reason if they excite you.

Finally, get out there and try them on some new prospects. Remember, the more you use them, the quicker they will evolve into something better. The point is, just get out there and start using them! You can always fine-tune them as you go.

The chart that follows is a checklist to ensure that each reason you create is, in fact, compelling enough for maximum impact. Create your own checklist using this chart as an example. Use column 1 to write out your compelling reason. In columns 2, 3, 4, and 5, identify the type of compelling reason that you are creating. Please note that each compelling reason will not possess every characteristic that we previously discussed. As long as you can check off at least one of the columns, that's all you need. Keep in mind that each compelling reason does need to pass the "so what?" test, which is identified in column 6.

To assist you with this process, I've included a few of the compelling reasons that I shared with you earlier so that you can see firsthand how to use this tool.

Cold Calling Conundrum

Perfection is paralysis. Do not attempt to make your compelling reasons "perfect" the first time around. Remember, they are not etched in stone. The more you use them the more they will evolve. You will always have the opportunity to refine them after you begin using them and have a chance to gauge their effectiveness as well as the reactions from your prospects.

Compelling Reason Checklist

Compelling Reason	Includes the end result of the benefit	Speaks to their ear (what's in it for them?)	Includes testimonials or measurable results	Exploits their greatest pain (states the pain or problem eliminated)	Passes the "so what?" test
Eliminate your stress so you can end the day with a smile on your face.	X	X		X	X
XYZ Company increased their sales 300 percent as a result of using our system.	X		X		X
We've helped ABC Company reduce costs by 20 percent.	X		X	X	X
Exceed your sales quota.	X	X			X
Jane Doe, a neighbor in your community, lost 30 pounds in three weeks.	X		X	X	X
Eliminate three hours of your workload every day.	X	X	X	X	X
Spend more time enjoying your life and your family.	X	X			X

The Least You Need to Know

♦ A prospect buys what your product or service will ultimately do for them, not your actual product. People buy based on their reasons, not yours.

♦ Your compelling reasons need to pass the "so what?" test. Make sure that one of your compelling reasons conveys a personal benefit that your prospect can realize.

♦ While testimonials are great to stimulate interest and establish credibility, use them carefully.

♦ Once you articulate the challenges a prospect experiences, they are more willing and ready to resolve them.

♦ When crafting your compelling reasons, interview your customers to determine why they bought from you.

♦ If you have only one benefit statement, you might be reinforcing the wrong message when speaking with your prospects!

Chapter 6

Winning the Prospecting Championship with Your MVP

In This Chapter

◆ Uncover what distinguishes you from your competition

◆ Repackage obvious features to become a unique offering

◆ When it's appropriate to use your ace in the game

◆ Leave a lasting impression

Okay. You've taken the time to reinvent and redesign the benefits that get to the core of what your prospects really want. This will certainly separate you from every other salesperson and will dramatically increase your cold calling effectiveness.

In this chapter, you will learn how to create a unique value offering that will enable you to rise above your competition.

What Makes You Unique?

As you move deeper into your sales process, your prospects are going to want to know more about your product or service. Unfortunately, simply stating that you have a great product, service, staff, company, or price point is no longer enough. Although important, this information is not unique and often falls on deaf ears as most salespeople, including your competitors, are saying the exact same thing.

What if there was something else that you can claim or offer that your competition cannot? What value can you offer that would distinguish you from the rest?

Cold Callingo

Your **most valuable proposition (MVP)** is a unique or distinguishing feature that leaves a lasting impression on every prospect you speak with while placing you and your product in a class by itself.

Your *most valuable proposition (MVP)* is a unique or distinguishing feature, product, service, or benefit you offer that clearly separates you from your competition and will enable you to overdeliver on the value that your customers expect.

If nothing comes to mind right now, that's okay. Like your compelling reasons, developing your MVPs will take some time and creativity.

Exploit the Obvious

When you hear the phrase, "30 minutes or less—guaranteed!" What company comes to mind? Domino's pizza! They capitalized on being able to deliver a pizza to your doorstep in 30 minutes or less. This MVP clearly distinguished them from their competitors and resulted in a dramatic increase in their business.

Interestingly, other pizza places may also be able to deliver in 30 minutes or less and may have been doing so long before Domino's ever came into existence. However, Domino's took this concept and exploited what may have been considered obvious. Regardless, it became a determining factor that made Domino's unique.

Were they delivering pizzas in 30 minutes or less before they began to broadcast this guarantee? Chances are they were! In essence, they took something they were already doing, transformed it into a unique feature, and then guaranteed it. The fact is, you probably have several MVPs waiting to be shared with your prospects and you don't even know it yet!

 **Cold Calling Conundrum**

The following statements or variations of these statements are not MVPs. Avoid using them! 1) We have great service. 2) We have a great company. 3) We have a great staff. 4) We have great products. 5) We have a great price.

Mike was a loan officer who came to me looking for ways to separate himself from his competition. Being in a highly competitive industry, Mike was looking for something that would give him the edge when speaking to prospects.

After learning more about Mike's business and his work ethic, it was clear to me that Mike was fully committed to delivering the best value and service to his customers. On the surface this was far from unique. Many loan officers may feel the same way.

Because Mike generated much of his business through referrals and, more specifically, through real estate agents, we started thinking about ways that he could separate himself from the other loan officers who were all competing for the same business that real estate agents could give them.

As we explored this in more detail, Mike shared with me many of the problems that can essentially destroy a loan. Interestingly, many of the reasons why a loan wouldn't close had more to do with the loan officer and less to do with the client. He said that poor customer service and communication between the client and the loan officer had caused many deals to go bad, even at the closing table, the very day that the customer was supposed to get their loan and become the owner of their new home.

Mike then shared with me all of the reasons why most of his loans got approved and actually closed.

"What if you could put this in writing?" I asked. As such, we were able to invent his first MVP, which was, "We guarantee closing your loan or we pay you $500."

Anyone can make a lofty claim or guarantee. However, Mike not only put it in writing but there was a cost to him and a conciliation to his customer if he couldn't deliver.

After a month of promoting this new and unique guarantee, his business took off. Essentially, Mike communicated to his prospects what he was already doing, which was providing exceptional customer service. The only difference was that he positioned it in a way that sounded unique and then wrapped a guarantee around it.

Imagine how his clients, as well as the real estate agents, received his new guarantee. They loved it! Especially the real estate agents. Now, they had one less thing to worry about that could kill their sale. He was able to offer his prospects something that other loan officers could not: guaranteed peace of mind. Mike not only guaranteed each closing but put his own money on the line if he couldn't deliver on his promise. Wouldn't you want to work with a salesperson that has so much faith and confidence in his process and abilities that he is willing to put it in writing?

Bear in mind that Mike never had to pay out the $500. Not because every one of his loans closed but because he was smart enough to include some stipulations in his guarantee that protected him in the event that a loan didn't close for reasons that were outside of his control. (The client didn't prepare the correct documents, the client's income changed, job status and debt ratio changed, documents weren't submitted on time, the client changed their mind, and so on.)

Cold Calling Conundrum

If you are going to develop your own MVP in the form of some type of guarantee or warranty, make sure you develop your own "fine print" that covers you in case you are not able to honor it for reasons outside of your control.

The bottom line is, if you are going to deliver exemplary service and superior products anyway, why not guarantee it?

To stimulate your creativity, your MVP can be …

◆ A unique service you offer.

◆ An unheard of warranty, guarantee, return policy, trial period, customer service, or referral program.

◆ An exclusive client list.

◆ Unique features and benefits of your product.

◆ An added value that you deliver to your clients. (Free support or training, an additional feature, product, or service offered at the time of purchase at no cost to the client.)

For the World to See

TRACO is a manufacturer of quality commercial and residential windows. Their website features a story about how they proudly participated in the $30 million restoration of the Statue of Liberty. TRACO was commissioned to manufacture and replace the 25 miniature windows that sparkle from Liberty's crown.

Talk about a unique MVP that no other window manufacturer can claim!

When you develop and share your MVPs with your prospects, you will find that they will be even more attracted to you as opposed to continually having to promote features and benefits.

Here are some other examples of MVPs that you may be able to use. Fine-tune them so that they best fit for you.

◆ **Guaranteed On-Time Delivery.** You can also guarantee a start date, project completion date, a product's performance, your level of service, an end result, and so on. For example, "We will refund each customer x amount of dollars for each day that goes beyond the completion date."

◆ **Fair Price Assurance Program.** We guarantee that you can't find a better price for the same product or service or we will refund the difference. Staples, the office superstore, offers a 110 percent price match guarantee. Not only will they match a lower price from another vendor, they will also give you an additional 10 percent off of the price difference. Is Staples in business to give away money? Of course not. However, they have so much faith in their pricing model that they are willing to guarantee it.

Creating Your Most Valuable Proposition

There is a three-step process to developing your MVP:

1. Take each component of your company (service or product, company, employees, guarantees, warranties, pricing, and customer service) and write each one on the top of a separate piece of paper. You can also use the table that follows as a template.

2. Divide the page into three columns. In the first column, list what your competition is saying as it relates to each category. (If you don't know exactly what your competitors are saying, then make an educated guess.) In the second column, list the things you are saying as it relates to each category. You will notice many similarities.

3. Now, get creative! Review the five suggestions at the end of the previous "Exploit the Obvious" section. Refer back to the examples of what other companies have done to develop their unique edge. Use the third column to list the factors that make you unique as it relates to each category that other companies cannot claim or is very rare in your industry.

Developing My MVPs

	What My Competition Is Saying	What I'm Currently Saying	My MVP
Product or Service			
Company			
Employees			
Customer Service			
Guarantee			
Warranty			
Pricing			

Like your compelling reasons, your MVPs will take some time and creativity to develop.

Put Me In, Coach!

We've established in the last chapter that you will be using your compelling reasons in your prospecting template, follow-up calls, voice mails, and introductory letters. As mentioned earlier, MVPs are typically used when you are deeper into a conversation with a prospect, after you've grabbed their attention and confirmed interest. However, there is always the exception. If your MVP is compelling enough, such as an unheard of guarantee that would make your prospects jump for joy, then certainly use it up front to stimulate their interest.

Cold Calling Conundrum

You do not have to create one MVP for each category. Having one or two unique and exciting MVPs that clearly distinguish you from every other salesperson is better than having seven dull ones.

Not only do these MVPs come in handy during a prospecting conversation, but you can also utilize them in your marketing materials, sales tools, during a presentation, or even as a response to an objection.

You know you have created your MVP when you get a response from your prospects that sounds like, "Wow, that's interesting!" or, "I have never heard of that before," or "Hey, that's really great and exactly what I need." You can bet that your name recognition will skyrocket because your prospects are now less likely to forget you.

The Least You Need to Know

- To create your most valuable proposition (MVP), take what you are doing and exploit the obvious so that you are now offering something unique.

- If you are going to offer a guarantee, protect yourself from situations that are outside of your control.

◆ Your MVPs can be used during practically every stage of your selling process.

◆ If you don't take the time to develop your MVP, then you'll probably sound like every other salesperson.

◆ Use your MVP in your marketing materials and sales tools.

Chapter 7

Developing Your Prospecting System

In This Chapter

- ◆ Creating your prospecting system
- ◆ Becoming process driven rather than result driven
- ◆ Uncovering new vehicles to deliver your message
- ◆ Warming up cold calls
- ◆ How to write a compelling introductory letter
- ◆ Get real with what you can expect

No amount of travel along the wrong path will bring you to where you want to be. Therefore, you must navigate a path that takes you to your desired destination.

Have you ever lost a sale due to poor follow-up? Do you feel overwhelmed when you sit at your desk and are unsure about what activities to engage in? Are you making mistakes that can cost you new business, or find that you are making sacrifices in order to reach your goals? If you answered "Yes" to any of these questions, then consider that it may be the result of poor planning and a lack of a comprehensive prospecting system.

In this chapter, you will be uncovering and evaluating your current prospecting system so that you can identify the additional components you need that will comprise and fuel your system in order to reach your goals.

Become a System-Oriented Thinker

Think about the steps you take when engaging in an activity. It could be a sport, a hobby, or playing an instrument. How do you know what to expect as an end result? Because you've consistently performed the same way over and over again.

The prime objective of any system is to produce a consistent and fairly expected result. Someone who is a system-oriented thinker has upgraded their thinking to believe that everything they do actually operates from a system. Businesses, communication, (even how we argue with people) learning, relationships, technology, a self-care regimen, sports, even our quality of life all operate from a certain system.

While many systems have been created with a conscious intention, most of the systems we use are actually operating in the background of our life. We are not even aware they exist! Therefore, the real benefit of becoming a system-oriented thinker is the realization that you have the ability to create, modify, eliminate, or entirely revamp any of the current systems you are using.

Similar to the on-board navigation systems that you find in cars today, your prospecting system will help you navigate through your day, keeping you on the course that will take you to your desired destination.

Identify the Components of Your System

Every system contains identifiable components. For example, when you flick on a light switch, you expect the light to go on (another system). If it doesn't, there is clearly a malfunction in one of the identifiable components that make up this system (blown fuse, faulty wiring, no power, bad outlet, broken bulb).

This book is another example of a system that guides you through the process of developing your cold calling skills, managing an effective prospecting mind-set, as well as creating a highly effective prospecting and voice mail template. These are just some of the components that are woven into the fabric of your prospecting system.

A prospecting system may contain several components or activities, such as cold calling, sending an introductory letter or e-mail, developing your target prospecting list, making a follow-up call and leaving a voice mail. If you ever find it challenging to adhere to certain activities in a system or generate your desired result, rather than assuming your system is "broken" or ineffective, consider this difficulty to complete certain tasks or attain your measurable objectives is an indicator, a warning or a "red flag" in your system that's letting you know something needs to be adjusted.

Identify the components you need that comprise and fuel your prospecting system so that it becomes systematic. Is it producing the results you want? If not, it simply needs an adjustment, an upgrade, a modification, or possibly a total overhaul.

How do you determine if your system is working? An effective system produces consistent results with the least resistance. An effective system is aligned with your goals and lifestyle. It operates as if on autopilot and will support the changes in your schedule as well as in your life. Plus, you'll know if it's functioning properly if you experience peace of mind, calmness, and clarity throughout your day.

Your system will enable you to develop and consistently engage in the productive habits that will automatically maintain balance, harmony, and order in your life while pursuing your goals. So allow your system to become your own automated process that keeps you in check and accountable for producing the results you really want.

When you finish implementing the strategies included in this chapter, you will be more aware of what it takes to develop an effective prospecting system. As such, instead of scratching your head trying to figure out why your prospecting strategies aren't working, your system will enable you to determine exactly where the breakdown is so that you can make the necessary changes and repairs.

There is a saying, "Begin with the end in mind." If you begin your prospecting efforts with a defined path that you are going to travel on and can even envision all of the steps that will guide you through the process, you will have much more control over the outcome. It's like running a race. You know where you start and you know where the finish line is.

The Result Is the Process

Are you hitting your numbers? How many follow-up calls did you make today? How much good volume did you book this month? How many appointments did you schedule this week?

These questions are relentlessly driven into our heads, and for good reason. Like many sales professionals, there's often pressure to reach quota or a certain level of acceptable performance. Although having a monthly sales goal keeps your eye on the prize and your focus on the end result, it may actually do more harm than good.

I often hear salespeople say, "Results aren't showing up fast enough." At the end of each selling month, frustration and stress run rampant as salespeople scramble to do their best to close sales and meet their numbers.

If selling is transference of feeling, imagine the feeling that you are transferring to your prospects. The stress of having to close more sales and the anxiety you're feeling inadvertently puts undue pressure on every prospect you speak with, fostering an unhealthy relationship from the start.

The irony is, this constant push to reach sales numbers keeps you hooked on the goal, diverting your efforts away from refining the selling process needed to generate more business. The quandary then becomes, "I'm too busy to work on my process. I have numbers to meet!"

Goals should contain advisory labels that read, "Warning! Goals may be hazardous to your success." After all, who would have thought that the very goals you create can actually sabotage your selling efforts?

Consider this paradox: The result *is* the process. In other words, what if you shifted most of your attention away from your goal or the end result and onto the process?

After all, what's the point of eating a bowl of chocolate ice cream, to get to the end or to savor every bite? How about the goal of a self-care or an exercise regimen? Unless you are in it to compete professionally, it's to *maintain* a level of health, vitality, and personal satisfaction. The same holds true for measuring productivity, maintaining your peace of mind and experiencing a sense of achievement at the end of each day.

After all, you don't *do* the result; you execute the process, which produces the result as a natural byproduct of your efforts. That's the paradox. By honoring the process, you can enjoy the benefit of knowing that you will attain your goals, because it's the process that will get you what you want.

From New York to L.A. in One Hour

To generate better results, you're either changing what you do or changing how you think. To continually exceed your sales goals, better manage your mind-set, and eliminate any anxiety that surrounds the process of attaining your goals, change your thinking to *become process driven rather than result driven.*

Ask yourself, "Do I have a (sales, prospecting, follow-up, time management, customer service) process in place that I can trust?" "Have I upgraded my thinking to become system-oriented?" When you look at your daily schedule, does it outline the specific and measurable tasks and activities you need to engage in that will move you toward your goal?

Cold Medicine

If you can measure it, you can manage it.

Chances are, salespeople who are solely focused on the end result don't have a process they have faith in. As such, they concentrate more on trying to control the outcome, pushing for what they want rather than managing their process. After all, you can't trust and manage the process if you don't have a process in place to do so!

Trying to achieve more without a process to guide you would be equivalent to driving from New York to California without a roadmap while wearing a blindfold. Not only can it be stressful, but you're bound to wind up somewhere other than your intended destination.

Schedule a time with yourself to develop your process for attaining each goal or task that needs completing so that you can see the path you will be traveling on. Look back on the successful sales you've made as a starting point for developing your process. For example, if you are looking to generate a certain number of sales each month, what activities do you need to engage in on a *daily basis* to do so? What skills or tools need further development? (For example: Pre-call planning + introductory cover letter/e-mail + prospecting and voice mail approach/template + frequency of calls/follow up + presenting and closing the sale = process driven.)

Once you have outlined a path and a success formula to follow, allow the *doing* or the process to be the reward and where the pleasure resides, not just the end result. For example, x number of calls produces x number of prospects, which produces x number of sales (more on this in Chapter 16). This way, you can be responsible for your future goals without having to worry about them. If you continue your quest with your eyes focused on the finish line, you'll miss out on the journey. Therefore, be careful not to hook yourself onto the future so that you can enjoy the process of reaching your goals today. (Remember the section, "Detach From the Outcome" in Chapter 4?)

Knowing when enough is enough each day and the specific activities you need to engage in provides you with the freedom to trust the process you've put in place. After all, there's always more to do. There is always more that can be done at the office, at your home or in your life, another call that can be made, or another e-mail that can be read.

When you become process driven you now have the opportunity to honor the realistic timeline that it takes to finish something, more specifically, the time it takes to generate new prospects. This will eliminate the chance of continually feeling frustrated that "results aren't happening fast enough." You can actually trust your process and enjoy the peace of mind that comes from letting the process do the work for you. You will be able to achieve your goals and complete your tasks once they are part of your system rather than always running out of time, leaving tasks incomplete, or wondering when your next sale will come.

The fact is ...

◆ You can't safely drive from New York to Washington, D.C., in two hours.

◆ You can't play a great round of golf in one hour.

◆ You can't train your body for one week and expect to be in great physical shape.

The point is, if you have an eight-hour workday, you can't effectively complete ten hours of tasks in that time period, even with all of your good intentions. For example, look at what you currently have in your schedule and what you need to complete in order to honor your entire prospecting system. Then, total up the time that it would realistically take to complete your daily to-do list. I'm sure that you will notice a disconnect between the hours you invest in your typical workday and the time it would take to complete your daily tasks.

By following this strategy, you have created a great way to continually beat yourself up, feel guilty about what you are not getting done, and make yourself wrong for not completing what you said you would, even with your best effort. And this just doesn't sound like a tactic that's enjoyable, working for you, or enhancing the quality of your life.

Let's recap your choices. You can continue to pile on more activities and tasks that you won't get to anyway, which will make you feel bad for not completing them at the end of the day. Or, you can begin to underpromise to others and to yourself by putting realistic timelines on the activities you engage in so that at the end of the day you feel great.

Exceeding your monthly sales quota will be the result of the cumulative efforts you make and the activities you consistently engage in every day. When you're mindful of the process, you now have the opportunity to recognize and celebrate your accomplishments on a daily basis (even the little ones) rather than pushing for or waiting until the "End." (And when does *that* happen?)

Mapping Your Prospecting Path

As we've discussed, the shotgun approach to prospecting does not provide you with the ability to become consistent in your performance. If you are constantly trying something different every time you prospect, you are never allowing yourself the opportunity to become skilled in using a certain system. Therefore, systemize your approach by developing your own prospecting system.

> **Cold Medicine**
>
> If you train for the race then you don't have to worry about being able to cross over the finish line.

Salespeople who follow a system are not only successful in generating new business but also exert a lot less effort because they know what results to expect every time they cold call. Salespeople who are disorganized in their approach often hang up from a cold call unsure of where they stand. This happens because they don't know where they have been, what the next step should be, or where they need to go.

Following a specific sequence and honoring the steps throughout this phase of your selling process is vital to an organized, professional sales effort. A system is what takes you from point A to point B with the least amount of risk or error. A system spells out what you need to accomplish from the time you make your initial effort to contact that potential prospect until the time you have developed a new, qualified prospect. It is your strategy that provides you with the freedom in knowing what the outcome will be. When you have a system in place, there is no need to second-guess your efforts and approach.

> **Warm Wisdom**
>
> To track calls, manage your tasks, and organize your prospect list, I would suggest using some type of contact management or time management software such as Outlook, Act!, or Goldmine. Depending on your profession, there may be some industry-specific software that you can use instead of these more generic, yet effective programs.

To begin creating your prospecting system ...

◆ List the chronological total number of steps in your prospecting approach. Define the steps or stages of your entire prospecting and follow-up system (perhaps, steps 1 through 10). How are you going to make your initial contact with each prospect? What communication platform will you use (face-to-face, e-mail, voice mail, snail mail)?

◆ List the duration of time between each step (how many hours/ days until you move to the next step?). For example, Day 1—send cover letter; Day 3—follow up with a phone call.

◆ List the number of attempts before moving to the next step. For example, if you don't get the response you are looking for from your first voice mail, how many unique voice-mail messages do you leave before moving to the next step in your prospecting system?

What follows is an example of a prospecting system that was developed for a salesperson that sells a product targeted for small businesses. Remember, this only serves as an example to provide you with a sense of how to craft your own prospecting system. As such, please modify this example so that it becomes the perfect fit for you and is aligned with your company's selling philosophy and product.

Step 1: Day one. Send out your cover letter via snail mail (U.S. mail).

Step 2: Five days later, if no response, follow up with an e-mail.

Step 3a: Three days later, initiate the first call. If you're able to contact the prospect, use your prospecting template.

Step 3b: If no response or you can't reach them "live," leave your first unique voice mail.

Step 4: Three days later, if no response (or you can't reach them "live"), leave your second unique voice mail.

Step 5: Three days later, if no response (or you can't reach them "live"), leave your third unique voice mail.

Step 6: Four days later, if no response (or you can't reach them "live"), leave your fourth unique voice mail.

Step 7: Five days later, if no response (or you can't reach them "live"), leave your fifth unique voice mail.

Step 8: Five days later, if no response (or you can't reach them "live"), follow up with a fax template.

Step 9: Four days later, if no response (or you can't reach them "live"), leave your sixth unique voice mail.

Step 10: Five days later, if no response (or you can't reach them "live") follow up with an e-mail or letter.

Final Step 11: Declare this lead a non-priority. Put in a separate file for future contact and prioritize your call list to target more qualified prospects.

Notice that this particular system honors the belief amongst top producers that it takes a minimum of eight touches or attempts to contact a prospect before they respond.

The Top Ten Signs of a Highly Functional System

After you develop your prospecting system, what are the gauges you will use to determine if your system is effective?

What follows are the top ten signs of a highly functional system. Use this as your checklist for the system you've created to determine if it passes the test and qualifies as a highly functional system.

1. It operates as if on autopilot. You've already created it. Now, all you need to do is follow the process (thus enabling you to become process driven rather than result driven).

2. It frees you from having to worry about what to do next. As such, you experience peace of mind, balance, calmness, order, and clarity throughout your day.

3. It keeps you in check and holds you accountable for producing the results you really want.

4. It has a feedback mechanism built in to let you know that a component in your system is not working or is not working effectively.

5. You have maximized your potential as it relates to your level of efficiency and productivity.

6. It supports change and evolution.

7. It is aligned with your goals and lifestyle.

8. Because you trust your system to produce the desired result, you've let go of having to control the outcome.

9. It produces consistent results with the least resistance.

10. It can be duplicated.

Choose Your Vehicle for First Contact

E-mail, fax, telephone, networking events, seminars, face-to-face; there are a variety of ways to connect with your prospects. The question is, which one is best for you? Just as each industry and profession differ, so will your initial method of contact.

For example, many of my clients send out an introductory letter via U.S. mail to begin their communication and attempt to connect with a prospect. However, I've also heard from other clients who live on the west coast and say their prospects would never even open a letter, because most of their written communication is done via e-mail. And yet I've heard from other clients who swear that sending out an initial communication via snail mail is a waste of time. Instead, they go right for the cold call as their vehicle for first contact. Therefore, it's up to you to determine the communication vehicle to incorporate into your prospecting system that would be aligned with how your prospects prefer to communicate.

Make a Cold Call Warmer

Deborah was a new salesperson who was responsible for selling insurance products for individuals and businesses. While she was open to cold calling and knew it was her main conduit for generating new appointments, she was concerned that she would experience a large amount of resistance when calling on new prospects.

Deborah felt that if she could prepare her prospects better, they, in turn, would be less resistant to speaking with her. As such, Deborah drafted a letter that she sends to her targeted prospects before she attempts to call them on the phone.

Deborah noticed a change in her prospect's attitude when she sent out the letter before contacting them by phone or in person. They were less reluctant to speak with her. When Deborah attempted to contact her prospects after they received her letter, her prospects were more prepared for her call.

Here are some of the benefits Deborah realized when sending an introductory letter to a prospect:

1. Prospects are more inclined to open and read your letter rather than embrace a cold call because prospects can read their mail when it is convenient for them. Letters are less intrusive than a phone call because the prospect will decide when and where they want to read a letter. This honors the prospect's agenda and schedule rather than a cold call, which can be perceived as more of an interruption.

2. Informing a prospect via your letter that you will be calling them diminishes their resistance when you finally call.

3. Deborah's letter was informative. It addressed the timely issues and changes that were occurring in her prospect's industry and how her product can support those changes. This demonstrated to the prospect that she understands their business.

4. She shared several compelling reasons (refer to Chapter 5) as to why her prospect needs to speak with her.

5. Deborah informed the prospect of her next step to better prepare them for her next contact. This way, her prospect was aware that she would be contacting them on a certain day and time.

6. With potentially dozens of people calling on the same prospects that you are calling on, sending out an introductory letter separates you from most of the other salespeople who are not warming up the prospect before making their first cold call.

Cold Calling Conundrum _____

> If you've tried using introductory letters and they didn't work, be careful not to learn the wrong lesson. Instead of learning the lesson that "introductory letters don't work and they are a waste of time," what if you changed that assumption to, "The introductory letter _I used_ didn't work. Therefore, if I change my letter, I will change the result."
>
> Second, what were you expecting to happen when the prospect read your letter? If you expect to send out an introductory letter and receive an influx of calls, you may be setting yourself up for disappointment. Instead, consider that the intention of your cover letter is to simply warm up the prospect in preparation for your next communication with them.

E-mail, Snail Mail, or Fax?

After a few weeks of using her letter, Deborah called me to discuss her prospecting system. She told me that she typically sends out an introductory letter and follows up with a phone call. I asked her if there were any other vehicles she used to deliver her communication to her prospects. She mentioned that she used to send e-mails but didn't get the response that she hoped for.

She then shared with me that her response rate from e-mails ranged from one to three percent where her response from letters sent via U.S. mail was a bit higher.

"So, why did you stop using e-mails?" I asked. What about those prospects who do respond to e-mails and not to regular mail? By not using e-mail as a prospecting tool, it sounds like Deborah just _decreased_ her response rate by one to three percent!

The lesson here is this: It will be your cumulative efforts that will yield the results you're seeking.

The fact is, you really don't know which communication medium each prospect will respond to. Sure, you can look at aggregate results to gauge what may be _most_ effective. However, if your least effective methods of communication generate less prospects than your most effective methods, then aren't you still generating more prospects collectively?

Cold Medicine _____

Be cognizant of the "do not call list" as well as the laws surrounding the use of the fax as a sales and marketing tool. For example, "spamming" or doing unsolicited fax blasts may not be legal in your state, depending upon the audience you are targeting (businesses or consumers). However, in most cases, using the fax to follow up with a prospect that you have contacted is perfectly legal.

As we continued our conversation, I asked Deborah if she ever used the fax as a prospecting tool. "Why should I use the fax," she replied. "No one uses the fax as much as they used to, now that they can use e-mail." I didn't say a word until she listened to what she had just said. I then saw the light bulb go on over her head.

If most salespeople look at the fax the same way you do, then haven't you just uncovered a new method of communication that may separate you from everyone else? Look at using the fax as the rebirth of an old communication tool that can be used to get your message to the right prospects. How many salespeople do you know who incorporate a fax in their prospecting and communication efforts? The fewer people you know who are using it, the more of an advantage it becomes for you!

Use as many vehicles of communication as you can. You never know what a prospect is going to respond to.

How to Write a Compelling Letter

I know this book isn't titled _The Complete Idiot's Guide to Writing a Compelling Letter_. However, I've included several key points you should be aware of when writing an introductory letter or e-mail to a prospect. Use the following guidelines when creating your letter:

1. Speak directly to your audience. The more personal and targeted your letter is, the more of an impact it will have. The letters that have the greatest impact are the ones that are crafted for each prospect, rather than a form letter that's being sent to many prospects. Targeting your letter has some huge advantages.

You can discuss the timely issues that are occurring in that prospect's industry. If the company has recently appeared in the news or has a website, you can align your letter with what is occurring within that specific company. This way, you can tie in your product and what it can do for them with what the prospect is currently experiencing.

2. Give the reader a reason to read your letter. If you want to ensure that your letter winds up in the circular file (their garbage) begin your letter with information about your company and services. Think back to when we discussed crafting your compelling reasons (Chapter 5) and developing your MVP (Chapter 6). Why should they read this letter? How can you add value to each prospect by sending them a letter? Begin your letter by letting the prospect know what's in it for them or discuss a common challenge or problem they may encounter that your product or service can solve.

3. Include a call to action. What do you want the reader to do after they read your letter? Are they on standby mode waiting for you to contact them? Should they be expecting something else from you, another contact via mail, a phone call? Do you want them to contact you?

4. Keep the letter to one page. Remember, your prospects don't have much time. The more information you send, the better the chance of the prospect putting it aside until they have time to review it. (And when does *that* happen?) You know you have a great one-page letter if you can scan the page and have the key points jump out at you.

5. To use or not to use your company or personal stationary. Look through your mail. Chances are, you can identify the origin of each piece of mail simply by looking at the return address. If that doesn't give it away, the company name, address and logo on the top of their stationary would. Unless the prospect was expecting something from a certain company or person, these identifiable mailings won't even make it out of their envelope and onto the prospect's desk for further review.

If you plan on sending a letter using regular U.S. mail, you may want to avoid announcing who you are by having your return address on the envelope as well as on your stationary. This tells the prospect who you are before they even read the letter. Removing this from your mailing can further reduce the chance of the prospect formulating any preconceptions about you or the letter and filing it with the rest of their junk mail. If the prospect wants to know who sent them the letter, they will have to actually read the letter! (That is the point, right?) At the very least, they will scan the letter down to the signature, which is still better than not opening the letter at all.

> **Cold Calling Conundrum**
>
> In some industries, it may be against the rules, even illegal, to offer presents or perks to prospects with the intention of earning their business. Make sure this does not apply in your industry.

6. Use quotes, statistics, and testimonials. Similar to the guideline when crafting your compelling reasons, here are some things you can do to make your letter stand out so that it grabs your prospect's attention. If you have a compelling enough testimonial from a satisfied client or a statistic that you want your prospects to see, you can position it directly on the top of the page, formatted in bold lettering. Letting a prospect know specifically how another client of yours has benefited from your product will stimulate their curiosity and interest in what they can learn by reading the remainder of the letter.

That's it! Hey, I tried to keep it simple. I've included several working templates on the next page so that you can see how these six points can be incorporated into an introductory letter that would be sent to a prospect. Just be sure to fine-tune them so they fit for you, your product, and your audience. You will notice that each letter has its own style and objective. While some salespeople take more of a formal approach to drafting a letter, other salespeople take more of a creative, even humorous approach to warming up a prospect. While both styles are included, use the one that you feel would be the best fit for your audience. (If you are unsure, then speak to your boss or another salesperson to see what has worked for them. You can also do a beta test and try them all out to determine which one works best.)

The "sample introductory letter" that follows on the next page is an example of what you could send before initiating your first call. In this example, the product is sales training. The target audience is sales managers.

The second introductory letter is another template you can use to make the prospect more receptive to your next attempt at connecting with them. Remember, the more unique you are in your approach, the greater the chance you have to capture the prospect's attention. As you can see with the lottery ticket example, it's a safe bet that the majority of your competitors are not sending out a letter like this. This is your chance to be creative and stand out above the rest.

Finally, the "jumping through hoops" letter is an example of what a salesperson did to capture the attention of their key targeted account. If you and your prospect have a good sense of humor you can also try this approach. Send a hula-hoop to your most important prospects with the "jumping through hoops" letter enclosed. Does this approach categorize as silly? Yes. Corny? Sure. Over the top? Maybe. Unforgettable, humorous, and puts a smile on someone's face? Definitely.

You can even use this approach for any new face-to-face prospect meeting as an icebreaker to put them at ease, create a more comfortable, relaxed atmosphere, and defuse their resistance.

Keep in mind that you may need to fine-tune the language in each letter so that it best fits for you and your audience. It is up to you to identify the prospects who would be receptive to this unique approach.

"I've increased my sales 400% since I started working with a sales coach!
But that was just the beginning ... " —Joe Client

Date
Name/Title
Address

Dear Mr. Prospect,

Unproductive salespeople cost companies millions of dollars each year. And that doesn't include the time and effort that's wasted on ineffective training and development. **Are you maximizing the ROI from your sales team?**

What if there was a way to ensure that your training initiatives are linked to your company's strategic objectives and can **achieve a measurable ROI**? The funny thing is, Mr. Client didn't think it could be done! Yet he was open to the possibility. Maybe you are in a similar situation, always on the lookout for ways to do things better.

The bottom line is, if you have ever been in a situation where you are ...

- Losing customers that should be yours because a competitor had the lower price.
- Failing to generate the results you need from your current training initiative.
- Wasting your precious time on recruiting efforts to combat high turnover rather than building a world-class sales team.
- Lacking an effective systemized sales approach that your sales team uses to generate unprecedented results.
- Stressed out and overloaded; spending more time solving problems rather than developing strategies to generate new business.

then it may be worth just a few minutes of your time to learn how we can help you dramatically accelerate your sales team's productivity.

Recently featured in XYZ magazine, our top-rated firm specializes in designing proven, result-oriented **sales training and coaching solutions** that help salespeople become top producers quickly so that you can ...

- Watch your team exceed their sales quota.
- Generate more sales by positioning your sales team in front of new customers in virtually untapped markets.
- Improve your meeting rate with qualified prospects while driving your cost per sale down by as much as 35%.
- Accelerate your sales cycle to generate more sales in less time.
- Eliminate at least three hours of your workload every day.

Mr. Prospect, with your direction and our proprietary training technology, we can assist your company in achieving similar results so that you can end your day with a smile on your face.

With just a twenty-minute meeting scheduled around your timetable, I can give you a good idea of what we can do for you. Feel free to contact me anytime at 123-456-7890 or e-mail me at me@companyname.com. I'm sure you're busy, so if I don't hear from you I'll follow up with a phone call next Thursday at 3 P.M. EST. I look forward to speaking with you.

Wishing you continued success.

Sincere regards,

Name
Title
Company

A sample introductory letter.

Date
Name/Title
Address

Dear Mr. Prospect,

Please accept the enclosed lottery ticket for the next drawing. I have found that there are three ways to achieve greater levels of success:

Hard work, planning, and a commitment to delivering value to your customers.

Luck and timing. (See enclosed lottery ticket. I hope you win!)

Partnering with leaders in the (XXXXX) industry.

You take care of the first one; I'll handle the rest. You can expect a call from me later this week to discuss why it would make sense to explore the possibility of working together.

Side note for the reader: You can also replace the above line to read as follows. "You can expect a call from me later this week to discuss how we can develop a mutually beneficial (alliance, partnership, relationship, etc.)."

Depending upon what you are doing now, I can show you how you can:

Side note for the reader: Here's where you tie in the benefits they will realize as a result of working with you and of utilizing your product.

Compelling Reason or MVP

Compelling Reason or MVP

Compelling Reason or MVP

I will be in touch within the next few days to see if you have the need or an interest in our (services, product, etc.) and whether there is anything we are doing that you could benefit from.

If you would like, feel free to contact me at 123-456-7890 or e-mail me at me@companyname.com any time. I look forward to speaking with you.

Kind regards,
Jon Smith
Title
Company

The lottery ticket example.

Dear Mr. Prospect,

This is just one of the hoops that I'm prepared to jump through in order to earn your business.

I will be in touch within the next few days to see if you have the need or an interest in our (services, product, etc.) and whether there is anything we are doing that you could benefit from.

If you would like, feel free to contact me at 123-456-7890 or e-mail me at me@companyname.com any time. I look forward to speaking with you.

Kind regards,

Jon Smith
Title
Company

P.S. If there are any additional hoops that I will need to jump through in order to schedule a meeting with you, please let me know and I would be happy to do so.

Jumping through hoops for your prospects.

Cold Medicine _____

Need to get someone's attention, fast? Send your letter or package priority mail or via Federal Express. If it's sent and packaged as if it were a priority, it will be treated as such. The packaging creates the perception that whatever is included is important. Who wouldn't open up a package like this? Try this approach when you absolutely, positively must grab your prospect's attention.

The Least You Need to Know

♦ Because everything we do operates from a system, become a system-oriented thinker.

♦ Take the time to map out the activities you engage in when prospecting to crystallize your system. Identifying the components of your system enables you to achieve greater, long-lasting, consistent results.

♦ Become process driven rather than result driven. Align your prospecting system with an effective weekly routine that supports your goals.

♦ The purpose of an introductory letter is to warm up the cold calling process by reducing the prospect's resistance to your next communication.

♦ Because you don't know where your next sale is coming from, use a variety of communication vehicles to connect with your prospects.

♦ Develop realistic timelines for the activities you engage in so that at the end of the day you feel a sense of accomplishment. Honor the length of time it takes to generate one new prospect.

Chapter 8

Pre-Call Planning

In This Chapter

- ◆ The activities that prepare you for prospecting
- ◆ What else you can do to bring in more business
- ◆ How to maximize every prospecting effort
- ◆ Time blocking for hyperefficiency and greater results
- ◆ When enough prospecting is actually enough
- ◆ Automating your system

When talking with salespeople who have prospected for a while, they can remember how challenging it was to take that first prospecting step. This is still a common theme amongst salespeople who have to learn how to prospect to build their business. They tell me that taking the first step and making that first cold call is exactly where they freeze or get stuck.

Many salespeople define the first step as the first cold call they make. That is, the first time they are picking up the phone and attempting to connect with a prospect. However, the first step isn't what you might think.

Warm Yourself Up

If you've ever honored a workout regimen, getting on the treadmill or hitting the weights probably isn't the first thing you do. Instead, you ease into your workout by first stretching and warming up your body. Why? To avoid injury. Warming up lets your tight muscles know that they are about to be torn down, exercised, and challenged. Stretching and warming up your muscles makes you more limber and your body more responsive and open to what you're about to put it through. It's a great way to ensure you'll get a good workout and most important, avoid an injury that can lay you up in bed for weeks.

Cold Callingo

Pre-call planning encompasses the activities you engage in before you begin prospecting that involve action and intellect in order to achieve the maximum return on your prospecting efforts.

The same holds true for prospecting and cold calling. Imagine that your *pre-call planning* phase is when you take the time to warm yourself up before the big game. View pre-call planning as your warm up for cold calling or other prospecting activities. The only difference is, the primary muscle that you are stretching and preparing for prospecting is your brain; that is, your mind-set and the activities that require your focus and attention.

This chapter will introduce you to the process of pre-call planning and what you need to accomplish *before* you even pick up the phone or begin your prospecting efforts. Pre-call planning is an essential step in your prospecting system that will enable you to plan effectively, get into the prospecting mind-set, eliminate any fear or reluctance, boost your confidence, learn about your prospects, tap into your drive and motivation, and target who you are calling. Finally, pre-call planning will enable you to become limber and hyperfocused on your objective. All of these activities are the preliminary steps you take to avoid injury or challenges during your cold calling, I mean, warm calling efforts.

The Five Degrees of Pre-Call Planning

Ken, a client of mine, called me the other day and told me that during the one-hour timeline he allocated each day for cold calling over the phone, he was only able to make a few calls. When I asked him to break down exactly what he attempted to accomplish in that hour, he shared with me the following tasks:

◆ Getting into the prospecting mind-set.

◆ Reviewing his action plan and approach.

◆ Compiling, reviewing, updating, and developing his prospecting target list.

◆ Calling back customers, prospects or other people that returned his call.

◆ Making calls to new prospects.

Without realizing it, Ken identified the five degrees of pre-call planning. Ken then shared with me that during the one hour he put aside for prospecting, it was taking him forty-five minutes just to prepare his targeted list of prospects to call, not leaving him much time for actual prospecting.

In other words, Ken was collapsing several other activities into one and calling that "cold calling." In actuality, he listed five distinct activities that need to be managed independently.

The jewel here is be sure that each task or activity you engage in is broken down into its most simplistic and measurable form. In other words, if prospecting is one of the activities you engage in, it is not enough to simply list "prospecting" as an activity. As we've discussed, prospecting involves a variety of distinct activities. Therefore, prospecting, as defined by Ken, needs to be broken down even further.

Mapping your prospecting strategy, getting into the prospecting mind-set, compiling your call list, returning or taking phone calls, and cold calling for new customers are five distinct and measurable activities that need to be managed separately when creating your schedule. If you find that you need to handle some of these activities at the same time, then make sure you have allocated enough time for each activity.

Additionally, each one of these activities calls for a different mind-set. You'll know if the activity you are engaging in needs to be broken down into other activities if it requires a different level of thought, skill, and focus.

You'll know if the task is broken down into the absolute smallest denominator when asking yourself the following questions. "How am I going to achieve that?" "What steps do I need to take to finish that task?" "What specific outcome will be produced?" If the answers to these questions open up another task, process, or strategy that would generate a unique end result then you'll need to narrow down that activity even further. For example, compiling your target-prospecting list not only produces a different outcome than when you pick up the phone and make cold calls but it requires a different thought process, strategy, and skill set.

Another symptom that will let you know whether or not you can narrow down the task into a smaller denominator is this: If you block out a certain amount of time for an activity and you find that you are not completing it, there's a chance that you have collapsed more than one activity into that block of time. Identifying each distinct activity that you engage in will enable you to be more realistic with the time lines that you allocate for each activity, making your prospecting efforts highly effective and more easily manageable.

In addition, this exercise will strengthen your ability to think in terms of detailed, measurable activities and tasks, rather than in vague, broad strokes. So, if you've ever been in a position where you have underestimated how much time a certain task or project would take, this process will also assist you in establishing more realistic timelines around your daily activities so that you can "get it all done" rather than constantly leaving tasks incomplete or overbooking and over committing yourself.

As you list all of your prospecting activities and tasks, don't get caught up in *how* you are going to complete them. That comes later on in the book.

Get Out of Your Own Way and Into the Prospecting Mind-Set

Because pre-call planning occurs before you begin to prospect, this is the time you put aside to recondition and realign your thinking to achieve a healthier mind-set. Review the first part of the book and take some written notes you can refer to that will enable you to quickly shift into the line of thinking you need to prospect effectively.

The amount of time you should spend on this activity is more of a function of how long it would take you to get into the proper mind-set. While some salespeople may need fifteen or twenty minutes, others may need only a few minutes to get focused enough to begin prospecting.

I'd suggest timing each degree of pre-call planning so that you will know exactly how much time you need to put aside before you actually prospect. As we mentioned earlier in this chapter, pre-call planning requires a distinct amount of time that you are carving into your schedule, which is separate from the actual time you are putting aside for cold calling or other prospecting activities.

Review Your Action Plan and Approach

Now that you are excited to cold call, what path are you going to travel on? The following questions will assist you in developing your prospecting action plan and approach. What are the measurables you want to accomplish during the time you put aside to cold call? Who is your ideal prospect? What do you need to know about your prospect before you call on them? Is there something timely going on that would affect them?

Is there any additional research about a prospect's company or industry that needs to be done? Who is the person you are calling on and what is their position? How will you find the decision maker? If you have follow-up calls to make, how many are you going to make? If you want to schedule appointments with new prospects what is your goal or the number of appointments you want to schedule? Conversely, if your objective is to make a certain number of dials, what is the number?

Take a few minutes to clarify in your mind and on paper the answers to these questions and what your intentions are going into the time block you put aside to prospect. This exercise will also provide you with the insight you need to determine if your intentions are realistic as they relate to the amount of time you put aside for prospecting.

For example, if you are a new salesperson trying to identify your target prospect in order to determine whom you should call on, it's going to take you more time in the beginning to aggregate your prospect call list. Because you may not have the luxury of working straight through the day (or week) until your list is compiled, simply make a conscious decision regarding the amount of time you are going to put aside, say every morning, to begin building your list.

This way, if you use a timeline as your barometer rather than the number of people you ultimately want on your call list, you can then determine when enough is enough each day, rather than beating yourself up for not completing your entire list. You can recognize and celebrate your accomplishments on a daily basis (even the small ones) rather than waiting until the "end."

Finally, this degree of pre-call planning also includes reviewing exactly what you are going to say or do when you finally connect with a prospect. And if you only succeed in connecting with their voice mail, what are you going to say then? (Lucky for you, Chapter 12 focuses on how to craft a compelling voice mail message that generates more returned calls.)

This pre-call planning exercise is absolutely essential. Just think about the last time you said the wrong thing and the second you said it, you could see it was the wrong thing to say. Imagine if you had the opportunity to know it was wrong before you said it? Proper pre-call planning will prevent this experience from occurring!

Who Ya Gonna' Call? Compiling Your List

At this point during your pre-call planning, you may be mentally prepared to prospect, know exactly what to say when cold calling, and have developed the measurables you want to achieve. However, cold calling isn't very effective if you pick up the phone and then ask yourself, "Whom shall I call first?"

There are a variety of ways to compile your call list. I've highlighted a few strategies here:

♦ Purchase a list. There are a variety of companies that will provide you with targeted call lists. Before you go out and spend your money, spend some time researching the company beforehand. Let's face it, there are a lot of scams out there. Speak to some of their references. See if they would be willing to do a trial run for free, share with you a sample list, or provide you with your first lists at a reduced fee, before you make the full investment. Two sources that I've seen to be reliable are Hoover's and D&B (Dun and Bradstreet, Inc.).

♦ The Internet. Search the web using the keywords that would be associated with your target prospect and grab the information from their corporate website. I happen to be a fan of Google to conduct my searches. While this approach may be a bit more time-consuming, you are sure to wind up with a highly targeted list of ideal prospects.

♦ Pay-per-lead services. Just because you are prospecting doesn't mean you can't find someone else to complement your efforts. There are companies out there who will do the cold calling for you. Some charge by the hour, others charge by the lead. Once again, make sure that you are dealing with a reputable company before making the investment.

♦ Your company. If you are lucky, your company will provide you with a list of targeted prospects to call on.

♦ Strategic partners. If you can find companies whose product or service is complimentary to yours, leveraging off of their established client or prospect list would be a salesperson's dream.

♦ The phone book. While I may be stating the obvious, salespeople still use this as a tool to find new prospects to call on. There are also several "yellow pages" that you can find on the Internet that list individual consumer information as well as businesses. These yellow pages vary from free to fee-based ones.

- Family and friends. Otherwise known as your circle of influence, for many salespeople, this is the first place they turn to aggregate their target list and begin their mining efforts.

- Trade groups, chambers, and professional associations. Some groups are willing to sell their list of members but it may require you becoming a member yourself. Many groups offer a member directory both in print and online. If you can find an association that makes up your target audience, it will wind up saving you a considerable amount of time, rather than compiling each prospect separately.

The amount of time you invest in compiling, reviewing, updating, and developing your prospecting target list is dependent on many factors, which I've outlined in the upcoming pages. But before you can even consider these factors, you must first determine who your ideal client even is.

Identify Your Ideal Client

Take the time to identify the characteristics you would want in an ideal client. If you are targeting businesses, what size business is ideal for your product or service? How many employees? Are you selling something that targets all of a company's employees or only managers, HR or salespeople? If so, do you need a minimum number of a certain group in each company, such as salespeople to make the company's investment into your product or service worthwhile? On the other hand, are you targeting businesses that can use your product to complement or enhance the quality of their end product or deliverable? Does the company you are targeting have to produce or sell a specific product or service in order to be compatible with your offering? Do they have to be in business for a certain number of years or are you targeting only new companies? Does your ideal client need to serve a particular market, demographic group or geographic area? Because of the timeliness of your product, are there only certain times throughout the year that your target prospect makes this type of purchase? As such, due to limited windows of opportunity, do you concentrate all of your prospecting efforts during these times only?

Conversely, are you selling a product that targets consumers? What criteria do these end users need to display? Do they have to live in a certain geographic area in order to benefit from your product or service? Do they have to be homeowners, be married (or divorced/single), employed, unemployed, have children, be of a certain age, income class or gender? Do they need to be affiliated with a certain organization or religious group? Do they have to hold a certain job title or be in a specific profession? Is your product a necessity or a luxury to them?

While I've shared with you some measurables or criteria you need to establish to determine who makes it on your call list, there are other criteria to consider as well. While we've unpacked *what* you want in an ideal client, *who* do you want to work with? What I am referring to here is the type of client you enjoy working with. Some examples are honest, high integrity, good sense of humor, flexible, open to suggestions and change, a great communicator, organized, professional, empathetic, responsible, understanding, friendly, value driven rather than price driven, and the list goes on.

There is a very important reason as to why I am suggesting developing a comprehensive picture of your ideal client. In most cases, (unless of course you are calling on a finite number of prospects in a specific geographic area) if you dig deep enough, you'll always find more prospects to call on. As such, you have a choice. You can find the prospects you enjoy working with or you can find the prospects that are going to make your life difficult.

The bottom line is this: If you are looking for a way to absolutely loathe, detest, and hate your job and getting up each morning, then only work with the prospects that you can't stand working with. It's a surefire strategy to be miserable. Why do you think that the primary objective of prospecting is to determine if there's a fit between you and the prospect? Notice that I said "you and the prospect" rather than "your product and the prospect." Hey, it's challenging enough to become a top producer. By targeting the prospects you really want to work with, you'll have more fun while you work, making what you do much easier!

Here are some other elements to consider when deciding on whom to target and some questions you can ask yourself to uncover the right prospect. If you are selling consumer direct, then some of the following guidelines may not apply.

- ◆ Product: Who will benefit the most from utilizing my product or service? Who have other salespeople in my industry targeted? Does my product appeal to a mass audience or only to a niche group of prospects?

- ◆ Company Philosophy: Do certain standards already exist regarding whom I should be calling on?

- ◆ Company Support: Will my company be providing me with a call list, do I have to create one myself, or is it a combination of the two?

- ◆ Decision Maker: Who is ultimately making the decision to purchase my product? Where can I find this person? Are there other avenues I can explore in terms of how I can meet this person? Are there places outside of the prospect's work environment that would allow me the opportunity to connect with them?

- ◆ Title: Can I rely on a person's title alone to tell me whether or not they are my target prospect?

- ◆ Sales Process: Am I selling my product over the phone, via the web, or is it something that ultimately has to be done in person? (Is it a combination of all three approaches?)

- ◆ Sales Cycle: How long does it actually take from the time I connect with a qualified prospect until the time a sale is made? What are the phases of my sales cycle (that is, the process involved and the time it takes from uncovering a qualified prospect to converting them into a client) that I need to be aware of?

- ◆ Price: Who can afford my product? Who can't?

- ◆ Industry: Is my product industry specific? Are their specific industries or professions that would only benefit from my product?

Later on in this chapter under the section, "Prospect, Prospect Everywhere," you will find a table that will assist you in identifying additional activities you can engage in and places you can prospect when looking for your ideal client.

Following Up and Returning Calls

The fourth degree of pre-call planning that requires a different mindset and approach is making follow-up calls. These are the calls you are making to prospects that you have connected with at least once and are now wanting to continue the communication that you began with them. This also includes return calls you need to make to prospects that may have contacted you to request more information about your product or who returned one of the calls (or e-mails) you made to them. And don't forget about your current or past customers you are in communication with because they may be in a position to make another purchase.

As such, it's better to make these calls separately rather than combining them with new prospect calls. Reason being: The approach you take when prospecting someone for the first time is going to look and sound different from a conversation you would have with someone who has already expressed interest in your product, someone you have already spoken with, or someone you have already sold to.

If you feel comfortable balancing and engaging in these different types of calls at the same time (both the cold calls and the warmer follow-up calls), that's fine. However, if you find that it's more of a challenge to keep shifting your approach, then consider separating these calls into two distinct activities. (Three, if you want to call on past customers during a different time as well.)

Calling New Prospects

Just like the title suggests, this time is devoted strictly for calling on new prospects. This is the time that you've put aside to call on those prospects who's only interaction with you thus far may have been an introductory letter or package you have sent to them (refer to Chapter 7).

This activity requires the most attention. When calling on new prospects, you need to be at your best. Your focus and objective must be clear and concise. You'll have your prospecting template ready so that you know where you want to take the conversation. Finally, you will feel certain that you can handle any concerns or objections that come your way. You are ready to get in the game!

You may have noticed that following up and returning calls preceded calling on new prospects. The reason is simple. Engaging in the activities that are more promising and position you closer to a sale are less of a challenge. Achieving a degree of success during these calls will in turn boost your confidence when calling on new prospects.

Smile Before You Dial

A smile is the universal expression of happiness. If you've ever been exposed to any level of sales training, this concept was probably introduced to you. Put a smile on your face before, during, and after your prospecting efforts.

This serves two purposes. First, if you are smiling then you can't be frowning. It's impossible to be in a bad mood when you are smiling! Even faking a smile or forcing a grin makes you feel better and actually fools your body into feeling more cheerful. The very act of smiling raises your endorphin level, the body's natural opiate. The benefit is, the more you smile, the healthier you become.

Second, a smile is contagious, even over the phone. When talking to a prospect, they can sense the mood you are in. It's a safe bet that people would rather do business with happy salespeople. Therefore, make sure you are coming across in the most positive light possible.

Some salespeople go as far as keeping a mirror in front of them when cold calling, just to make certain that they are, in fact smiling. So, just smile! Not only will it make you healthier, it will make the prospecting process more enjoyable, especially when you notice the results of smiling (more smiling customers).

Cold Medicine

There's one more thing that I would strongly suggest you do before you pick up the phone and begin to cold call. Get a reliable headset. You will be amazed at how much more comfortable and efficient you will be. You now have two hands available to type, dial, or take notes, rather than having to use one to hold the phone to your ear. Moreover, keeping your head up straight is healthier and much better for your posture. Say good-bye to those neck and back cramps you get from wedging the phone between your neck and shoulder!

Scheduling Time Blocks

While this book does not focus much on time management and its importance, this is one topic that's critical to discuss in order to ensure a highly successful prospecting campaign. That is, getting comfortable with the strategy of *time blocking*.

Time blocking is the art of creating blocks of designated time for specific activities or tasks throughout the day that are aligned with your goals and the realistic number of hours you have each day. If you haven't already, I would strongly suggest that you make a list and prioritize your tasks and activities to be included in your daily routine along with established timelines for each.

If you have a nine-hour workday, you realistically have about eight hours (or less) to use for activities that you can create designated blocks of time for and then position within your schedule.

Cold Callingo

Time blocking is the art of allocating blocks of designated time for every task, chore or activity you need to accomplish throughout your day that are either non-negotiable or move you closer to your goals, while keeping your life in balance. The more effective you are at time blocking, the greater the quality of your life will be.

I say only eight hours of actual task time for the following reason. Build in some buffer time throughout your day for those activities that either take longer than expected or the activities you have to complete that would typically fly under your radar undetected when planning your day (unscheduled meetings, traffic, emergencies, proposals, client demands).

You may encounter certain sporadic, yet consistent activities that take up a portion of your day such as personal errands, phone calls, e-mails, prospecting, administrative duties, managing employees, writing proposals, training, meetings, or other work-related tasks. Consider allocating blocks of time for each activity during certain intervals throughout your day to handle them rather then having these activities get in the way of your prospecting efforts. For example, instead of being interrupted by incoming calls or e-mails throughout the day, try blocking out specific portions of your day to make and return calls or respond to e-mails.

How much time do you spend on the phone or responding to e-mails? Many people complain that their workflow is constantly being interrupted by phone calls or incoming e-mails. As such, they feel compelled to either take those calls or respond to an e-mail as soon as it hits their inbox, which distracts them from the initial activity they were involved in and disrupts their focus.

Cold Medicine

Become someone who is driven by goals rather than driven by distractions.

Are You Interrupt Driven?

Do you become easily diverted or distracted by situations, new tasks or people rather than maintain the focus on your goals and initial objective? Consider for a moment that if your e-mail program is set to download e-mail every five minutes, in essence, you are *scheduling an interruption* or a distraction for yourself and get diverted from your initial path every five minutes.

While many people feel the need to multitask, there are many similarities between managing your mind-set and managing your schedule. Each activity or task that you engage in requires a change in your direction, both in action and in thought. As such, each task or activity requires a shift in your ...

- Mind-set and thought process

- Focus

- Action and energy

- Skills and resources

- Desired outcome

That's why I suggested earlier to separate new prospect calls with follow-up calls. When you shift the focus of your energy and thoughts, you are taking up time. Whether it's 10 seconds or 10 minutes, that time is compounded over days, months, and years.

For example, let's say for every five minutes that you check your in-coming e-mails, you are losing one minute. That's 12 minutes per hour. In an eight-hour workday, consider that you are losing at least one hour and thirty-six minutes, every day!

If you are a creative person, there's a different mind-set that's required when creating a marketing piece, writing an article, and answering a phone call or an e-mail. Allowing certain interruptions can surely stall or block the flow of creativity, affecting your level of productivity. Imagine trying to play golf, tennis, and baseball all at the same time.

Consider this solution. Change the time that you have your e-mail program set to receive e-mails from every five or ten minutes to every four hours. While this may sound excessive, I've heard of some people treating their response time to e-mail like regular postage/snail mail.

Sure, e-mail is a great tool for communication, collaboration, and cor-respondence, enabling you to communicate quickly and conveniently. The point here is to ensure that this tool continues to be productive and efficient for you. Managing your e-mail like snail mail may sound a bit extreme for your situation. Even checking your e-mail every four hours may sound challenging.

To determine a realistic frequency when it comes to checking your e-mail, ask yourself these questions:

- "Are the bulk of my e-mails time-sensitive? Does my ability to quickly respond to an e-mail determine whether or not I will earn a new customer's business?"

◆ "Can I still honor my prospecting campaign, provide the same level of service to my customers, and not compromise my ability to attract new customers or perform my job effectively if I respond to e-mails only twice a day?"

If creating blocks of time to respond to e-mails or phone calls would compromise your ability to do your job effectively, then this strategy may not fit for you. However, if you have a degree of flexibility in your job to do so, consider this. Instead of checking and responding to e-mails and phone calls every four hours, make it two. If two hours still doesn't work for you, try doing so every half hour.

Take the next week to determine if there's a specific time throughout your day when you receive the bulk of time-sensitive e-mails. There still may be an opportunity for you to block out designated times for responding to calls and e-mails at less frequent intervals than you are doing now.

The fact is, even if you change the frequency of when you check your e-mail from every five minutes to every ten minutes, you have just cut the time you can lose from this distracting tactic in half!

Remember, this same strategy can be used for telephone calls. If you have other responsibilities aside from making or returning phone calls, consider blocking out time throughout your day to do so. Whether it's once, twice, or three times a day, you would allocate a designated block of time to make or return calls.

Finally, if you are responsible for attracting and retaining your customers, your ability to manage your customers' expectations is a direct reflection of your ability to not only manage your schedule but your mind-set as well.

Determine When Enough Is Enough

Get comfortable with the principle of enoughness. We've discussed the importance of not only assigning a specific start time for tasks but also a completion time to ensure that you have blocked out enough time to finish what you began. This way, you won't mistakenly schedule something else during that time.

In addition, it may help if your tasks, as well as the results you are seeking, are specific and measurable so you know when you have completed them. For example, if one of your goals is to generate new business or ask for referrals from your current customers, make sure that you have narrowed down these intentions so they are specific and measurable.

 **Cold Medicine**

Specific and measurable actions produce specific and measurable results.

What would be an example of a specific and measurable action to take? How about calling 10 people in your network or circle of influence who you know who can provide you with a list of potential customers. Is this specific? Yes, your specific action is picking up the phone and making calls to a select group of people with the intention of generating referrals. Is it measurable? Of course, because you have set the measurable number of 10 people to call in order to determine when this specific activity will be completed.

Now, think about the result. The result that you are looking for is not a vague result but a specific and measurable result. After taking this action you will be able to measure the result of your initiative, which will be a list of potential customers. By taking the specific measurable action of calling ten people, you generated the specific measurable result of a certain number of potential prospects.

Making cold calls = vague

Making ten cold calls in one hour = specific and measurable

While some tasks can be measured, some cannot. So, if you have allocated one hour to develop your target calling list each day, that's it. Don't get caught up in having to finish it (unless you have a deadline) to the point where it consumes you and becomes a weeklong activity that takes you away from your other responsibilities.

While putting time aside throughout your week for a specific ongoing activity is one way to determine when enough is enough, here are some other examples of measurables that you can use to determine when enough cold calling is enough. Your selling strategy and sales goals will often dictate which of the following measurements are the most appropriate for you.

1. Number of dials

2. Number of contacts (with live prospects)

3. Number of appointments

4. Number of sales

5. Number of requests for proposals

6. Number of demonstrations

7. Number of free trials

8. Number of recurring sales (residual/repeat business)

There is always another call that can be made or another e-mail that can be responded to. The key here is to recognize that it's an ongoing process of taking consistent, measurable actions so that you can truly enjoy the journey while achieving bigger goals.

Make Prospecting a Non-Negotiable Activity

Forgive me for such a personal imposition but I'm assuming that you find the time each day to go to the bathroom. How about taking a shower or brushing your teeth? And of course, we can't forget about eating something throughout the day. Would you even think about *not* taking part in any of these activities each day?

Therefore, to ensure that you are using your time to engage in the activities that are aligned with your goals, rather than becoming distracted or consumed with activities that may not move you toward achieving what you want, I would suggest adding prospecting to this list of goal-oriented activities and make it non-negotiable. As we have discussed earlier, build this activity into your schedule by assigning a designated block of time for prospecting throughout your week.

There are also other activities that would fall under this list of non-negotiables regardless of whether or not you want to do them. These include your commute (if any) to work, drive time to appointments or pre-defined functions that you have to perform at work, which include your primary responsibilities or administrative tasks (time sheet, weekly sales activity report, expense reports). This list of non-negotiables can also include tasks that must be done which will determine your level of financial success, such as prospecting and continued training or talent development. Finally, this list can also include those personal responsibilities that you may not be able to eliminate or delegate to someone else (your children's carpool or after school activities, and so on).

Expose Your Diversionary Tactics

Have you ever done something that you know is not in your best interest? Have you ever avoided doing something that is in your best interest? In either of these scenarios you were able to justify your behavior as well as your line of thinking and most of all, avoid being accountable.

Allow me to introduce to you a definition for this type of behavior. A *diversionary tactic* is an action, excuse, or belief you hide behind that justifies your behavior and performance.

Other examples of diversionary tactics are as follows:

Cold Callingo

Diversionary tactic is an action, excuse, or belief you hide behind that justifies your behavior and provides you with the out so you do not have to be accountable for your performance, responsibilities, goals, or the situations you put yourself in.

♦ An excuse for the behavior you really don't want anymore.

♦ An action, a lack of action or a belief that keeps you from being accountable or looking at the real truth in a situation.

♦ A persistent or constant complaint.

♦ A source of energy. (Even though it may be a negative energy source, human beings tap into any available energy source even if it causes additional problems, stress, and difficulties.)

♦ A justification for doing something you are better off not doing that isn't aligned with your goals and objectives.

As we've just pointed out, some non-negotiable tasks, activities, and priorities in your life may be obvious, such as your commute, showing up for work, engaging in your favorite hobby or pastime, and spending time with family. However, some may not be so visible, such as prospecting, practicing self-care, or putting time aside for professional development.

If there are activities that you need to engage in that support your lifestyle and will truly determine whether or not you will reach your personal and professional goals, it's essential that you make these tasks non-negotiable rather than optional. Otherwise, you'll find that they have tendency to take a back seat to other activities that may need to get done and have some degree of importance.

You know, the activities or tasks that you may be more comfortable doing (such as cleaning your office, doing paperwork, responding to e-mails, helping other people, compiling data, customer service, working on making your marketing material perfect) but don't significantly move you forward. Instead, they keep you stuck in maintenance mode, allowing you to do just enough to stay afloat. Then, you may have conversations with yourself that sound like, "That's okay, I was busy today. I'll do that tomorrow." Or, "I just wasn't able to find the time to get to prospecting today." And wouldn't you know it, something else always seems to comes up! I don't suppose this has ever happened to you (wink, wink).

This busy work will disguise the truth, creating the illusion that you're working hard, simply because you feel busy. These diversionary tactics enable you to do everything else but the activities that would dramatically accelerate your success.

Just ask any salesperson who has to prospect to build their business. They can justify practically any and every activity that will take them away from prospecting, allowing them to major in the minor activities that act as a diversion to doing what's truly needed to build their business.

So you just can't seem to "find the time"? In my experience, I have yet to stumble across time that I just happen to "find." It becomes a never-ending search, an exercise in futility. Consider that these non-negotiable activities must become as habitual as waking up in the morning, taking a shower, brushing your teeth, and breathing. These are the activities you do, (hopefully) without a second thought.

Uncover your diversionary tactics. Once you do, you'll then be able to make the choice whether or not to continue to take part in them or the activities that serve you best. To further illustrate the importance of uncovering and eliminating your diversionary tactics, consider the cost you incur by *not* making certain activities non-negotiable. What does it cost you if you don't prospect? (Example: professional satisfaction, selling opportunities, peace of mind, income, your career)

Get Automated

If you find that your workspace is a bit chaotic and cluttered and you're still digging through piles of notes and paperwork to find the information you need about your prospects, now may be a good time to begin using a time or contact management software such as Outlook, Act!, or one of the web-based contact management solutions. (Although Act! and Outlook have similar functionality, Act may be considered more of a database management software and is a bit more robust.) You can also use the contact management software that comes with your PDA to plan your schedule.

There may also be a contact management or CRM (customer relationship management) software that is specific to your industry, so it may be worth looking into. I happen to be a fan of Outlook, because it allows me to manage my e-mails, contacts, tasks, and schedule all in one program. There are some other great features in this program as well. You have the ability to create categorized task lists and recurring reminders so that you don't have to continually enter weekly or biweekly appointments into your schedule; journaling; and the ability to link files, contacts, meetings and tasks to other Microsoft documents such as Excel and Word files. Outlook is also compatible with your Palm Pilot and most PDAs.

If you are an Outlook user, the following strategy will be very useful. If you are using another program, I'm sure there is similar functionality;

just check the help section in the program to see how you can integrate this.

Cold Medicine

Align your specific tasks, activities, and appointments with their designated blocks of time that you have created in your schedule.

Once you have scheduled a time for each task or activity, you may find that one of your allocated time blocks is labeled, "follow up with potential clients." The question is, where is the list of people that you are following up with and how can you tie it together with your schedule? In other words, what are you doing specifically during that block of time you have allocated?

You want to ensure that your routine is not only reminding you about the general activity or task you have blocked out time for but also the specifics of exactly what needs to be done during that block of time. In other words, you want to be able to look at your routine and say, "Here is the general task (cold calling) that I have allocated for this block of time and here's what I will complete (calls to specific prospects) during this time today."

When creating a reminder to follow up with someone, whether it's a new client, a potential client, a long-time client, or a vendor, here are two options.

Option One: Schedule the person or the follow-up time with that person as an appointment on your calendar during the time you have allocated for making follow-up calls. For example, if you have allocated every day between 4–5 P.M. for follow-up calls, then schedule the person you need to follow up with as an appointment during that time.

> Benefit: When checking your schedule for that day, the appointment will be adjacent to the time block you have created for that activity.

> Drawback: If you have dozens of follow-up calls to make, your routine is going to look incredibly daunting and cumbersome and will visually crowd your daily schedule.

Option Two: Schedule the person or the follow-up time with that person as a task in your task list during the time you have allocated for making follow-up calls. For example, if you have allocated every day between 4–5 P.M. for follow-up calls, schedule the person you need to follow-up with as a task during that time.

> Benefit: This will eliminate the clutter in your daily schedule. If you miss the pop-up reminder, the task is still in your task list. You can also assign these tasks to specific categories, which will make it easier to access and track rather than going back through your calendar to see what appointments you may have missed. (You can still assign categories to your appointments but working with tasks seems a bit easier.)

> Drawback: It won't appear on your calendar, only on your task list. However, as long as you review your task list daily or create a pop-up reminder for each task, it shouldn't be an issue.

 Cold Calling Conundrum

When scheduling your appointments, don't get hung up on trying to schedule every specific task at a different time interval during the block of time you have allocated for that activity. For example, if you have scheduled the time between 4–5 P.M. for follow-up calls, schedule each individual task or follow-up call at the start time for that activity and check them off as you complete each one. Refrain from scheduling each follow-up call at a different time. (Example: Call Jett at 4:00 P.M., Nicole at 4:15 P.M., Jessica at 4:30 P.M.) Otherwise, you're a perfectionist, and this exercise will paralyze and divert you from your initial intention.

On a technical note, if you are using the pop-up reminder feature, each pop-up reminder that is open on your computer consumes a percentage of your computer's resources. If you have many pop-up reminders open and notice that your computer is slower than normal or you are running into some problems with the software, try closing the reminders and rebooting your computer. In addition, if you have many reminders opened at once then reschedule them, complete them or consider that you may have overbooked your schedule.

Creating and assigning categories to each appointment, project, and task is a great way to keep track of all of your activities as they relate to a specific category. Whether it's a task or an appointment, you can create your own categories for each one. For example, if you have a list of prospects to call, you can create a category called "Prospects." This way, when you go through your task list, you can view each task by category and due date, as well as by other custom fields that you can create. You can even create categories for the tasks that involve your family, home, and so on.

If you are a Netscape, Yahoo!, AOL user, or simply prefer a web-based application, you can use their time/contact management software. However, you may need to be connected to the Internet in order to access it.

Prospect, Prospect Everywhere

If you never want to cold call or if cold calling isn't an option for you based on what you sell, here are some other activities you can include in your prospecting efforts and places you can go where you can mine for more prospects.

As you can see in the following table, I'm also suggesting wrapping some measurable goals around each activity that you choose to participate in. If you get stuck on how to craft the proper goal, do not worry. In Chapter 16, you will have the opportunity to create a formula that will let you know exactly how much prospecting you need to do. Also, in Chapter 15 you will have the chance to craft the appropriate language or "laser introduction" when meeting new people or for those activities that qualify as networking. So, if you want to wait until then to complete the goal setting part of this exercise, feel free to do so.

My Prospecting Strategy and Action Plan

Prospecting Activity	Monthly Goal (List the Desired Number of Prospects You Want to Generate for Each Activity)	Actual Number of Prospects Generated per Activity	Percentage of Goal Attained
Telephone Prospecting			
Face-to-Face/ Walk-in Prospecting			
Social Functions			
Trade Shows You Attend			
Trade Shows (As an exhibitor)			
Networking Meetings/ Lead Groups			
Structuring Alliances/ Partnerships			
Meeting with Networking Sources (Alliances/Partners)			
Seminars/Workshops You Attend			
Seminars/Workshops You Deliver			
Giving Referrals			
Asking for Referrals			
Follow-up Calls			
Press Releases, Annual Reports, Articles on Company			

continues

My Prospecting Strategy and Action Plan (continued)

Prospecting Activity	Monthly Goal (List the Desired Number of Prospects You Want to Generate for Each Activity)	Actual Number of Prospects Generated per Activity	Percentage of Goal Attained
Professional or Trade/ Industry Associations			
Internet/Websites			
Other Salespeople			
Internal Contacts/ Advocates			
COI (Circle of Influence/Friends, Family)			
Additional Prospecting Activities			
1.			
2.			
3.			
4.			
5.			

The Least You Need to Know

◆ Pre-call planning is your game plan for selling success, making you more confident and knowledgeable in the eyes of your prospects.

◆ Be sure that each task or activity you engage in is broken down into its most simplistic and measurable form. Make prospecting a non-negotiable activity and build specific time blocks into your schedule to prospect.

◆ Identify your ideal prospect in order to uncover the places where you can find them outside of the office.

◆ Expose your diversionary tactics that limit your growth and productivity so you can achieve greater results.

◆ Get automated and empower your schedule to hold you accountable for doing the things you need to do.

◆ If you don't want to cold call, uncover other avenues that will put you in front of your targeted prospects.

Part 3

Transforming Cold Calls into Warm Calls

There are a variety of ways for you to get from New York to L.A., just like there are many ways to achieve the same end result. This section takes you through a process to ensure that your prospecting approach and communication style are aligned with your personality, values, strengths and talents. This is accomplished by uncovering and building on your natural abilities that complement and enhance your personal style of selling.

Chapter 9

The Seven Types of Prospectors

In This Chapter

- ◆ Learn about the seven different types of prospectors
- ◆ Identify the type of prospector you are
- ◆ Develop a prospecting style that best fits you
- ◆ Avoid the common pitfalls in communication

In all of my years of training and coaching salespeople, one thing is for certain. Each salesperson has a unique communication style and approach. That's a great thing and something I certainly encourage each salesperson to develop based on who they are or their personality, their unique skills, strengths, and talents, as well as how they come across.

The more you can personalize your prospecting approach, the more comfortable and confident you will be when prospecting. This way, your approach will come across more as a natural conversation rather than a canned pitch.

Although developing a unique approach to prospecting is encouraged, there are some pitfalls to be aware of and a few exceptions to this rule. The bottom line is, there are some styles of communication that you are better off avoiding rather than modeling.

What follows is a description of the seven types of prospectors, along with their unique style of cold calling and communicating. Regardless of your industry or profession, you will find that at least one type of prospector is going to resemble your current cold calling style. Keep in mind that this chapter focuses on how to communicate effectively when cold calling a prospect, as opposed to what you actually say or the steps you take when cold calling. If you can come across in a way that puts a prospect at ease to the point they will actually want to listen to you, rather than pushing them through the conversation, they will be more inclined to do business with you.

While each style encompasses qualities that seem to work and produce results, you will quickly notice that there's only one style worth modeling. The others, well, you'll probably want to stay away from them. As you read through this chapter, if any of these styles resonate with you or if you feel that a certain type of prospector describes you to a tee, here's your opportunity to adjust your communication style for maximum impact.

The Pusher

Also known as "The Intimidator," this type of prospector relies on old school high-pressure selling tactics to generate the results he seeks. The Pusher operates under the misguided belief that he is selling a product that cannot be sold any way other than to push it and his presentation onto his prospects.

The Pusher focuses more on the sale than anything else. To him, the sale and "what's in it for him" take precedent over the customer and the value his customers can expect from purchasing his product. The Pusher often puts his personal needs and objectives above his customers'. As you can imagine, The Pusher has more returns and cancellations than any other type of prospector.

Whether he feels pressure from his competition, internal pressure from his supervisor to perform, or believes that his product is a commodity in an oversaturated market, he relies on fear tactics and other manipulative tools to turn a prospect into a customer. This prospector typically shows no regard for the prospect or their best interests.

The Pusher isn't too concerned about developing relationships because he believes that once a sale is made, there's no opportunity for future sales or referrals.

To pull off this approach to the point where it would demonstrate some measurable results, The Pusher is typically an assertive and confident individual. However, he is typically driven by his ego to look good and outperform the rest of his team.

Ironically, with all the confidence this prospector possesses, The Pusher doesn't have enough faith in himself or in the product to attempt to cold call any other way. This belief is often fostered within a sales culture that has been a long-time promoter of this particular style of selling. At one point or another, The Pusher was told, "This is how our product has always been sold. This is how the top producers do it and how it has to be done. There's no other way to sell it." As such, this prospector truly believes that this is the only way for him to sell his product.

The Pusher is a hard, relentless closer and feels he only gets one shot at each prospect. He adheres to the "one call close" mentality, which is, "You only get one chance to sell each prospect." He believes that there will be no other opportunity to sell them again. While his enduring persistence can be appreciated, he will continue to try to sell each prospect he speaks with up until the point the prospect has had enough. Ultimately, The Pusher will wedge his foot in the prospect's door until they kick it out.

The Pontificator

Have you ever started a conversation with someone that you may have regretted ever starting? Not because they weren't interesting to talk with, engaging, personable, or even fun, but because they kept going and going and going and going and going! Like the Energizer Bunny, this prospector just doesn't know when to stop! And that's often due to the fact that they don't remember where they even started.

The Pontificator will admit he doesn't follow any type of cold calling template, outline, or presentation. According to him, each prospect and cold call is unique. Instead, he shoots from the hip, making it up as he goes along. As a result, he often finds himself in a selling situation that he is unprepared for. Interestingly, The Pontificator thrives on situations like this. Now, he has an opportunity to once again create a new approach off the cuff!

Like many of these prospectors mentioned, The Pontificator feels that his approach actually works. And quite frankly, it often does but not for the reasons he thinks. The results The Pontificator realizes are more a function of this person's other admirable traits that compensate for the weakness in his prospecting system and where he falls short.

This type of person is often fun to talk with and be around. The Pontificator is the type of prospector that can talk to anyone and immediately make another person feel comfortable. This character strength becomes a crutch to his prospecting approach, often blinding him from the need to further systemize his approach. As a matter of fact, the only thing consistent about this prospector is his inconsistency regarding his cold calling approach.

> **Cold Medicine**
>
> Enthusiasm sells. Enthusiasm plus a prospecting system sells even more.

The Pontificator is all about exploiting his charming and gregarious personality. He possesses a strong belief about what he is selling. His conviction and passion about what he does and the value he can deliver come across in his communication. The excitement, energy, and exuberance this prospector displays is contagious! The Pontificator's enthusiasm does most of the selling for him. As a result, people love to do business with him.

Because there are many salespeople with great personalities who are engaging, friendly, and love to be in the spotlight, this type of prospector is the most popular of all. While this approach seems to work for many salespeople, the lack of a strategic cold calling system puts a ceiling on his performance.

The Sprinter

If The Sprinter had a mantra for prospecting it would probably be, "From 'Hi' to 'Bye' in 30 seconds." The Sprinter is the athlete of prospectors. Acting as if cold calling is a race, it's as if this prospector's goal is to beat the time he invested on his last call. Unfortunately for him there are no extra points for getting through a cold call at back-breaking speed or in the shortest amount of time.

Also known as, "The Regurgitator," this "marathon runner" believes that if he can just get his pitch out, the prospect would be more in-clined to buy from him. The Sprinter will spit up his entire presenta-tion all over the prospect, without stopping for a breath or even for some feedback from his prospect. Would someone get out a mop and clean up this mess?

The Sprinter is oblivious to the fact that going faster doesn't get the prospect any more interested in what he has to say. If anything, it turns a prospect off because whatever this prospector is saying comes across more as a pitch rather than a conversation. (The prospect often misses what The Sprinter is saying anyway because he is talking way too fast!)

The Sprinter is a fast talker and focuses more on quantity rather than on the quality of each cold call. Because of his approach, his results are also skewed. Because he can make a large number of cold calls in such a short amount of time, he's sure to run into a sale every now and then. After all, even a blind squirrel is bound to trip over an acorn at one point or another.

This type of prospector has been known to offer unsolicited informa-tion to his prospects, because he isn't taking the time to truly listen to and understand each prospect's situation, goals, problems, or concerns.

The Sprinter holds the belief that if you give the prospect an opportu-nity to say "No," they will. Therefore, he won't give the prospect the opportunity to do so!

There may be a fear on The Sprinter's side that sounds like this. "If the prospect does in fact say 'No' I will be unable to turn them around to the point where they say 'Yes.' As such, I would rather dump as much information on them hoping that my pitch will do the selling for me."

The irony here is that his approach is achieving what he wants to avoid the most. Not taking the prospect's pulse and forcing unsolicited information on the prospect puts the prospect in a defensive posture. The more you put a prospect on the defensive, the more objections and "No's" you are bound to create.

Cold Calling Conundrum

The quality of each call you make is always more important than the quantity of calls. Each call deserves the same care and attention that you put into the first call you make each day. Cold call and treat each prospect as if they were the most important prospect on your call list. If not, you'll find your call list dwindling into oblivion with no measurable results to speak of.

Let's face it. To make the volume of calls that The Sprinter makes in one hour, you've got to be highly organized. However, what this prospector needs to understand the most is this—cold calling is not a race. You don't get points for your intentions, only for your results.

The Copier

The Copier is one of the more elusive types of prospectors. What makes this type of prospector so elusive is that The Copier possesses some wonderful traits. This prospector is open to change, innovation, coaching, training, and personal growth with the intention to continually improve and evolve as a sales professional, yet almost to a fault. This wonderful trait often becomes his weakness.

You see, The Copier is on a quest for the perfect presentation.

This prospector is a voracious reader. Often self-taught when it comes to developing his core selling competencies, The Copier is excited to try any new cold calling approach that he can get his hands on as often as possible. In his search for the latest and greatest prospecting approach, like The Pontificator, he never gets to experience the benefit of consistency.

By continuously refining his cold calling approach, he never gets comfortable with one. The Copier has not yet become confident enough to trust his own communication style, strengths, and talents. Instead, he relies on other people's proven methods to achieve his goals.

The Copier is seduced by the fancy closes he reads about that other salespeople have used with a great deal of success. As such, he often tries to memorize other salespeople's techniques verbatim without considering whether or not it fits his style or personality.

Unfortunately, The Copier tries to incorporate everyone else's style but his own. It's amazing this prospector gets any results at all because he never stays with one approach long enough to gauge its effectiveness.

The Copier has been known to be a perfectionist, often using his inability to find the perfect prospecting approach as an excuse for his performance. Moreover, The Copier tends not to prospect as much as he should be. Instead, the story he tell himself is, "I don't want to mess up a cold call and lose out on a potential sale. Therefore, I will only cold call once I can get my presentation down perfectly."

This prospector's intentions are sound, always wanting to better himself by investing his time in professional development so that he can maximize his cold calling potential. However, finding the ultimate cold calling approach becomes an exercise in futility.

The Copier comes in at number three on the list of the most popular types of prospectors.

The Pleaser

The Pleaser takes the concept of customer service to a new level. This prospector has one ultimate goal; to make people happy. While this is certainly an admirable trait, it acts as a barrier to his cold calling efforts.

Because all The Pleaser wants to do is please, he is more timid in his approach. This prospector will do anything to avoid confrontation and stir the waters. As such, he collapses objections with confrontation. In other words, if The Pleaser hears an objection or a concern that the prospect voices, rather than viewing this as a sign of interest, (we will discuss this more in Chapter 11) he takes the prospect's word at face value, without exploring their concerns at a deeper level. At the first sign of what he perceives as conflict, The Pleaser will do anything to appease his prospect. It's no wonder that this type of prospector has the longest "callback list" of any other type of prospector! Persistence is not one of The Pleaser's strong points.

This prospector is quick to send brochures or collateral material to his prospects hoping that his support material does the selling for him. (Is he missing the key word "support" in support material?)

As you can surmise, The Pleaser is a bit intimidated by his prospects as well as the cold calling process. Because of this fear, The Pleaser is reluctant to lose a prospect by asking the tough questions or attempting to overcome objections. Instead, he winds up keeping all of his prospects as prospects rather than moving them into the next step of his sales process so they can become customers.

Because The Pleaser is willing to do almost anything for a prospect to keep them happy, he winds up delivering incredible value to his prospects. You see, The Pleaser is all about giving. Therefore, he rarely asks for anything in return, especially for the sale or the appointment. He's hoping that by providing so much value, the prospect will tell him that they are ready to buy or take the next step in the sales process.

Because of this, The Pleaser is the type of prospect that any salesperson would love to sell against!

In his desire to keep his prospects happy and not upset them, The Pleaser actually winds up doing a disservice for his prospects and a service for his competition. Sure, he's educated the prospect, answered all of their questions, and filled any requests. However, by not encouraging the prospect to take the next step, he has positioned this prospect to be taken away by the next competitor who calls on them. In essence, The Pleaser has just done all of the selling for his competition.

No one likes a pushy salesperson. However, there's nothing wrong with a little nudge once and a while. After all, there's a difference between being pushy and being persistent. With all of the good-hearted salespeople out there, The Pleaser comes in at number two on the list of the most popular types of prospectors.

The Educator

The Educator is a master of their trade, product, and profession. If you need to know technical data, statistics, and how the product works, he's the person to call.

This prospector is a true master of industry knowledge. He can tell you the who, what, when, where, why, and how as it relates to his product. The Educator can even share information about his competitor's product and how they differ. It seems as if this prospector knows more about his competition's product than the competition does!

If there's an Educator on your sales team, chances are he has been called upon by management to help with product training and to provide industry knowledge for the new recruits.

This prospect is a talking spec sheet. After all, The Educator wants his prospect to make an informed and educated purchasing decision.

The Educator relies on his vast amount of product knowledge to hopefully impress a prospect into a sale. While he may be heavy on product knowledge, he often falls short on developing his selling and cold calling skills.

While product and industry information is certainly a crucial factor for most prospects to consider when making a purchasing decision, this "baffle them with brilliance" approach has been known to backfire on this prospector. In his quest to educate his prospects, he actually overeducates them by providing too much information. The more information a salesperson provides, the more information that needs to be processed and considered by the prospect. The more information the prospect needs to consider, the longer the selling cycle becomes.

Cold Calling Conundrum

Be cognizant of the amount of information that each prospect requires. Ask them what information they want to hear. Assuming they need to know everything is a surefire method to talking yourself right out of a sale.

In addition, by providing a deluge of information, what might have once been considered an easy purchasing decision has now been compromised and complicated. Instead of the prospect making an easy purchasing decision, they may now feel as if they don't have the time to make an informed decision until they get a chance to process all of the information this salesperson has provided.

As you can see, The Educator has the tendency to talk himself out of a sale. Similar to The Pleaser, The Educator often sets up a prospect for the next salesperson to come in and take away his business but only after he has taken the time to educate the prospect and do his competition a favor.

The Advisor

Finally, let me introduce the last type of prospector we will be discussing and the icon of professional prospecting: The Advisor.

This prospector is a model for what every sales professional should aspire to. The Advisor encompasses all of the good qualities that the other types of prospectors possess, yet without all of their foibles and pitfalls.

The Advisor possesses the ...

- ◆ Persistence and confidence of The Pusher.
- ◆ Enthusiasm, passion, and charm of The Pontificator.
- ◆ Efficiency, organization, and focus of The Sprinter.
- ◆ Drive for continuous improvement, lifelong learning, and innovation of The Copier.
- ◆ Desire to serve, respectfulness, and sensitivity of The Pleaser.
- ◆ Product and industry knowledge of The Educator.

The Advisor encompasses all of the positive attributes that encapsulate the ultimate prospector! The Advisor is a true doctor of the trade. The Advisor relinquishes all of the self-imposed pressure to perform or look good and manages a healthy prospecting mind-set.

This prospector not only possesses the right mind-set, but also the right tools and approach. Like a good doctor, he *first* asks questions and *then* listens to his prospect's responses. Before he offers a solution, he takes the time to understand each prospect's situation, goals, and greatest challenge or problem rather than providing unsolicited information or advice. It is only then when The Advisor suggests some possible solutions to his prospect, solutions he knows will be a perfect fit for them.

The Advisor takes the time to prepare for prospecting. He has a path to follow that encompasses his entire prospecting system. He's taken the time to craft the right questions in order to get the prospect involved in the conversation. Instead of memorizing fancy closes, The Advisor seeks to deliver value in every conversation and serve his prospect's best interests, regardless of whether or not they buy from him. As such, he encounters very little resistance and only minor objections when it's time for him to invite the prospect to move forward.

Cold Medicine

Honor your authenticity. Ultimately, people buy from you because of you! Ask any of your customers. They buy from you because of who you are and the way you come across, which always take precedent over what you do.

Most important, The Advisor is authentic. He is true to himself without attempting to become someone who he is not. Rather, he utilizes the tools and approach that complement and are aligned with his personality, values, strengths, and talents.

As you can probably see, this book provides you with the tools that will enable you to become a true advisor to your prospects and clients.

If you are still unsure about the type of prospector that you most resemble, try this. Audiotape yourself giving your presentation. You can also ask your peers what type of prospector they think you most closely resemble. I'm sure they would be happy to tell you. Once you uncover your dominant style, you will then have the choice to fine-tune your approach.

The Least You Need to Know

◆ While your style may resemble one or more of these prospectors, uncover your dominant style and adjust accordingly.

◆ Become a doctor of prospecting in order to fill the needs of your prospects.

◆ Cold calling is not a race; you don't get points for your intentions, only for your results.

◆ Make sure that your approach and communication style are aligned with your personality, values, strengths, and talents.

◆ Be authentic and true to yourself, rather than trying to become someone else.

◆ Genuine enthusiasm combined with a prospecting system, a well-needed quality product or service, and a passion to serve will make you unstoppable.

10

The Anatomy of a Prospecting Conversation

In This Chapter

◆ Learn the five objectives during an initial cold call

◆ Develop your own seven-step prospecting template

◆ Grab a prospect's interest in seconds

◆ Have a conversation instead of pitching them

◆ Defuse a prospect's resistance

◆ Generate more sales in less time

Congratulations, you're practically halfway there and on your way to winning the prospecting game! Here's a good time to take a moment and acknowledge how far you've come. So, pat yourself on the back. You're doing great!

The work you do in this chapter will continue to build on what you have learned. Now that you know the reasons why your prospects should speak with you it's time to determine exactly what you are going to say during a prospecting conversation when you actually connect with the person you've been diligently attempting to contact.

Developing Your Prospecting Template

When you finally connect with a live prospect, your *prospecting template* is the language or verbiage you use during an initial prospecting conversation.

Cold Callingo

Prospecting template is the language or verbiage you use during an initial prospecting conversation when you finally connect with a live prospect.

Now, I know that some salespeople are not comfortable reading from a script let alone memorizing one, while others require this level of structure and organization. Conversely, some salespeople are more comfortable "winging" a prospecting conversation where other salespeople find it intimidating.

Please note that your template is not a script to read from or memorize (unless you choose to use it this way). It's more of a guide or an outline to follow in order to generate consistency in your approach and to ensure you maintain your focus and intention during each prospecting call.

Think of your template as a mapped out path to travel on during an initial prospecting conversation that contains great degrees of flexibility, which will enable you to incorporate your personal style of selling and communication. While your template will provide you with the freedom to adjust your approach during a conversation with a prospect, it will also eliminate your chance of being diverted from your objective or feeling as if you have to wing it.

The Five Objectives of a Cold Call

During any initial cold calling conversation with a new prospect, there are five objectives that must be accomplished.

1. Introduce yourself and identify who you are.

2. Provide the prospect with a compelling reason to speak with you. Create a new possibility for them to take advantage of a new feature, benefit, or a solution to a problem that would enhance their success. (What's in it for them?)

3. Defuse their resistance. Create a pressure-free environment by getting permission to proceed with the call.

4. Guide them to the questioning or the diagnostic/needs analysis part of your call so that you can get them involved and determine if there's a fit.

5. Determine the next step.

Here's a friendly tip from your sales coach. The first four objectives must be accomplished within the first minute of your conversation. Sound like a tall order to fill? Let's see.

To illustrate and overcome some of the challenges that you may face when speaking with a prospect, we're going to create a skill practice scenario. I'm going to share with you a recent conversation I had with a salesperson.

Then, I'm going to ask you to put your sales coaching hat on to determine what you hear.

This salesperson's name is Jack and he really needs your help. Listen carefully to the following scenario. You will then have an opportunity to identify the holes or the parts in Jack's approach that he needs to improve upon in order to find a solution to Jack's challenges.

Jack and I were talking one afternoon about how to improve his prospecting skills. He's been a salesperson in the same industry for about ten years. Like many of us, Jack feels that business is not what it used to be. Sales activity has slowed down.

Jack targets and calls on new prospects in the territory that he manages with the intention to schedule an appointment to meet with them in person. He was telling me how unmotivated he was because he wasn't getting as many appointments as he used to. People weren't returning his phone calls. The few people he did speak with just weren't interested in meeting with him.

When I asked him to describe his current approach to prospecting this is what he told me. "Once I got the prospect in the phone, I would typically 'wing it' or keep the structure of my approach very loose. I feel this is the best approach because I have to get a sense of the type of prospect I'm talking with before determining a course of action."

Jack also shared with me that he often felt as if he were caught off guard when he finally connected with a live prospect. When cold calling, once Jack got someone face-to-face or on the phone, these are the things he would do.

First, he would introduce himself. Second, he would talk about his company and service. Third, he would do his best to push as much information onto the prospect as possible. He would share with them the features and benefits of his product. Sometimes he would even ballpark pricing and fee structure. Finally, if he were feeling brave enough, he would ask for the appointment. If he did not, he would ask if he could send out some literature and would then let the prospect know that he would be following up at a later date.

If you've been in sales for a while, I don't suppose you know anyone who has ever taken this approach, right?

Okay, here's your chance to help Jack sharpen his prospecting skills. What are you hearing in this scenario? Where is Jack stuck and what needs to change? While you may want to ask Jack more questions to see how you can best assist him, let's break down his approach and see what he needs to adjust immediately to increase his effectiveness.

Let's review what Jack shared with us and see if we can make some suggestions that would help him refine his approach.

♦ **Jack's current approach:** He would typically wing it, or keep the structure of his approach very loose because he believed that he must first get a sense of the type of prospect he's talking with before determining a course of action.

Tip from the sales coach: Jack needs to develop consistency in his approach by creating his own prospecting template to ensure he maintains his focus and intention during each prospecting call.

♦ **Jack's current approach:** Jack then told us that he would talk about his company and service. He would share with the prospect the features and benefits of his product. In some cases, he would tell the prospect that he would be sending them some literature in the mail.

Tip from the sales coach: Jack didn't bother to ask the prospect if he or she wanted to even hear about his company. As a matter of fact, Jack didn't ask the prospect any questions that would classify as a needs analysis. Offering unsolicited information is a great way to turn off a prospect's listening, because you are providing them with information they did not request. This has now become Jack's agenda rather than the prospect's agenda. Once a prospect hears something they are not interested in, he shuts down his listening for the remainder of the conversation.

◆ **Jack's current approach:** Jack mentioned that he would ballpark pricing and fee structure.

Tip from the sales coach: If he's providing information about his company, benefits of his services, as well as a pricing model, are there any reasons left for the prospect to meet with Jack? No, there are not. Jack actually talked himself right out of the appointment.

◆ **Jack's current approach:** Finally, Jack would do his best to push as much information onto the prospect as possible.

Tip from the sales coach: If you feel as if you are pushing through a sales pitch rather than having a conversation with a prospect, consider that the more you push, the more resistance you create. This fosters an adversarial position from the start, putting undue pressure on both you and your prospect. A more effective path of least resistance would be asking questions to uncover their needs, goals, and challenges rather than regurgitating information about your company and product.

Therefore, a prospecting conversation would begin by gaining permission from the prospect to have a conversation in the first place. In other words, cold call with the intention of having a conversation rather then feeling as if you need to pitch a prospect.

While there are other things that may be limiting Jack's ability (such as his inability to schedule a specific time to reconnect with that prospect and offering to send out collateral material), we've unpacked some key points. Now that you've heard what Jack is doing that's keeping him stuck at the same level of performance, let's take what you've learned and develop your own step-by-step prospecting template to generate more appointments and more sales.

Using this template will enable you to develop your unique and personal approach to cold calling and will allow you to drop in the information that relates specifically to you and your product.

The Anatomy of a Prospecting Conversation

When you're speaking to a prospect, do you know the number of steps you follow in your prospecting approach? If you are now attempting to count the steps you take in a prospecting conversation, therein lies a wonderful opportunity to uncover and fine-tune your process so that you can bring it to a conscious level of awareness. As we have discussed, if you can measure it, you can manage it.

Now that we've established the five objectives of a cold call, let's break them down into seven, easy-to-follow action steps that will compose your prospecting template and enable you to have a successful initial conversation with your prospects.

1. Develop Your Opening Approach

2. Deliver a Compelling Reason

3. Get Permission to Begin a Conversation

4. Conduct Your Analysis

5. Summarize to Create Consensus

6. Reconfirm Interest

7. Confirm the Next Step

Imagine that you are beginning your workday and have carved out time to make cold calls. You're in full prospecting mode. You've dialed a number, the phone rings, and the right person on the other end of the phone actually answers. Now you have a prospect on the phone.

What follows are the seven steps of a prospecting conversation, the objective of each step, and sample language you can use when crafting your own prospecting template.

Step 1. Develop Your Opening Approach

Objectives:

◆ Introduce yourself.

◆ Respect their time.

◆ Start a dialogue and have a conversation rather than pitching them.

Example dialogue:

You: *"Hi Mr. Prospect (state the prospect's name)."*

Prospect: **"Yes."**

You: *"(State your name)_____ here from _____ (Company name). Did I catch you at a good time?"* (Another option would be to ask, *"Do you have a moment [a quick second]?"*)

There are conflicting schools of thought as to whether or not to ask this type of question. Some salespeople believe that asking this question gives a prospect the opportunity to say, "No."

While this may be true, providing a prospect with the opportunity to say, "No" doesn't mean that they won't say "No" as you attempt to forge ahead and push your presentation on them.

Cold Medicine

While there is no hard and fast rule when it comes to using their first name or last name when addressing a prospect for the first time, addressing them using their last name is always the safe bet. Otherwise, unless you know them personally, it's a judgment call on your part.

The more important upside to asking this question is that it demonstrates your respect for their time and that you realize your phone call is not the only thing on their plate for the day. The general feedback that I hear from salespeople who ask this question is, "Most prospects

I speak with comment about how much they appreciate the fact that I was courteous enough to ask this question out of respect for their time and their daily agenda. As a result, they are actually more inclined to speak with me." That's why I would suggest asking this question.

What follows are the four general responses you will get when you ask a prospect this question and how you can respond to each one.

"Yes." Great! Move forward.

"No." If you hear this, don't give up yet! Instead, respond with another question. For example, "I apologize for the imposition. What would be a better day and time to contact you regarding (state one or two compelling reasons)." Here's one opportunity to use your compelling reasons! After delivering this question, keep in mind that you may still have an opportunity to continue this conversation after they hear your compelling reasons.

"No, but go ahead." You've still gotten permission. Keep going!

"Click" (They hang up). There's nothing you can do here except to move on to more promising prospects.

Once you can determine whether or not you will be continuing this conversation, move to the next step.

Step 2. Deliver a Compelling Reason

Objective:

◆ Generate interest.

◆ What's in it for them?

Example dialogue:

You: *"Thanks! Mr. Prospect, I'm sure you're busy, so I'll be brief. The reason for my call is this …"*

Another approach may sound like, *"I'm calling you/contacting you today because we specialize in _____ (Below are some examples of what you can say as it relates to this blank space.)"*

Examples for the prior sentence:

- Working with (state industry or profession. For example, accountants, business owners, managers, salespeople)
- Filling the needs of small business owners
- Providing unique solutions for HR professionals
- Assisting companies such as yours
- Developing systems (that enable you to)

You: *"So that you/they can:*

1. State Compelling Reason #1
2. State Compelling Reason #2
3. State Compelling Reason #3
   (Note: Use three compelling reasons only if your compelling reasons are short. Otherwise, only use one or two.)

Notice at this point in your prospecting conversation, I still did not mention what I do or how I do it. Remember, at this stage prospects don't care what you do or how you do it. They only want to know what they can expect as an end result.

Step 3. Get Permission to Begin a Conversation

Objective:

- Get them involved.
- Get permission to have a conversation.

What follows is an example of the dialogue you can use to gain permission to begin a conversation.

You: *"Mr. Prospect, depending on what you are currently doing, I don't know whether or not you have a need or an interest in our (training, consulting, IT, placement, financial, marketing) services."*

"But with your permission, I was hoping to ask you a few questions and see if there's a way to assist you in _____ (state one compelling reason.)"

You can also use a more general statement as an alternative to the prior sentence. *"But with your permission, I was hoping to ask you a few questions to determine if there's anything we offer that you could benefit from."*

Then, continue with this question.

You: *"Would you be comfortable spending just a few minutes with me if I stick to my timetable?"*

This approach accomplishes several objectives.

1. **You Are Creating a Healthy Atmosphere:** This approach diffuses the prospect, lowers their resistance, and brings down their guard. As such, it creates a healthier atmosphere rather than pushing your way through the call. Making the statement, "I don't know whether or not you have a need or an interest in our product" lets them know you are not trying to force something down their throat that they may not need or may not be ready for, such as trying to sell them something or make an appointment with them.

2. **You Are Asking for Permission:** Pushing through a sales pitch creates resistance on the other end. Resistance generates friction, which creates a defensive or adversarial posture from the start. Asking this question opens up a dialogue, making it possible for you to gain confirmation from the prospect that they are indeed willing to have a preliminary conversation with you. You are now able to move them into the needs analysis or questioning part of your prospecting conversation.

3. **You Are Establishing a Timeline:** By asking, "Would you be comfortable spending just a few minutes with me if I stick to my timetable?" you let the prospect know that you are honoring their time and that you're not going to keep them on the phone for longer than a few minutes (or the timeline you've established), eliminating the chance of the prospect making the assumption that this call will drag on for 30 minutes or longer.

Step 4. Conduct Your Analysis

Objective:

◆ Ask questions to uncover the prospect's current situation, objectives and challenges and determine if the prospect has a need for your product or service.

◆ Establish if you and this prospect make a good fit. (Do you want this prospect as a customer?)

Cold Calling Conundrum

In some instances, prospects may be reluctant to answer any questions as they relate to their company or themselves. After all, in most cases they don't even know who you are! Therefore, consider setting the stage for confidentiality by making the following statement before moving into your needs analysis.

"Mr. Prospect, I want you to know that, regardless of whether or not you become one of my valued clients, please know that as with all of my clients, everything we talk about will always be held in the strictest of confidence."

Diagnose Rather Than Dump

At this point during your conversation with a prospect, instead of getting permission to continue and begin asking questions in order to get the prospect involved in the conversation, salespeople have a tendency to dump information on the prospect.

There's a big difference between diagnosing and dumping. Providing unsolicited information to a prospect is a great way to turn off their listening for the remainder of the conversation. Whether you're offering a solution or sharing information about your company or product, you are providing information that has not been requested!

Besides, how can you offer a solution before understanding their unique and specific problem, concern, or long-term objectives? Doing so would be equivalent to a doctor prescribing medication or treatment to a patient before they even meet with them and have a chance to diagnose their problem!

Moreover, if you give them all of the information that you would normally provide during a follow-up meeting, then what is their motivation to meet with you? By sharing too much information up-front, you may wind up forfeiting the chance to meet with them. So, be careful not to talk yourself right out of the next step in your cold calling strategy, such as scheduling a follow-up meeting.

Your needs analysis consists of carefully crafted questions that will accomplish several objectives.

Questions will ...

- ◆ Uncover new selling opportunities that you may never have been able to identify otherwise.

- ◆ Get the prospect involved.

- ◆ Uncover the prospect's current situation, needs, goals, and objectives.

- ◆ Uncover the prospect's pain, problems, and challenges.

- ◆ Determine whether or not there's a fit.

- ◆ Determine whether or not you want this prospect as a customer.

- ◆ Raise the prospect's awareness when asked to reevaluate something while challenging their current negative perceptions and patterns of behavior as they relate to their industry and your product or service.

- ◆ Enable you to align your product's benefits around the prospect's specific needs so that your solution becomes a perfect fit for them.

Whether you are selling a product or service that your prospect has not used before or want to position your product or service so that you can become the prospect's primary vendor and take the place of the their current vendor, what follows are some examples of questions you can use during a needs analysis.

1. What's working well?

2. What's not working well or what areas would you like to see improved?

3. What do you like about your current (vendor/solution provider, product, service)?

4. If you could create the ideal (solution, product, service) what would you like to improve or change about the current product/service you are using?

5. What solution would my product have to offer that would motivate you enough to explore working with us?

6. If you could magically eliminate three of your biggest problems, headaches, or stresses what would they be? (If there were three problems that you would want to see resolved with your current [vendor, product, service] what would they be?)

7. How do these challenges affect your (business, bottom line, performance, profitability)?

8. How does this (current problem, headache) affect you and your job? (What is it costing you?)

Here's a key point regarding question eight. Notice what this question accomplishes. You are tying the challenges that the prospect experiences directly to them and their position. By doing so, you are having the prospect identify their own cost as a result of these challenges and how it personally impacts them.

Once you have a prospect articulate their personal cost as a result of certain challenges and problems, you now have someone who is more motivated and willing to make changes and eliminate these challenges.

Cold Medicine

People resist what they hear but believe what they say. By asking questions, your prospects can then share their goals and challenges with you. As a result they will be more inclined to support and act upon what they say, rather than a salesperson telling them what they need to do or what they perceive the prospect's needs and problems may be.

To Ask or Not to Ask

The number of questions you ask is dependent on the length of time you have with each prospect as well as the quality of the information you receive. If you have a prospect who has shared an obvious need they have or a problem that needs immediate attention, it's up to you to decide if you have enough of the right information to take the next step in your cold calling conversation.

Therefore, it's critical that you take the time to develop the most effective questions that will enable you to obtain the appropriate information you need. Once you do so, keep them in front of you when speaking with a prospect.

When you craft the questions you will be asking each prospect, ask yourself this, "What do I really, really want and need to learn about each prospect?" Realize that it's going to be those tough questions you ask that will create greater selling opportunities.

Maximize Your Prospecting Time

Another prospecting philosophy that has been debated by salespeople is the question of how many questions do you ask a prospect during an initial contact? How detailed should your needs analysis be?

The answer is, it depends on your sales process. If the objective of your prospecting efforts is to book a face-to-face meeting with that prospect, some salespeople tell me, "Keith, I intentionally avoid asking all of my questions during an initial conversation, even if I did have the opportunity to do so. The reason being, if I ask all of my needs analysis questions during my first prospecting conversation with them, then what questions do I ask during my second exploratory meeting with them?"

In theory, this may make sense. However, as a salesperson, your most valuable non-negotiable commodity is time. Picture this scenario. Lori is a new salesperson who recently finished reading this book and designed her prospecting system accordingly. As a result, her prospecting efforts were finally paying off! She was feeling great about the results she was generating.

Lori spent a considerable amount of time on the phone cold calling and using her new approach. And because of the high number of in-person meetings Lori scheduled, she now had prospects interested enough to review a proposal from her that would outline the initiative she would set out for them. A few months later and Lori was on her way to becoming a top producer.

Now that she had some more sales under her belt, she began getting calls from her clients requesting her support and assistance. Referrals from her new clients began trickling in. Lori now had the additional responsibility of managing client expectations while providing them with the information or service they needed as it related to her product.

As you can see, Lori began with one activity, cold calling, which generated a minimum of four additional activities that she needed to find the time for. These new activities included in-person meetings with new prospects, writing and submitting new proposals, customer service and managing client expectations, and following up with the referrals she received.

While Lori's sales numbers were reaching an all-time high, at the same time, she noticed the new challenge of balancing and completing all of these additional activities that were now on her plate as a byproduct of her cold calling efforts.

Ironically, she began to struggle with honoring the timeline she put aside for cold calling, the very activity that generated these other tasks. Not wanting her cold calling efforts to suffer or be compromised, she found herself having to juggle her daily routine and move other appointments and tasks around because of the sheer number of in-person meetings she had scheduled.

Right Activities, Wrong Prospect

As Lori forged ahead in her quest to drive up her sales numbers, she began noticing that the quality of the appointments or, more specifically, the prospects she was meeting with were not as qualified as she would like. She started becoming frustrated, unsure of what to do. The more she met with prospects that were not in a position to even review a proposal from her, the more discouraged and aggravated she became.

When Lori finally came to me, it was clear that something had to change. I asked her, "How much time do you spend meeting with prospects that you feel you are better off not meeting with in the first place?" After she factored in her meeting preparation time, drive time to and from each appointment, and the actual meeting time, she reluctantly responded, "Between 10 to 12 hours each week, if not more. That's almost two full workdays!"

Quality Rather Than Quantity

Lori was suffering from the belief that quantity was better than quality. Somewhere, it was driven into her head that the more appointments you make the better. And considering that her sales team was praised for filling up their schedule with appointments each week and reprimanded when they did not, I wonder where she learned this.

Unfortunately, this strategy produced a residual, negative effect. Lori wasted a minimum of one day each week meeting with prospects that she was better off without.

"What if you used your prospecting time more effectively? What if you were able to eliminate these unproductive appointments from your schedule?" I inquired. By this time, Lori was all ears. We then discussed what would happen if she wove in the critical needs analysis questions into her initial prospecting conversation rather than keeping them as her "Ace" only to be used during an in-person meeting. Lori was willing to give it a try.

Besides, what's the point of having a second exploratory meeting with a prospect if you could accomplish what needs to be done and gain the essential information you need about that prospect during your initial call? And if you're hesitant to ask these "second meeting" questions during your initial conversation, the same questions that would better qualify each prospect, you run the risk of booking an appointment with a prospect who may not be a fit. It all boils down to this: What's the point of spending your valuable time having a second meeting (the cold call was the first meeting) with a prospect if they aren't a fit for you anyway? The only way for Lori to break this cycle was to give her sales process an overhaul.

Very soon, Lori was back on top and feeling great. She learned the very important distinction between the quantity of appointments and the quality of them. As a result of reducing the number of in-person meetings and expanding upon the initial needs analysis she conducted with each prospect, Lori was able to shorten her selling cycle dramatically. She was now able to meet with truly qualified prospects. By focusing on the quality of appointments, Lori freed up an additional day each week to fit in all of her appointments.

Sure, the number of appointments she scheduled each week may have dropped a bit. However, you can't argue with results. Besides, she wasn't getting any closer to her sales goal by meeting with unqualified prospects. Now that Lori's attention was directed on prospects that warrant a meeting, she was able to balance all of her responsibilities with ease, become hyperefficient, and bring in more sales.

Step 5. Summarize to Create Consensus

Objective:

♦ Confirm that you have an accurate understanding of the prospect's specific needs, goals, and challenges.

♦ If you misunderstood the prospect's core goals or needs, you can now create the opportunity for the prospect to clarify their intended message, which prevents costly misunderstandings and communication breakdowns.

♦ Make the prospect feel as if they are truly being heard, listened to, and understood.

♦ Reinforce what the prospect knows to be true about their situation.

To effectively summarize and confirm what the prospect has shared with you, use a *clarifier*. It is crucial to demonstrate to others that they are being listened to and understood. To make a prospect feel heard during a conversation, use a clarifier when responding to what they shared with you. If what you rephrased was inaccurate, you now have created the opportunity for the prospect to clarify their intended message, which prevents costly misunderstandings and communication breakdowns.

Cold Callingo

A **clarifier** is a statement that rephrases, in your own words, the message that someone communicated to you. This is done to assure the person you are speaking with that you not only heard, but also understood them. Then, you can confirm the next course of action. The advantage of using a clarifier is that it makes the person you are speaking with feel heard. Feeling heard is a level beyond just being listened to and few of us, especially in the selling profession, ever cause the other person to feel as if they were truly heard.

Here are a few examples of clarifiers that you can weave into your response to a prospect.

◆ "For my own understanding, what you are truly saying is ..."

◆ "What I am hearing is ..."

◆ "So, if I understand you correctly, you are currently experiencing a situation (challenge) where ..."

◆ "If I'm hearing you right ..."

Once you recap what you have heard, continue with the following question to confirm that the information you heard was the information that was sent by the prospect.

You: *"Is that accurate/correct?"*

Step 6. Reconfirm Interest

Objective:

◆ Confirm that the prospect is interested in moving forward with the goal of eliminating their challenge(s) or improving their current condition by taking advantage of the benefits that your product or service can offer.

What follows are two examples of a reconfirming question. Notice that in both examples you are filling in the blanks with the information you have gathered from your needs analysis.

Example 1

You: *"Mr. Prospect, would it be safe to say that if there were a way for you to:*

_____

(Restate biggest obstacle. Example: Overcome the challenge/problem of …) and

_____

(Restate their most important goal or objective they shared with you.)

It would be worth exploring/discussing in more detail?"

Example 2

You: *"Is solving the problem/challenge of _____ and/or reaching the goal of _____ important enough to invest 20 minutes (state approximate timeline of your meeting) of your time to explore the possibility of having us assist you in this process?"*

 Cold Calling Conundrum _____

You do not get an appointment with a prospect until you have a problem that's important enough for the prospect to solve or a need that's a priority for them to fill. You must provide the prospect with a reason to meet with you or to take that next step, rather than meeting just for the sake of meeting and then hope there's a fit.

Step 7. Confirm the Next Step

Objective:

◆ Determine the next course of action. Invite the prospect to move into the next phase of your sales process. (Scheduling an appointment, product demonstration, submitting a proposal, free trial, on-site meeting, beta test, becoming their primary vendor, or close the sale and ask for their business.)

The language you use here is dependent upon the next step in your selling strategy, as we just illustrated in the objective. If your next step is to book an appointment, here are some examples of the verbiage you can use.

You: *"Then let's get together for (state timeline. Example: 20 minutes) to see if there's a fit. I will answer your questions, share with you several options, as well as demonstrate how our product will specifically address your challenges and objectives."*

You: *"Mr. Prospect, do you have your calendar handy? What day would be good for you, towards the beginning or the end of the week?"*

You: *"Do mornings or afternoons work better for you?"*

Cold Medicine

When asking a question, it is always useful to provide your prospects with a choice between two options. This will make them feel as if they are making the decision rather than you telling them what to do. It will also increase their feeling of control over the conversation. Finally, asking a question that involves a choice instead of asking a closed-ended question or a question that elicits either a "Yes" or "No" response reduces the chance of hearing a "No." Whatever option they choose, it's moving you closer to a sale.

You: *"By the way, is there anyone else that you can think of who would be part of this evaluation and decision-making process and therefore should be included in this meeting?"*

This question is crucial and certainly communicates the importance of your time as well as the prospect's time. The fact is, you need to make sure that everyone who is responsible for this decision will be at the meeting. The last thing you want to do is schedule an appointment with the so-called decision maker, present your little heart out and then hear, "Wow! This sounds great! I wish Mr. Smith were here for this meeting. He is the other person who is in charge of making this decision. I guess you're going to have to schedule a meeting with him as well."

If you need to qualify your prospect even further, you can ask the following question after you've scheduled the appointment. *"Mr. Prospect, let's say that at the end of our meeting, you absolutely love what we can offer and want take the next step. In order for me to provide you with the information that you are most interested in hearing about, can you share with me the process you follow when making a decision like this and the criteria you use to do so?"*

This question demonstrates your respect for their decision-making process as well as your commitment to deliver the information they need to hear in order to make an educated purchasing decision. This way, you can adjust and align your selling approach around how they buy, rather than how you buy or attempting to figure it out on your own.

Mind Your Manners

Once you determine the meeting time, and you are ready to wrap up the call, continue with the following statement. A simple "thank you" will do.

You: *"Thanks again for the opportunity to meet with you and for taking the time to discuss how we may be able to _____ (restate the benefit of meeting. Example: make your job easier, reduce your overhead, boost your sales). If anything changes on your side or if you need to reschedule, please take down my phone number and e-mail address. Otherwise, I'll reconfirm this meeting with you on _____ (state date prior to appointment). I'm looking forward to meeting with you on _____ at _____. Have a great day!"*

It is essential that you practice using your template until you are comfortable and it sounds like a natural conversation, rather than a pitch. It is not uncommon for a salesperson to role-play with someone or rehearse their template out loud a minimum of 30 times before using it. If you have to make changes, make sure that when you practice using your template, you are practicing it the same way consistently, after you make all of your changes. Once you do this, you are ready to make your first cold call with your fabulous new approach.

The Least You Need to Know

♦ Put aside a few hours to develop your own prospecting template. Craft the right questions that will provide you with the information you need most to propose the best solution.

◆ During a cold call, you have less than one minute to capture a prospect's attention.

◆ The quality of the prospects you generate is more important than the quantity.

◆ You don't get an appointment until you've provided the prospect with a reason important enough to warrant a meeting.

◆ You can talk yourself right out of a meeting with a prospect, so be cognizant of how much information you provide.

◆ Let your prospect do the selling for you by asking him the right questions so he can convince himself that there's a need for what you are selling.

Chapter 11

Defusing and Preventing Initial Objections

In This Chapter

- ◆ Learn to love objections
- ◆ Become more proactive and responsive
- ◆ You'll never have to close a sale again
- ◆ Questions that open up new selling opportunities
- ◆ Collateral materials that kill a sale
- ◆ Tapping into unlikely referral sources

Objections. You just gotta love 'em! You can't sell with them and you can't sell without them. It's been a love-hate relationship ever since the first salesperson began roaming the earth in search of their precious sale.

While good salespeople hunt for new selling opportunities in the most unlikely of places, their search for objections is far from diligent.

Instead, salespeople tend to avoid objections at all costs, crossing their fingers and hoping with all of their heart that if they just do everything right, they won't run into any objections. In their eyes, objections are immense obstacles that prevent or stall the sale.

What if you began seeking out objections right from the start? What if objections actually assist you in your selling efforts rather than act like a barrier to your next sale? What if your perception of objections and the role they play in your selling process is actually hindering your selling efforts more than any actual objection ever could?

Before you go running to the dictionary to uncover what an objection truly is, in this chapter you will find a new, more appealing definition of what an objection is so that you can use them as a conduit to a new sale rather than an obstacle to overcome.

Become Responsive Rather Than Reactive

If you took a survey amongst sales professionals, many of them would know and could articulate what needs to be accomplished during their initial contact with a prospect as well as during a follow-up meeting with a qualified prospect. When asked to list a few of the important steps and strategies while delivering a masterful presentation, they might respond with the following:

- ◆ Ask the prospect questions to uncover his or her needs and concerns in order to provide the most appropriate solution for them.
- ◆ Actively listen for buying signs as well as preliminary objections or concerns that may get in the way or stall the sale.
- ◆ Create the space for the prospect to do most of the talking during the meeting.
- ◆ Sell on value not on price.
- ◆ Differentiate my company from my competitors.

Although many sales professionals
have some blueprint or selling
strategy to follow when cold calling or during their meeting with a
prospect, most admit that they don't
always apply these techniques during
every cold call or sales presentation.
It seems that when salespeople experience their first *objection* or obstacle,
something happens that throws them
off their initial path: They start performing unhealthy sales practices
and revert to old ineffective selling
habits.

 Cold Callingo

An **objection** is a sign
of interest, a request for
additional information, a prospect's concern or fear that
needs to be acknowledged
and satisfied in order to continue guiding the prospect
through your sales process
and to its natural conclusion
(a sale).

When salespeople feel a possible threat to their selling efforts, they
become concerned that they will lose the sale and at that specific
moment salespeople do something that creates a barrier between their
prospects and themselves. That is, they *react*.

Reacting is the aggressive and often abrasive action or posture a salesperson takes which quickly erodes the relationship between the salesperson and prospect.

Think about the word. Reaction is an action you have taken before.
When you react to what your prospect says or does, you are acting
from your instincts or past experiences, surrendering all your personal
power to act by choice.

For example, something happens during a cold call and you think back
to what had transpired during a previous situation. Whether it's a similar cold call you made, another prospect you met with, or a common
objection you've heard, you react the way you did before. Reacting to
these situations only succeeds in keeping you stuck in survival mode, re-
creating the same experiences and results over and over again.

One of the greatest barriers to prospecting success is that salespeople
spend much of their time reacting to a prospect.

Reacting to a prospect based on old habits creates pressure for the
both of you, fostering an unhealthy relationship from the start.

Are Your Selling Skills Revolving or Evolving?

As we discussed in Chapter 4, when a salesperson makes a cold call, he or she goes into that call thinking about either a past experience or a future expectation. If you're focused on what transpired during a previous situation, you will react the same way as you did in the past.

Conversely, you may be focused on the end result of your conversation with the prospect. If you are thinking about the end of the call, then you are concerned about the outcome or whether or not you will sell. And if you are concentrating on the outcome, then you can't be in tune to or truly listening to the prospect. A preoccupied mind does not allow for the space to create the best solutions for your prospects during a prospecting conversation.

If you're a golfer you'll appreciate this analogy. Have you ever missed a shot and carried that feeling of frustration over to the next shot? Essentially, you're living in and still focused on the past. Even though the past may have happened moments ago, it is still the past and that is where your focus is when preparing for that next shot. The simple truth is, your outlook on the next shot will determine the outcome. So if you are telling yourself, "Don't turn your head" or "Don't swing too hard" or "Don't miss this putt," there is a very strong chance that whatever you are focusing on is exactly what will happen.

The End of the Sales Slump

Think about a time when you may have experienced a dip in your performance. This occurs because you are continually reacting the same way you did during previous appointments, presentations or prior cold calls.

Reacting to a selling situation or to what a prospect says keeps you stuck where you are, preventing you from moving forward. When you finally sell or achieve your desired result when prospecting, you have taken new actions or responded to the prospect in a different way, whether you realize this on a conscious level or not.

If you enter into a sales call reacting from either a past experience or a future expectation, what is missing? The present. Imagine what would be possible if you had the ability to act by choice to each situation in the moment, without concerns about the outcome and without limiting or unconscious reactions based on your past experiences or beliefs.

For starters, you will hear more about what your prospects really want. You will develop a greater level of awareness, become more sensitized to your prospects' needs and feelings, and learn how to best serve them. You will no longer be concerned whether or not something will threaten your sale. Instead, you will be fully present and engaged in helping your prospect make the right choice or purchasing decision. Finally, you will enjoy the selling process more, as it becomes less of an effort and more of a natural process.

If your goal is to create a mutually beneficial relationship with your prospect, it requires conscious action. One created by reaction is based on past experiences, future expectations, fear, limiting beliefs, or negative assumptions.

To generate greater results during the selling process and prevent costly selling mistakes, learn to respond to your prospects rather than react from the past.

One responds to a prospect when he or she is fully present with them, not thinking about what happened in the past or thinking about how the conversation will end. Becoming responsive means viewing each appointment or cold call as a fresh, new experience with boundless possibilities, uninhibited by what had happened on a previous sales call.

Cold Medicine

Exercise your power of choice. When you are in reaction mode, your actions are responses to external circumstances or other people. Exercise choice over how you respond to events in a healthier way. Until you practice responding, you are always in some form of reaction, surrendering your personal power to act by choice. If you are responding then you can choose how you are going to act or think. If you are reacting, you can't!

So, how can you determine whether you are responding or reacting? If you act from your instincts or from your ego, it's a reaction, likely based on some fear or threat. We react instinctively to bright lights by squinting. Our body reacts to the cold weather by shivering. The difference between our body's reaction to certain external forces and our reaction to our prospects is that we have the power to control how we react during a cold call.

Responding is adapting to what is occurring without feeling threatened. You know you are responding if you feel less distracted and have plenty of time to make changes in order to create a new selling opportunity.

To begin making this shift from reacting to responding, practice responding to what the prospect says rather than reacting to what he or she is saying.

The Question Is the Answer—The Power of Questions

The greatest salespeople know how to respond to what the prospect says with a question in order to have the prospect support what it is she had stated.

These salespeople actually *listen* the sale out of the prospect by asking the right questions.

> **Cold Medicine** _____
>
> Although you need the right answers to keep up, to get ahead you need the right questions. Therefore, focus more on the question than on the answer, solution, or refuting the statement to the prospect's objection. This way, the prospect can uncover the solution to their concern. And if the prospect creates it, they are more apt to own it and act on it. The question *is* the answer.

On the surface, it's apparent what questions accomplish. A question is the tool of inquiry you use to gather information. While this might be fairly obvious, questions actually accomplish much more. In Chapter 10, I shared with you several advantages of asking questions during a prospecting conversation. Here are some additional benefits you can realize when asking the right questions:

- ◆ Offer a possible new perspective.

- ◆ Honor the prospect's intelligence. (They really do have the answers.)

- ◆ Slow down automatic thinking and responses.

- ◆ Raise awareness when stopped to rethink something and challenge current perceptions or behavior.

- ◆ Enable the person to illuminate, crystallize, and clarify their thoughts.

- ◆ Stimulate new answers and possibilities. (Questions make a person think!)

- ◆ Encourage ownership by empowering a prospect to come up with their own solutions that are a perfect fit for them rather than being told what to do.

- ◆ Create more of a "pressure free" and consultative environment. Questions let the prospect sell themselves and do the selling for you!

The most brilliant thinkers, innovators, and explorers of our time emphasized questions more than answers, a characteristic of all highly evolved individuals. Note the root of the word question, "quest"—the act of seeking or pursuing something. This desire to search and journey beyond what is already known and seek out that which would enhance the quality of our lives or broaden our wisdom is what has enabled humanity to continually evolve over time.

Curiosity stimulates questions, and questions then evoke change and exploration, arousing our desire to create and discover even more.

All the answers we ever get are responses to questions. However, because our society has become answer-oriented, we often wind up with ineffective solutions because we fail to construct the right questions that generate greater results or possibilities, focusing more on the solution, rather than on the question.

Questions precede change. They are the foundation for creating that which we want or that which we want to avoid. (Some questions actually create more objections.) Therefore, it's important to be aware of the words you use in the questions you ask.

Stop Closing, Start Opening

In a perfect world, we would be able to get through our entire prospecting conversation and at the end the prospect would say something like, "Sure! Come on out to my office. I can't wait to meet with you!" or "I'd love to buy that. Where do I sign?" However, something is missing. Those little things that get in the way during our prospecting and selling efforts—objections.

One of the most popular concerns amongst salespeople who have to cold call is sounding too pushy or putting too much pressure on a prospect. This concern expands when the topic of "closing the deal" is discussed. I often hear salespeople say, "I'm not a strong closer," "I don't handle objections very well," or "I don't want to push a prospect into doing something before they are ready."

As such, salespeople become hesitant to ask for the sale or at the very least, invite the prospect to the next step in their sales process. Then they wonder why their competition is taking all of their business away!

Cold Medicine

Salespeople don't overcome objections, prospects do. The only person who can truly overcome an objection is the prospect. Salespeople create the opportunity for this to occur through their effective use of questions. Selling is therefore the art of asking questions, listening openly and intentionally, and gaining information, not giving it.

The word "closing" has certainly gotten a bad rap because of the negative connotation associated with it. After all, look at the root of the word, "close," which is synonymous with shutting, locking, finishing, final, and end.

Here's a little known secret that the top salespeople are aware of. Never close again! You will never have to worry about sounding like you are "selling" (as in pushing) a prospect again. The alternative action that I'm suggesting results in more profitable sales with less effort.

Many salespeople believe that their product or service should speak for itself. Once they encounter any resistance, they are quick to ask for a time best suited for a follow-up call. Unfortunately, this "dead time" is when many selling opportunities are lost.

Instead of closing, create a new opening without having to close. You can accomplish this in a simple conversation that does not threaten your integrity by sounding too "pushy."

The word "closing" is really the wrong title for this phase in the selling process. This phase should be considered the "opening." It is at this time when you are suggesting a new possibility in the form of a question for your prospect to consider that might better suit his or her needs.

Here are the most generic and common obstacles to selling: "I need to think about it, the price is too high, I want to shop around, I need more information, the monthly installment is too much, I'm already working with another vendor, I'm not the only decision maker, we have no budget, I'm not interested, this is a bad time, and so on." How can you create a new opening that can overcome these concerns?

Cold Medicine

Top producers aren't great closers, they are great openers. As opposed to closing the opportunity for a sale to occur, you are opening up a new possibility to work with that particular prospect. Instead of referring to the art of overcoming objections as the closing strategy, consider it your opening strategy.

Remember the new definition of an objection. It's a sign of interest or a request for more information. Therefore, what the prospect is not saying in the prior examples is "No, I don't want to and never will use your product or service." What they are really saying is, "I'm saying 'No' or a form of 'No' because you haven't given me enough of a compelling reason to explore what you have in more detail."

In other words, instead of fearing objections, embrace them. Every objection provides you with a new opportunity to share the right information with a prospect that can move them into the next step in your sales process.

The key for this conversation to work without you sounding like a high pressure or "cheesy" salesperson is to get permission by asking the following question. You can create a new opening to overcome a prospect's concern by asking for permission to do so.

Here's an example of the verbiage you can use when gaining permission. "Mr. Prospect, if the possibility existed where we can (state the solution to the objection) is that something you would be interested in talking about?"

If you refer to the list of common objections I shared with you earlier, here are several examples of how you can respond to the objection, "We don't have a budget for this. (We can't afford this.)"

The intention behind the following responses is to first ensure that you are, in fact dealing with an actual objection rather than a smokescreen. Therefore, isolate the objection down to its core to see if the initial objection they shared with you is really the truth or if it's something else. The "something else" could be that they don't believe you, don't trust you yet, don't believe you or your product can help them, they may not be the decision maker, they have been burned before, they are simply having a bad day and you are their new target, and so on.

Prospect: **"We don't have a budget for this."**

You: *"Mr. Prospect, I certainly understand that. It seems as if everyone today is more sensitive about operating within their limited budget, only making investments into proven (products, services, strategies, processes) that they know are going to work."*

Here's another example of a segue you can use before asking your responsive question: *"Mr. Prospect, thanks for being so upfront with me. I can certainly appreciate your position. I'm sure there's even more pressure to make certain that the limited funds you do have are being invested in the right place."*

What follows are some responsive questions you can ask in this situation.

- ◆ "May I ask, is it that you have no budget now, or no budget ever?"

- ◆ "May I ask, is it that you don't have a budget at all or is it more about the hesitation to try something new and different that has not yet been proven to work for you?"

♦ "How much do you think my product would cost that would cause you to feel that there's no budget available for this?"

♦ "Has the budget been cut altogether or has it been dramatically reduced?"

♦ "Is it a budgetary concern or are you more concerned about the value you will receive?"

♦ "So then, is it more a function of not having the money to invest or is it more about making sure that your limited budget is being invested in the right place to ensure a measurable ROI?"

♦ "May I ask what factors you consider when choosing where to invest your (printing, travel, marketing, training) budget?" ("How do you make that decision?)"

♦ "So, if you don't have the money right now, who in your company does?"

After using these types of questions, you should be able to confirm whether the objection they shared is the core objection or if the real objection is actually something else. These questions will enable you to expose what their primary concern actually is.

Once this is accomplished, before offering a response, a solution, or a new possibility that would defuse their objection, now is the time for you to get permission to discuss a solution to their concern. Here are some examples:

♦ *"Mr. Prospect, at this point, I'm not sure if we can provide you with the ROI that my other customers have experienced. However, if the possibility existed where we can demonstrate a rapid ROI so that you can start profiting from (realizing the advantages of) our service within one month, is that something you would be interested in talking about?"*

♦ *"Mr. Prospect, if budget was no longer an issue for you, would you be open to exploring this in more detail?"* I love these "if" questions. All I did here was reverse or take away the objection to determine if "not having a budget" is the only thing that's truly getting in the way. Now that I've hypothetically removed this objection, their response should be a "yes." If not, then there's still something else going on that they haven't shared with you yet. So keep digging!

◆ *"Mr. Prospect, if I can demonstrate to you in just three minutes how the value you receive will far outweigh the manageable investment amount that I would propose, would you be open to hearing more about how you can achieve this?"* Notice how I include a timeline of three minutes to let the prospect know that this will not take up all of their precious time. Just make sure that you can accomplish what you are proposing in the timeline you stipulate.

If you feel that the prospect is giving you a very vague objection that you really can't grab on to, such as, "I'm not interested," or "I need to think about it" here is yet another opportunity to use a compelling reason in your permission question that would fit for this prospect: *"Mr. Prospect, if the possibility existed where we can (state compelling reason), is that something you would at least be interested in talking about?"*

Here are just a few examples of compelling reasons that you could add to the permission question: "Satisfy your specific needs, cut your overhead by at least 15 percent, increase your sales by 25 percent, position your product in front of more qualified prospects, reduce your stress level, make your life easier, improve efficiency and delivery time, show you how to develop a passive income stream working only three hours a week," and so on.

If they say "Yes," you now have a prospect who is interested in hearing more about what you can offer. So, go for the appointment (sale, demo, or whatever is the next step in your sales process)! Because you have gained permission to explore other options, the prospect is now willing to listen to your suggestions. If you fail to ask permission, and instead dump alternative solutions or more information on them even before you have a true understanding of what their primary objection is, you are running the risk of sounding too pushy, which causes a prospect to put up their defensive walls that prevent you from making a sale.

The next time you run into an objection, defuse it by getting permission to continue with the conversation. The result will be more sales with less resistance.

Remember, like all selling strategies, there are no absolutes. When some prospects say "No" they actually mean it! However, if you can convert even 35 percent of the "No's" you hear into selling opportunities, then this process would be considered wildly successful.

Defusing Initial Objections

Now that we have uncovered a new approach to closing or as we have now defined as "opening," what follows are two more examples you can use when responding to the initial objections you may hear that have been proven to defuse objections and create new selling opportunities.

Rather than react to an objection with a *statement* that creates an adversarial posture between you and the prospect (Example: defending your position, service, or product) respond to the objections you hear using one of the following approaches. Notice that each approach has a question woven into it.

First Approach—The Pleasure-Oriented Response

This response is similar to the approach we just discussed regarding how you can gain permission from a prospect to continue with the conversation.

You: "Mr. Prospect, with your experience and what you've seen, I know you may not believe this now (or "I know this may be hard to believe"), but what if there was a way to:

(Note to Reader: State your three top compelling reasons or state the three goals/objectives that the prospect shared during your needs analysis.)

1. _____

2. _____

3. _____

Would even the potential of (attaining these goals, achieving these results) be important enough to explore in more detail?"

Second Approach—The Problem-Oriented Response

This approach is a bit different. Here, you are actually pointing out the pain that other prospects and clients have experienced, problems that your prospect may not want to readily admit until you bring them to the surface. If the prospect you are speaking with has experienced one or more of the challenges you now brought to the surface, they will be more inclined to want to fix the problem or, at the very least, hear more about what you can do for them.

Moreover, it demonstrates to the prospect that you are a salesperson who truly understands their situation and the challenges they are faced with.

You: "When I speak to other (homeowners, people, parents, buyers/ business owners, sales professionals, managers, hr professionals, accountants), I have found that, although they may feel they (for example: are doing well and want to continually improve, are happy with their current vendor/solution provider, etc.), they still run into situations such as:

(Note to Reader: State the top three pains that your customers have experienced.)

1. _____

2. _____

3. _____

Then follow up with the following question:

Are any of these a concern of yours?" (Note to Reader: You can also replace the question above with one of the following two questions if you prefer.)

◆ "Is it safe to say that you've experienced one or more of these challenges at one point or another?"

◆ "Do any of these challenges sound familiar to you?"

Warm Wisdom

Questions are the type of language we use to get information that we wouldn't have gotten otherwise.

Once you hear a "yes" response to this question, go back to step 7 in your prospecting template (see Chapter 10) or refer to the permission-based questions in the prior section, "Stop Closing, Start Opening" that you can ask to gain permission to continue with the conversation.

Responsive Questions That Get to the Real Objection

To add more tools to your toolbox, I've unpacked several additional questions you can use when responding to an objection. These questions will enable you to gather more information in order to create an opportunity for the prospect to buy from you.

Some examples of responsive questions are:

1. If it were possible for us to satisfy and alleviate your specific concerns, would you be interested in discussing this in more detail?

2. (I can certainly appreciate how you feel.) May I ask why you feel that way?

3. What are the top three benefits you would want to realize if you were to make this investment?

4. What do you need to see in order to feel confident that you've made the best purchasing decision?

5. Is it possible that there is another approach/solution here?

6. What else do you think may be possible?

7. I'm not sure what you mean by that. Can you say more?

8. That's interesting. Will you share with me why you see it that way?

9. What solution would my product have to offer that would motivate you enough to explore working with me?

10. If a prospect says, "We're not ready now. Call back in a few months," here's a great question to respond with. "May I ask, what might be changing within the next few months that would then make it a better time to discuss this?" This question enables you to smoke out the real objection, just in case "we're not ready now" is not it. Moreover, you may uncover some additional information you can use that will allow you to reposition or tie in your product with those timely concerns or problems that were initially causing the prospect to delay his conversation with you for a few months.

Now, the responses you hear as a result of using these questions will enable you to create a new opportunity for a sale to occur. The prospect will either convince herself that she should hear more about what you have to offer or share with you the reasons why she does not want to continue with this conversation (or if you are at the end of delivering your presentation, the reason why she will not buy from you).

Either way, you now know exactly what the prospect is feeling as opposed to walking away scratching your head and wondering why she did not buy.

Notice the type of questions I listed. These questions are known as expansion questions, which are more effective in opening up a conversation to gain more information rather than closed-ended questions or questions that elicit a "Yes" or "No" response. (For example: Is that? Does that? Doesn't it? Isn't it? Will you? Doesn't it?)

Cold Medicine

What about those prospects that come right out and say, "No, I'm not interested." Here's a quick question that you can use to salvage any opportunity to convert this person into a viable prospect. "Is that 'no' for now or 'no' forever?" In many instances, you will get a response that would keep the selling opportunity alive and classify this person as a prospect. Here is the response you would love to hear. "I'm working on some other projects right now. Call me back in a couple of weeks (months)." If you notice in this example, 'no' was not the actual objection. By asking this responsive question, you have uncovered something under the 'no;' the real objection. As you can see, the objection was actually more of a timing objection ("Now is not the best time") that you can wrap your hands around and overcome.

Responding to an objection with a question reinforces your commitment to understanding the unique needs of each prospect and becoming their trusted adviser. By uncovering their true concerns, you can then provide a solution that's a perfect fit for them. This strengthens your relationship with your prospects, as you take the time to provide the information or solutions they want, not the ones you think they want. Now, you can determine exactly what is needed to best satisfy your prospect's needs in order to earn their business.

Questions motivate people to think and create solutions on their own. Besides, what do you think a prospect is going to believe more, what you say or what she says?

Being responsive creates more space within a conversation to explore a topic in more detail, providing a buffer to handle certain obstacles that may prevent the sale. This space will provide you with the room to develop new selling opportunities with your prospects that you may never have noticed before.

Cold Medicine

Be curious. Tap into that innate curiosity that all children have and question everything! Because you are in the business of providing solutions, invest the time to uncover the person's specific need or problem as opposed to providing common solutions that you assume may fit for everyone. For example, the words "Happy, frustrated, successful, satisfied, expensive, affordable and quality," can be interpreted in a variety of ways and often carry a different meaning for each of us.

When you hear a prospect make a comment like, "I want a quality product that will help me produce the results I want at an affordable price. Can you provide that?" use this as an opportunity to explore deeper into what they want or need most. Ask questions such as, "How do you determine whether or not a product has the level of quality that you are looking for?" "What features do you need to see which would ensure that you are getting the quality you want?" "What type of results are you looking for?" "What is affordable to you?" Questions allow you to clarify what you have heard or go into a topic in more depth so you can become clear with what they are really saying.

Patching Your Achilles Heel Permanently

Regardless of what you sell, one thing is certain—eventually you will hear an objection. To take this a step further, if you are selling the same product to the same type of prospect then you can count on hearing the same or similar objections from your prospects.

While many salespeople know this to be true, I find it interesting that most of them have not completed the valuable exercise that I am about to suggest to you. If you know that you're going to hear the same objections from different prospects, then wouldn't it make sense to write out the objections you hear and then craft a rebuttal or a responsive question for each rather than sounding surprised every time they surface?

Consider that one of the primary reasons why salespeople don't like objections is because they haven't effectively planned for how they are going to handle them.

Earlier in this book, I explained that most sales are lost at the beginning of the selling cycle, rather than at the end. Therefore, the more effective you are at uncovering and diffusing any objections up front, the easier it will be to close the sale.

Take the time to list all of the objections you typically hear when cold calling or during a presentation. Then, craft a response to each objection. Chances are, there is probably only a handful of objections that you typically hear.

By outlining your responses to each objection, you can now begin to create some benchmarks regarding what responses defuse the objections best so that you can consistently use what is working every time you speak with a prospect.

The alternative approach is to cross your fingers and hope that no objections come up. (And if you believe in this approach, I have a beautiful bridge to sell you, cheap!)

By the way, this approach to diffusing objections also works at the end of your sales process, after you present your product, demonstration, or proposal, or when you are asking for their business.

As we've discussed, most objections you hear can be responded to with a question. Rather than craft a long response to each objection, craft a question that enables you to extract more information from the prospect so that you can get to the real truth about what's getting in the way of the sale.

Objection	Response (Question)
1.	
2.	
3.	
4.	

Questions will make it possible for you to prospect more effectively, uncover what your prospects really want and provide more effective solutions to their greatest challenges.

Collateral Damage and How to Avoid It

Marty was well into his conversation with a prospect that he cold called minutes ago. The conversation was going great and the prospect was responsive up until the point where Marty was going to conduct his needs analysis to determine if there's a fit.

The prospect then asked the fatal question, "Marty, I'm in a bit of a rush now. Can you send me a brochure or some additional information about your services?"

When Marty responded with a resound, "Yes," he knew that he already blew this selling opportunity. Instead of scheduling another time to speak, Marty lost control of his sales process. He didn't have a chance to conduct his needs analysis to uncover the prospect's challenges and difficulties with their current process or service provider. He was not able to determine the advantages the prospect could realize from making a change.

Cold Calling Conundrum

Sending out a brochure does not overcome any objection. Rather it multiplies them.

Many salespeople look at a request for more information as a good sign. However, these are the same salespeople who have a mighty long list of prospects to call back and check if they received the information that was sent.

How many times do you follow up with a prospect who you've sent collateral material to only to find that they haven't gotten around to reviewing it? And if they did review what you sent them, how many times have you heard, "Thanks for the information. I've gotten everything I need from you at this point. If we have an interest, we will contact you in the future." It's no wonder the prospect responded this way. If they've gotten all of the information they need, then what do they need you for?

Sending out collateral material this early in the game accomplishes nothing more than creating another obstacle that will limit your chance of selling them. The irony is, the act of sending out material to a prospect actually creates an objection. The very thing that you are trying to avoid the most is what you've succeeded in creating. How utterly ironic.

Why should they call you back when they have all of the information they need about your company and product? Why should the prospect put time aside to meet with you if they feel that they have all of the information on paper that you would share with them in person?

The hasty and untimely use of brochures and other marketing material can easily spoil even the best prospecting efforts.

Here are three scenarios that would fool you into thinking that sending out collateral information is a good idea when, in fact, it is not.

1. You get through your prospecting conversation and the next step is scheduling an in-person meeting. The prospect says, "Before we schedule a meeting, is there any information you can send me that I can review?" Don't allow yourself to fall into this trap! (You will see an example of how to respond to this request later on.)

2. You don't get a chance to conduct your needs analysis. Do you even know what information the prospect is looking for? Do you know what their biggest headache is or what their specific goals are? Do you know how you can tie in your product with something timely that's going on with your prospect? No you do not. If you didn't have a chance to conduct a needs analysis, then how do you know what information to send them?

3. The prospect clearly stated that they have no interest and never will. If this is still the case even after you've conducted your needs analysis, then why would you still take the time to pack up and send information to that prospect if they don't have a current need for your product and never will? This is a pitiful attempt to stimulate any interest and is nothing more than an exercise in futility. Thinking that a package of information is going to overcome an objection is a false hope and a pipedream. This action can also be classified as a diversionary tactic. After all, if you are sending out information every time you hear an objection hoping that it stimulates some level of interest, you will never actually have to handle and respond to an objection head-on. For the most part, salespeople overcome objections, not fancy brochures.

Collateral information is so widely misused that it acts as a crutch for many salespeople who are using it to compensate for their failure to develop their selling skills.

The next time you find yourself in a situation where you can take the easy way out by sending literature in the mail, remember Marty. Situations where the salesperson is the one who actually destroys a selling opportunity are totally preventable. Instead of digging your own grave, try this approach the next time you get a request for more information or have the urge to send out your marketing material.

You: *"Mr. Prospect, I appreciate your interest in learning more about our product. To ensure that I send you the appropriate material, what information would you like to see that is most important to you when making a purchasing decision?"*

Prospect: **"Well, I'd like to learn a little more about your company and exactly what features your product offers that the product I'm currently using does not offer."**

You: *"Great! Thanks for letting me know. Based on what you are looking for, the last thing I want to do is put another task on your plate that you have to complete, such as reviewing the information I send you. I know how valuable your time is. My goal is to make your life easier, not more difficult. That's why I'm a bit hesitant to send you something that may do you more of a disservice without learning more about you and your current situation, goals, and experience with the product that you are currently using.*

Based on what you've shared with me, the best brochure I can send you is me! Being an interactive, walking-talking brochure, I can assure you that all of your questions and concerns are addressed. Because you were planning on putting some time aside to read the information I send you, let's schedule a brief meeting instead. This way, if you still have a need for additional information, I would be happy to tailor it around your specific needs and objectives, okay?"

Like every rule, this one also has its exceptions. Here are a few guidelines that will help you determine when it is appropriate to send out your collateral material.

1. The type of material you send to a prospect is generic. For example, if your material does nothing more than open up additional questions about your product or company that only you can answer, it should be okay to send it. Otherwise, it's really a judgment call on your part. I would suggest keeping track of those prospects who you've sent collateral material to and if you actually sold them something.

2. They don't have a need now but they may have a need in the future. If they plan on making a purchase at some point but refuse a meeting with you even after every attempt to schedule one, you can put them on your list of prospects to call back in the future. Your collateral material can then become a great tool to keep your name in front of them up until the point where they are ready to revisit your initial conversation, meet with you, or make a purchase.

3. The prospect needs certain information that is necessary to review prior to taking the next step, such as scheduling a meeting.

These are just a few situations that would justify sending out additional material. Otherwise, keep your materials at bay. If you follow the prospecting and selling system you have put in place, then you may never have to use your collateral material again.

While You Have Their Attention—Opt In

Wouldn't it be great if every prospect became a new customer around our timeline? Now that I'm back down to reality, it's a safe bet that some of the prospects you call on will not be ready to take that next step with you, at least not just yet.

So, like many prospects, they get put on the "callback" list of prospects to call on in the future. A typical conversation would sound something like this:

You: *"Okay, Mr. Prospect. Based on what you're telling me, it sounds like this isn't the best time to explore what we can do for you in more detail. When might be a better time to reconnect with you?"*

Prospect: **"Give me a couple of months to clear off what I already have on my plate. Then I'll be in a better position to discuss this with you."**

You: *"That sounds fair. So, if I quickly check my calendar, you are suggesting to touch base with you again in early March, is that correct?"*

Prospect: **"Yes, that sounds fine."**

At this point, you thank the prospect and create a reminder in your contact management software to call on Mr. Prospect in March.

In March, you reconnect with Mr. Prospect only to find that not only is he no longer with the company, but they bought a similar product that you sell from another vendor!

While there's no foolproof method to prevent this from happening, here's something you can do to dramatically reduce the chance of this happening again. Let's now continue the conversation between you and the prospect where we left off.

You: *"Mr. Prospect, thanks again for your time today. Before we wrap up this conversation, I've noticed that in the past, when I have attempted to reconnect with someone months after our first contact, many things have transpired. Changes in their position, in their company, or in their life often have tendency to divert even the best-laid plans. Because there are so many things that can happen in two months, I was hoping that I could stay in contact with you without stepping over the line and being annoying about it. With your permission, can I contact you from time to time with updates about our product or valuable information that you may find of interest as it relates to your business?"*

By asking this question and gaining confirmation that it's okay to stay in touch, you now have a prospect that has given you permission to continue to prospect them instead of sending out unsolicited information that will do nothing more than aggravate and turn off a prospect.

Sure, it may sound like they are not in a position today to explore your offering in more detail. However, that doesn't mean they will be in the same position in the future.

A monthly newsletter, a free trial, an article of interest, collateral material, or a great new product feature are just a few ways to deliver value during this "down time" and keep your finger on the pulse of every prospect you speak with.

This way, if things change on the prospect's side, you won't be the last person to find out.

Prospecting Your Prospects?

As much as I would love to make this claim, I'm sorry to inform you that even with your best intentions, every prospect will not become a customer.

At some point during your prospecting efforts you are going to determine whether or not that particular prospect is a fit for you and your product. Whether this prospect becomes a client of yours in the future or remains a prospect of yours for eternity, there still may be an opportunity to prospect them but not for what you may think.

I'm referring to prospecting your prospects for other prospects! After all, your prospects know prospects who know prospects and on and on and on.

If you want to ensure that every prospecting effort provides you with the opportunity to maximize your time and uncover a new prospect, then consider this your last ditch effort to find new prospects.

Let me explain. Let's say you contact a potential prospect who you initially feel could benefit from what you sell. You do everything in your power to try to convert this person into a qualified prospect. After speaking with them in detail, you've determined that there is not a fit. At this point, here are your options:

1. Thank them for their time and move on to your next call.

2. Because it is clear that this person will not become a prospect at any time, prospect them!

If you opt for choice number two, here is a sample of the language you can use when doing so.

You: *"Mr. Prospect, thanks again for taking the time to speak with me today. I've certainly enjoyed our conversation. Based on what you are currently doing, it seems that our product is not a good fit for you. However, I hope our conversation reinforced what a great job your current vendor is doing for you.*

While there may not be anything I can provide you that would make a measurable difference in comparison to what you are doing now, maybe there's another way we can work together. In your line of work, I'm sure you run across other people who have shared similar challenges that you had and might be looking for a better solution. If you know someone who is always looking out for ways to do things better and who you feel could benefit from our product, would you be comfortable referring them to me?"

Prospect: **"Sure."**

You: *"That sounds great. Then may I ask who you know that would be a good candidate for our product?"*

Hey, look at it this way. You've got nothing to lose and only more prospects to gain.

Cold Calling Conundrum

Timing is everything when asking for referrals from prospects. The strategy just discussed is to be used only when speaking to a prospect who you have determined is not a qualified prospect, cannot benefit from your product, or is someone who, for a variety of reasons, you will never be doing business with.

Conversely, for those qualified prospects who may turn into clients and who you want to use as a referral source, there is a different approach to use that we will discuss later in Chapter 15.

The Least You Need to Know

◆ Most of the time, objections are not a "no" but a request for more information that will get you to a "yes."

◆ Break out of any sales slump or limiting behavior by becoming more responsive rather than reactive.

◆ Respond to objections with questions rather than reacting with a statement that puts you and the prospect on the defensive.

◆ Instead of closing the sale, open up a new selling opportunity by gaining permission from the prospect to do so.

◆ Write down the most common objections you hear and for each one, craft a question as a response.

◆ If you have to follow up, get permission to stay in touch so that you can keep your name in front of that prospect.

4

Cultivating Your Selling Opportunities to Close More Sales

Now that you have a viable prospect, what can you do to keep the selling process moving forward so that you can eventually earn their business? If you have ever experienced the frustration of losing a sale that should have been yours or seem to be courting a prospect with no end in sight, rest assured that after reading this section, the only sales that will be lost are the sales that your competition is losing to you.

Chapter

12

Getting Your Calls Returned

In This Chapter

◆ Crafting voice mails that get more callbacks

◆ Treat your voice mail like your product

◆ Uncover the most common voice-mail blunders

When leaving a voice mail for a prospect, do you tease them with anticipated results or baffle them with your sheer brilliance? As a business owner, I've been prospected hundreds of times. Yet, as a sales trainer and coach, I look at these cold calls through a different set of lenses. That is, I use these cold calls as an opportunity to conduct market research. I notice the strategy that each salesperson uses to grab my attention and then determine which one actually worked!

I've gotten voice mails from some salespeople that clock out at just under three minutes and others that sound as simple as, "Hi Keith. It's Fred. You can reach me at (123) 456-7890. Thanks."

Is one approach better than the other? Actually, while both of these approaches can be defended and shown to work, they only possess a few characteristics of what would be classified as a highly effective voice mail. After reading this chapter, you will be able to utilize these guidelines for creating voice mails that are guaranteed to make your phone ring more than it ever has.

Crafting Compelling Voice-Mail Messages

To illustrate and overcome the challenges that you may face when speaking to your prospect's voice mail, we're going to conduct another skill practice scenario. This time, put yourself in your prospect's shoes for a moment. Imagine that you are an incredibly busy sales manager for an apparel company. You have the same old issue that many managers face today: trying to do more with fewer resources available.

It's 7:30 A.M. and you are already at the office ready to begin your day. You glance at your schedule. It's no different from any other day. Meetings in the morning from 8 A.M. until 11 A.M. Then, your day continues as usual, beginning with the typical barrage of service calls from existing clients. One of your salespeople requests a one-on-one meeting for additional support and training. Afterwards, you're off to work on the new product line and complete a few requests for proposals. Because one of your many responsibilities is to expand your distribution channel, you then begin to compile your call list of companies who you feel would be a great fit and therefore should carry your line of clothes. Before you know it, it's 6 P.M. and time to pack it in for the day.

You are clearly someone with many responsibilities and little time to do it all. While sitting at your desk, you notice the light flashing on your phone. Someone's left you a message. In the spirit of multitasking and juggling several other responsibilities, you begin to retrieve your voice mails. One call is from a client requesting a price list for one of your newer lines. Another call is from one of your salespeople who wants you to meet them at a prospect's office to assist in closing a sale. And finally, a voice mail from a Mr. Neil Daniels begins to play over your speakerphone. Neil is an account executive who represents a product that you happen to purchase from one of his competitors.

"Hi ahh, (Your Name). This is Neil from XYZ Company. We sell the software program you need to manage the inventory for all of your clothing lines. Um, I'm calling to check in with you and see if you have a need for our product and are interested in saving money. I also wanted to touch base and see if you received the brochure I sent you. Um, we are doing some great things with our product now. We, um, actually have a new web-based platform to process and track your orders and inventory online. You can also do all of your billing and invoicing online. In addition, we've adjusted our pricing structure so you can save an additional 10 percent off the pricing that I've already quoted you in the literature I sent. You can also get some more information on our website at www.xyzcompany.com. So, ahh, give me a call when you get a chance. I would love to schedule a time for us to meet in person. I look forward to hearing from you soon."

Once again, I'm sure you don't know *anyone* who has ever taken this approach, right? When I share this voice-mail example during a training event, it's inevitable that a few participants would approach me at the end of the event and say, "Oh my gosh. Are you in my office when I leave my voice mails? That's me! How did you know I say that?"

By the way, when you know the correct approach to leaving a voice mail, it's quite a challenge to purposely interject "um" and "ahh" into a voice mail. But then again, it's fairly easy to do so when you don't have a voice mail strategy in place that would let you know the objective of your message, the appropriate language to use, and where you want it to end.

Now, I know this may come as a shock to you, but Neil called me a few days after leaving his message asking for help. He didn't understand why he wasn't getting as many returned calls as he would like!

Let's face it, based on your hectic schedule outlined in this scenario, do you think you would take the time to actually listen to Neil's entire message, let alone take the time to call him back? Neil's current approach is destroying selling opportunities every time he picks up the phone and leaves a message.

Now that you had an opportunity to catch a glimpse of what it looks like through your prospect's eyes, we are going to dissect Neil's approach so that we can assist him in identifying the areas he can improve upon to dramatically increase the percentage of calls he gets returned from people he prospected.

This way, you can use these guidelines to develop a few compelling voice mail templates that incorporate your personal approach with your fingerprint in order to get more callbacks rather than deliver the same underlying message that your prospects tune into and hear. "Hi, I'm a salesperson and I want to first tell you about me and then sell you something."

> **Cold Medicine**
>
> Your voice mail is your product. Until your prospect has the opportunity to experience what your product or service can do for them first-hand, the only thing they have been exposed to is you! Imagine if you put the same amount of time, research, attention to detail, care, and value into your voice mail as you do with your product. If your voice mail is your prospect's first exposure to what you have to offer, realize the impression they get from your voice mail equates to the value they can expect from your product. If you stumble through your voice mail like Neil did and come across unprepared, ineffective, and disorganized, imagine the perception that your prospect has formulated about your final deliverable.

How Long Should Your Voice Mail Be?

Let's now explore Neil's current approach and uncover some strategies to make his voice mails more effective while at the same time assisting you in improving yours.

Neil's current approach: It takes Neil a little less than two minutes to typically get through his voice-mail message.

Tip from the sales coach: *The length of a voice mail should be approximately 30 to 45 seconds.*

Keeping your message short and concise accomplishes two things:

1. If your message is longer than one minute, you will lose the prospect's attention. People don't have the time to listen to a three-minute voice mail, let alone from someone who they don't even know. Putting a time limitation on your voice-mail messages prevents rambling.

2. Placing a limit on the length of your voice mails forces you to laser in on the most compelling language to achieve your secondary objective, which is typically a return call. If you know you need to grab the prospect's attention in a matter of seconds, this accentuates the importance of taking the time to craft the right wording in each message and putting it on paper.

Give Them a Reason to Return Your Call

Neil's current approach: If you read over Neil's voice mail, he did not provide the prospect with a compelling reason to call him back that a prospect would classify as important. Actually, the only reason Neil gave was to schedule a time to meet. Neil succeeded in making the voice mail about him and what he wants, rather than sharing a benefit that the prospect could realize. (Oh, that's right. He did mention that he could save the prospect money. How unique and utterly motivating!) How presumptuous to call on a prospect you don't know and then ask for something that satisfies your needs rather than giving value to them.

Tip from the sales coach: Each message must state a reason for them to return your call. (What's in it for them?)

What is the prospect's incentive to want to speak with you? What can you say to create enough urgency to motivate someone to return your call? What is it that is going to make a prospect take the steps to put aside what they were currently doing to make picking up the phone and calling you their new priority?

I can assure you, the following statements do not motivate a prospect to return your call.

♦ "I'm just calling to check in with you to see if you have a need for my product."

♦ "The reason for my call is to see if you received the information that I sent you last week."

♦ "I was hoping to schedule a time for us to meet."

Calling a prospect with the intention to confirm that they received your brochure is not compelling enough to cause a prospect to act. Besides, if you are asking for something from your prospect such as an appointment, then who are you making the sales process about? (Hint: you!)

Here's where your compelling reasons come into play. (Remember the ones you created in Chapter 5?) Your voice mail will contain at least one of the compelling reasons you have created.

For example, if you were to use a testimonial in your voice mail, it would sound like this:

You: "Hi Mr. Prospect. Keith Rosen here from Profit Builders. I thought you'd want to know that we just helped (STATE COMPANY NAME) in the (STATE/CITY) area reduce their expenses by more than 50 percent. The funny thing is, they didn't think it could be done! Let me show you how you can experience the same dramatic benefits while making your job easier.

If you're always on the lookout for ways to do things better, let's talk for a few minutes and see if you're a candidate for achieving these results. My number is (123) 456-7890. I'm sure you're busy and I want to respect your time, so if I don't hear from you, I'll follow up with another call on Tuesday at 3:30 P.M. EST. Otherwise, I look forward to your call. Have a terrific day."

Here's a quick side note. If you are reluctant to use one of your clients' names, then remove it from the example so that the second sentence reads, "I thought you'd want to know that we just helped a company in the (STATE/CITY) area ...." Then finish this sentence with a compelling reason as I did in this example.

Don't Give Away the Farm

Neil's current approach: Neil practically included his entire presentation in his voice-mail message. Aside from sharing all the new features of his product, he even directed the prospect to his company's website to gather even more information! Neil also sent his prospect unsolicited information in the form of a brochure and pricing schedule. Bad enough that Neil initially sent his pricing structure to the prospect. He took an ineffective approach a step further by actually discounting his pricing in his voice-mail message before even speaking to the prospect!

Tip from the sales coach: Remember, the primary objective of a voice mail is to get your call returned. If you tell the prospect in the voice mail everything you would want to tell them when you finally have the chance to speak or even meet with them, then what's their incentive to call you back? What information do they need to know now, that they haven't already received?

Weaving a compelling reason into your voice-mail message stimulates the correct response you want from your prospects, which is, "That's interesting. How are they actually going to do that?"

Create Five Unique Voice-Mail Messages

Neil's current approach: Take my word for it, the first voice mail Neil leaves with a prospect sounds pretty much like his second, third, and fourth voice mail.

Tip from the sales coach: Develop a minimum of five unique voice-mail messages.

As mentioned in Chapter 5, if you are prospecting someone for the first time, do you know exactly what his or her greatest challenges are? Do you know what their specific goals are?

Remember, there's a big difference between what you think is important and what your prospect thinks is important. You just have to work at putting yourself in their shoes to uncover what they want and need to hear rather than either assuming what you think they need to hear or saying the same thing that every other salesperson is saying. These statements simply fall on deaf ears.

If you are using the same voice mail over and over again, you're limiting the chance of getting your calls returned, especially if you continue to reinforce the wrong message!

Multiple approaches will increase your odds of hitting on what's most important to the prospect.

Developing five unique voice-mail messages provides a unique opportunity for you to reconnect with your product, to reinvent and reposition what it is you are selling, and to discover a greater value in your product that you can offer each prospect.

Here's one example of a great voice mail that I typically use if I know something about the prospect.

"Hi Mrs. Prospect. Keith Rosen here from Profit Builders. I understand you're now in the process of launching a recruiting initiative to build your sales team. Depending on what you're currently doing, we might have some ways to help you attract top producers and deploy a system so they can quickly exceed their sales quota, while keeping your costs down and complementing your current recruiting efforts. Let's talk for about two minutes so that I can share with you some ideas to cut your recruiting time down by at least 20 percent while making your job easier. My number is (123) 456-7890. I'm sure you're busy and want to respect your time, so if I don't hear from you, I'll follow up with another call on Tuesday at 3:30 P.M. EST. Otherwise, I look forward to your call. Have a terrific day."

On another note, you can also "relanguage" this example to exploit the pain or the challenges that your prospects experience, rather than the benefits they can realize from your product or service.

To recap, in order to create five distinct voice-mail messages, all you need to do is take the example I just shared and use that as a template. You can also use the example I gave in the prior section, "Give Them a Reason to Return Your Call."

" " Cold Medicine

Before calling a prospect, do your best to gather as much information about them as possible from the front desk receptionist or operator. This way, you can customize your opening to include the prospect's name so that your message appeals to them on a personal level (rather than generically calling on the "person in charge of marketing").

I actually wove in a few compelling reasons in the most recent example, just to provide you with a great working model. I also knew a little about the company I was calling on, as you can see in the second sentence, "I understand you're now in the process of launching a recruiting initiative to build your sales team." If you don't have detailed information about your prospect, then remove this type of sentence from your voice mail. However, if you can find out timely information about your prospect or their company (via the receptionist, the news, or the Internet), it makes for a stronger message.

Next, remove the compelling reasons that I created, (unless they fit for you). Finally, create five separate voice mails by simply plugging in one or two of your compelling reasons (depending on how long and how strong they are) in each voice mail. That's it!

Unlike Neil, I would suggest inserting your contact telephone number in your voice mail as I have done in this example to make it a bit easier for the prospect to get in touch with you.

Twelve Ways to Contact an Elusive Prospect

Neil's current approach: Neil shared with me that most of the time he uses the phone as his preferred communication vehicle when prospecting.

Tip from the sales coach: Because you are calling on this prospect for the first time and therefore are not sure of their preferred method of communication or the communication vehicle that they best respond to, take advantage of the variety of communication channels you have at your disposal.

In Chapter 8, I listed 19 strategies or ways you can prospect. What follows is a condensed list of 12 avenues you can travel down to contact a prospect that you are having trouble connecting with.

1. E-mail

2. Voice mail

3. Cell phone

4. Business phone

5. Snail mail (letter or direct mail)

6. In person

7. Fax

8. Networking or social function

9. Another vendor or salesperson

10. Trade shows and industry functions

Cold Medicine

Studies have shown that it takes a minimum of eight attempts to contact a prospect (voice mails, letters, e-mails, etc.) in order to trigger one return call from them.

11. Secretary or administrative assistant

12. Other internal advocates

Remember, the way you communicate with your prospects, including the frequency of contact, should have already been defined in your prospecting system (refer to Chapter 7).

Speak with Enthusiasm

In Chapter 8, we have talked about the importance of smiling. The same rule applies for voice mails as well. Smile when leaving your voice mail message. It comes across on the phone. If you are not excited about what you have to offer, then how can you expect a prospect to be?

Directions to Carnegie Hall

Just like your prospecting template, it's essential that your voice mail comes across as natural as possible. That's why I'd suggest practicing each voice-mail message a minimum of 24 times without making any changes to it.

There is a saying, "Perfect practice makes perfect." It's important that you practice your voice mails the same way, consistently. Otherwise, if you keep making changes every time you practice your voice mail, it's similar to changing your golf swing every time you attempt to hit the ball. The result? Consistent inconstancy.

The Least You Need to Know

◆ Your voice mail is your product so treat it with the same care and attention you give to your deliverable.

◆ Time your voice mails to ensure that they clock out at less than one minute.

- Each message must state a call for action and a reason for them to take action (for example, return your call).

- Rather than share information about your product or service, tease them with measurable results they can realize.

- Practice your voice mails until they sound like your natural style of communicating rather than a "canned pitch."

Chapter 13

Five Surefire Ways to Make the Gatekeeper Your Ally

In This Chapter

- ◆ Upgrade your relationship with the gatekeeper
- ◆ Make the gatekeeper a raving fan
- ◆ Help the gatekeeper help you
- ◆ Develop internal advocates
- ◆ The back door approach to connect with a prospect

"How do you get through the gatekeeper?" This question sounds like the beginning of a joke or riddle. Salespeople certainly invest a large portion of their time trying to come up with the right answer to this question. With all the time and energy that salespeople spend in their quest to conquer the gatekeeper, you may be surprised that the answer to this riddle is, "You don't."

Did I at least get a chuckle or a guffaw? You may already know that this answer is, in fact, the truth. In your quest to get through to your prospects, I'm going to dispel some myths and costly assumptions that create additional barriers to your prospecting efforts—barriers even bigger than the gatekeeper.

Forget Gatekeeper ... How About Concierge?

Throughout this book, I have reinforced the importance of developing a mutually beneficial relationship with each prospect by utilizing the strategies outlined in this book. We've discussed how to avoid making each prospect your adversary and instead, making them your ally.

Why should this objective change when speaking to the person who answers the phone that we have endearingly named "The Gatekeeper?" I can't imagine that I'm the only person who has a problem with this nickname. Why don't we just refer to all receptionists as "The Terminator" or "The Exterminator" or, while we're at it, let's just address them by their ultimate mission as depicted by the name "gatekeeper." That is, "The person who destroys all prospecting efforts."

Okay, so you get my point. In case you may have missed it, the word "gatekeeper" has a fairly negative connotation associated with it. What visual comes to mind when you think of a gatekeeper? I can tell you what I see; a 10-foot-tall ogre with a very big club that's used to squash any salesperson who attempts to get past them and into the prospect's office, home, or anywhere the prospect may be. And according to conventional sales wisdom, it's your responsibility to "get through" them. You don't even have the option to go around them, above them, or under them. Instead, you have to plow directly through them head-on. Oh, I can hardly wait (gulp).

When was the last time you "got through" something without force, resistance, an argument, or a struggle? Right from the starting line, you are preparing for a battle between you and the gatekeeper.

Hey, it's already a challenge to overcome cold call reluctance, develop your prospecting system, and then be disciplined enough to take the steps and follow your system. Now, you're telling me that in order to actually get to the prospect, I have to battle a viscous beast? What fun!

Talk about adding bricks to the wall of resistance when prospecting! C'mon, do salespeople really need this additional pressure? I don't think so.

That is why I am launching a worldwide initiative (okay, at least through this book) to change the nickname of "gatekeeper" to "concierge."

It's assumed that this gatekeeper is an evil ogre before you even get a chance to meet them. Maybe the lesson here is to recognize that this negative perception has tainted your approach and how you handle the gatekeeper. In other words, if you knew up-front that you were dealing with someone friendly who actually wants to help you, wouldn't that change how you approach, communicate, and respond to the gate-keeper? You betcha.

The Concierge Is Your Friend

Think about your reaction to the word "gatekeeper." What thoughts does it conjure up for you? Now, think about the word "concierge." What comes to mind?

When you go to the mall and you need to find a specific store, who do you ask? The concierge. When you are staying at a hotel on vacation and are looking for directions, the hotel's amenities, somewhere to eat or need tickets to a show, who do you ask? The concierge.

How good are you at making friends? Instead of "getting through the gatekeeper" how about "making friends with the concierge"? Now, doesn't that just sound (and feel) better?

Consider this for a moment. The concierge secretly wants to help you. (Concierge is synonymous with caretaker.) The only caveat is, you have to give them a reason to. After all, if you try to sneak behind their back and get busted for doing so, you have succeeded in creating an adver-sary. Not only that but you've now fueled their justification as to why they need to screen all incoming calls! Now, when you need them in the future, it's a safe bet that they probably won't welcome you with open arms.

Treat the gatekeeper more like a concierge. This way, instead of assuming you need to get though the gatekeeper with manipulative selling tactics, consider that the more honest you are, the more they will actually want to help you. What do you have to do to enroll them in helping you? Just ask rather than trying to get around them.

Cold Calling Conundrum

Never underestimate the power of the concierge.

What you will find on the following pages is more of a process to enroll the concierge in helping you rather than some manipulative tactics to "get through the gatekeeper." (Okay, maybe one or two tactics, just not the manipulative kind.)

Brutal Honesty

The old adage, "Honesty is the best policy" certainly holds true when trying to befriend the gatekeeper, I mean, the concierge. When calling to speak with your prospect or to find out exactly who the prospect is, try this approach in the following example.

You: "Hi, I'm calling to speak with the person who is in charge of all corporate training initiatives, would that be you?"

What You Have Accomplished: Asking the concierge, "Would that be you?" or, "Are you the expert in that area?" comes across as a complement and makes the concierge feel important. As such, they are now more likely to give you the name of the contact you are looking for. As you will see in the following dialogue, the concierge did in fact share the prospect's name with you!

Concierge: "Oh no. The person you need to speak with is Mrs. Mary Johnson. May I ask what this is in reference to?"

You: "Of course! I'm a salesperson and I want to relentlessly hound them until they take my call."

What You Have Accomplished: Let's face it. If you're talking to a seasoned concierge, they can smell a cold call a mile away. Instead of dancing around this issue, address it head-on, yet in a light and humorous way.

Warm Wisdom

Here's another approach that would cause the concierge to happily pass you on to the person you are trying to contact. First, prepare a question that you know only the person who you are looking to contact can answer effectively. For example, when calling to connect with the person who spearheads all training and professional development initiatives, I would first introduce myself. Then I would continue with, "I'm hoping you can help me. If I were to apply for a sales position in your company, does the training that the company provides include continuous product training, the psychology of selling, and a one-on-one performance coaching element that would help me continually develop and strengthen the core selling competencies needed to maximize my potential?"

If you sell printing or advertising, here's another example: "We're putting a sample brochure together for you and wanted to know the dimensions of the paper you use for your current marketing and sales materials, the color scheme and number of colors, or whether you use black and white." Because these questions are typically ones that a concierge may not be able to answer on their own, they will often connect you directly with the decision maker or the person in charge of that department.

This brutal, honest approach will get you to the decision maker more frequently than trying to manipulate, mislead, or sneak by the concierge. Instead, it gets right to the truth and intention of your call. Because the concierge is always on the lookout for sneaky salespeople, they will actually appreciate your approach. As such, this will defuse the concierge's reluctance to helping you.

Cutting right to the chase will actually catch the concierge off guard and often creates a laugh. At this point, the concierge would lower their guard and quite often connect you to the decision maker or, at the very least, provide you with the information you need for your next call.

Here's another version of how to respond when the concierge asks, "What is this in reference to?" However, this strategy will only work if part of your sales process includes submitting either a proposal or even a brief summary (pricing structure) detailing the solution that you are proposing.

"This is in reference to the confidential report and analysis we're putting together for your (sales, marketing, production) division."

Because you plan on delivering some type of proposal to a qualified prospect (once they become a qualified prospect) you can use this as a leverage point to get the concierge to transfer your call to your targeted prospect.

Using the word "confidential" implies that the information is for the decision maker only. As such, the concierge would be less inclined to question you about it.

Notice that I've also referred to my proposal as a "report and analysis." After all, a proposal is, for the most part, an analysis of the prospect's current condition and a report that details how they can improve their situation.

When the prospect takes your call and questions you about the report you are referring to, here's your lead to begin your prospecting conversation, letting the prospect know that this is something they will be receiving once an initial analysis is completed.

Feel free to adjust the language so that it best fits you, your approach, and your product.

Let's now continue with the dialogue.

Cold Medicine

This approach also works great as a voice mail. Here's what it would sound like: "Hi Mr. Prospect. Keith Rosen here from Profit Builders. I'm calling about the confidential report and analysis we're putting together for you. Please let me know how you would like this report delivered, whether by e-mail, FedEx, or in person. You can reach me at (123) 456-7890. Have a terrific day."

Concierge: (Chuckle.) "Mrs. Johnson isn't in today. Would you like to leave a message?"

You: "No thanks. I'll try to catch her next week. By the way, may I please ask your name?" (Or "By the way, who am I speaking with?")

Concierge: "This is Jane."

You: "Jane, it's been a pleasure talking with you. Thank you so much for your help. It is deeply appreciated. Have a great day."

What You Have Accomplished: Whether it's the secretary, gatekeeper, administrative assistant, or receptionist, make it part of your process to always ask for the person's name who answers the phone. Then, make sure you note their name in your prospect's file or contact. As you can see, I've also used her name when ending the call with a "thank you."

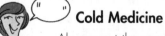

Cold Medicine

Always get the name of the concierge. This way, you can properly address them when you call again, making it a "warmer" cold call.

Ask for Help

Now that you have the prospect's name, you begin the initial steps of contacting the prospect. After several attempts, you still have not successfully connected with them.

Another avenue to revisit would be asking the concierge for help. Think about how you respond when someone asks you for help. Chances are, you do your best to help them.

Appeal to their humanity. Here's a sample of the dialogue to use.

You: "Hi Jane, Keith Rosen here. We spoke a few weeks ago and you were kind enough to help me then. Well, here I am again in desperate need of your help. I've been trying to get in touch with Mary Johnson, but have not been successful in getting her to return my calls. I'm sure she is very busy and I certainly don't want to keep filling up her voice mail with messages from me. Can you help? Any suggestions you can provide, whether it's an alternative way to get Mary to return my call, a different way to contact her other than voice mail, or a better time that I should try to reach her would be deeply appreciated."

You now have the opportunity to develop a relationship with the concierge and become the salesperson who gets preferential treatment that the other salespeople who are calling do not. Finally, you might find that once you ask for help, they will immediately connect you to the prospect!

Becoming friends with the concierge provides some immediate benefits that you can realize. As a matter of fact, you'll be surprised how much insider information you can get. This includes the name of the decision maker and their contact information, important information about the decision maker and how to best approach and appeal to them, company politics and procedures, company status and timely news, internal changes, initiatives, or challenges.

Connecting with them as a person rather than as an obstacle will make your cold calling efforts much less of an effort. So, acknowledge every concierge you speak with. It's safe to say these types of calls are not the majority of calls they receive. Some are just downright hostile! After all, the concierge is often the first point of contact and in the hot seat when dealing with certain problems. With the barrage of calls that a concierge fields daily, a sincere and authentic complement goes a long way. You now have an internal advocate on your side.

What's in a Name?

We have now established the importance of developing a relationship with the concierge. The first step is asking for their name.

As a result, you've been able to get the name of the person you need to speak with who could make the decision to purchase your product.

The next time you attempt to call that prospect, try the following dialogue.

You: "Hi Jane. Keith Rosen here. Is Mary available?"

What You Have Accomplished: After you address the concierge by her first name, ask for the prospect by their first name. The concierge will often make the assumption that you already know her as well as the prospect and have some type of relationship with them. Therefore, you have a much better chance of having the concierge put your call through.

An alternative approach would sound like:

You: "Hi Jane. Keith Rosen here. I need to speak with Mary, please."

What You Have Accomplished: Instead of asking a question, make a statement. If delivered with a confident, firm yet friendly voice, the concierge will often put you through to the prospect.

When Is the Meeting?

Like it or not, meetings are here to stay. Whether it's a planning meeting, marketing meeting, sales meeting, committee meeting, chapter meeting, executive meeting, client meeting, performance reviews, staff meeting or other, meetings dominate corporate America.

You can leverage your attempts to connect with your prospects by using meetings as your springboard that would catapult you into their office and onto the phone with them. Here's how.

Let's work from the presupposition that most meetings are held in the morning hours between 9:00 A.M. and 11:00 A.M. Therefore, this approach is most effective if you call first thing in the morning. What follows is an example of the dialogue you can use.

You: "Hi Jane. Keith Rosen here from Profit Builders. I'm hoping it's not too late to catch Mary before her meeting this morning. Any chance that I can catch her before her meeting begins?"

What You Have Accomplished: If your prospect is, in fact, about to go into a meeting, the concierge will typically attempt to connect you to her beforehand. Conversely, if your prospect does not have a meeting, simply follow up with. "Oh, great! Can you put me through to her please?" Finally, if she is not available, simply respond with, "No worries. If you happen to have her schedule handy, when would be a good time to catch her today?" You can also respond with, "When would be a better time to call back?"

" " **Cold Medicine** _____

If you happen to be calling on a prospect who has an assistant, try this approach. "Hi Jane, Keith Rosen here from Profit Builders. Mary and I have been playing the longest game of phone tag in history. If you have her calendar handy, can you please help me by scheduling in a five minute block of time that works for her so that I can answer her question regarding your sales training initiative?" You've now succeeded in scheduling a time to call a prospect when you know they are available and are expecting your call.

They're Expecting My Call

Whether you are following up at the request of your prospect or are following up on a letter that you sent, this simple yet effective approach also gets the job done.

As we've discussed in Chapter 7, when drafting an introductory letter, always include either an approximate time ("some time next week") when you will be calling on them or a specific day and time when they can expect your call. (This approach is a bit more effective if you include a specific day and time.)

When it's time for you to call the prospect back, use the following language to make your cold calls warmer.

You: "Hi Jane. Keith Rosen here from Profit Builders. Can you please connect me to Mary? She's expecting my call."

If your prospect told you during the prior conversation you had with them to follow up in a couple of weeks, take this approach. Once you are on the phone with the prospect, remind them that they asked you to call them back to continue where you left off in the last conversation.

The alternative approach is to work from the letter that you mailed the prospect. When you call them back at the specific day and time that you told them you would be calling, it's still safe to tell the concierge that your prospect is expecting your call.

The Back Door Approach

Before we wrap up this chapter, here are a few more innovative ways to connect with your prospects that don't require speaking to the concierge.

Call Before or After Hours: Call before or after a live person begins to answer incoming calls. Many businesses today have an automated voice mail system when the office is closed. The intention here is to get into their voice mail system and listen for the prompt that asks you to "Please spell out the person's last name." Once you do this, the voice-mail system will often tell you the prospect's direct extension before transferring your call. Now, when you call back during normal business hours, you can ask the concierge to "Connect you to extension 2345 please." In addition, if you want to circumvent the concierge who refuses to patch you through to their voice mail, calling before or after hours provides you with the opportunity to leave a message with your prospect.

Use Their Website: Many websites list contact information. Some go so far as to provide a picture, bio, and contact information for the top officers of the company and their position. If you don't have the luxury of finding all of this information, then find any person's e-mail address within that company. (Check out their "help center" or the "contact us" option in the menu.) Once you can see how the company formats their e-mail addresses, you can take an educated guess regarding what your prospect's e-mail address would be.

Return Receipt: This approach comes in very handy. When sending out an e-mail to a prospect, use the "return receipt request" option in the software you use to manage your e-mails. If the prospect opens your e-mail and sends a receipt, you not only know that they received your e-mail, but you also know when they have received it. This way, as opposed to trying to track down a prospect when they are at their desk, you know exactly when to call on them, because they are now in front of their computer checking your e-mail! Obviously, this strategy only works if you are in front of your computer often enough to retrieve your e-mails as they are sent.

The Least You Need to Know

- Never underestimate the power of the concierge.
- Always ask the concierge for their name as well as for help when you need it.
- Befriending the concierge provides you with valuable "insider" information and access to your prospects.
- The concierge becomes your own internal advocate when a prospect asks for their opinion on what vendor to choose.

◆ A concierge wants to help you; a gatekeeper does not. Because a good concierge can sense a cold call, take the honest approach, instead of using deceptive tactics which will ruin your chance to connect with that prospect again.

◆ Call before or after hours and use the voice-mail system to get the prospect's extension.

14

3-2-1 Contact! You've Made It ... Now What?

In This Chapter

- ◆ Become a master at follow-up
- ◆ Stop handing over sales to your competition
- ◆ Maintain your prospect's interest
- ◆ Prevent warm prospects from turning cold
- ◆ Craft a follow-up conversation

There are many roadblocks that can prevent or stall a sale. Typically these roadblocks show up in the form of some type of objection or concern that you hear from your prospect. While we can't control what a prospect says or does, we can certainly control how we respond to them. Chapter 11 provided you with some powerful tools to prevent and defuse the initial objections you hear from your prospects.

The irony is, the biggest roadblocks or barriers to the sale are actually created by you, the salesperson! After all, if a salesperson doesn't take the time to develop and sharpen their own skills, they are creating a situation where they can lose many selling opportunities because they just don't have the right tools and strategies available.

Have you ever lost a sale due to poor follow-up? Did you ever miss a selling opportunity because someone got to your prospect before you did?

The good news is, you have the power to control and eliminate the self-sabotaging behavior and self-imposed obstacles that will cost you sales daily. We are now going to discuss some highly effective follow-up strategies you can use so that you never have to utter the words, "I dropped the ball" again.

Are You Helping Your Competition Sell More?

Stop and think for a moment about all the countless hours you have invested in building your career and developing your selling skills.

Now, picture this scenario. Rob, an IT and computer salesperson, identified an ideal prospect. Rob continued with his due diligence during his pre-call planning stage. He sent out an introductory letter, step one of the prospecting system he's created. Several days later Rob began his follow-up strategy, starting with his first voice mail. One week and three voice mails later, Rob actually got a call back from his prospect! He had a great initial conversation with her. Together they had uncovered several opportunities that may warrant the purchase of Rob's product. As such, an in-person meeting was scheduled.

A few days later, Rob arrived at the prospect's office. The meeting went great! Rob's prospect requested a proposal from him. Rob even scheduled a follow-up meeting so that he could deliver and review the proposal with the prospect rather than sending it via regular mail or e-mail. At this point, Rob was feeling pretty good about his prospecting efforts and the progress he has made.

In the spirit of maintaining his momentum, Rob went back to his office and began drafting his proposal. He met with his prospect one week later to review the proposal with her. Rob's prospect loved it! She informed Rob that the next step would be for her to present this proposal to the board.

Rob let the prospect know that he intended to reconnect with her one week later, after they had time to review his proposal.

Then, for various reasons, Rob got caught up in some other activities at work, some client service issues, administrative duties, and other daily occurrences. Bottom line, Rob doesn't follow up. He doesn't call. He doesn't even e-mail her. A few weeks later, Rob happens to stumble across the proposal he sent his prospect and decided to call her at that time. To Rob's surprise, she went with another vendor!

After Rob shared his story with me, I asked him, "If you're sacrificing your valuable time engaging in pre-call planning activities, cold calling, driving to an appointment (twice), delivering a presentation, writing and reviewing a proposal, and then don't follow up, then who are you *really* helping?" Then it hit him between the eyes. "My competition!"

Rob was correct. And if it wasn't his competition that he is helping secure new business, it was the vendor or supplier that the prospect is currently working with. By not following up, Rob succeeded in reinforcing the belief in the prospect's mind, "If my other option is to work with salespeople who can't even follow up effectively or do what they say they are going to do, then I'm better off sticking with what I have!"

The Objective of a "Follow-Through" System

Okay, I'm not suggesting that you now refer to a follow-up call as a follow-though call (unless you want to.) Instead, I've added this distinction here to make an important point.

That is, following through is defined as "seeing something through to its completion." For now on, this is the proper mind-set to adopt when you think of "following up."

Cold Callingo

The **buying cycle** is the length of time it takes for a prospect to go through their process of making a purchasing decision, from the time they are introduced to a new product or service, up until the time when they make the purchase. The buying cycle for an existing client may differ slightly. This would be defined as the average length of time it takes for a client to go through their process of making a repeat purchase. You may be familiar with the traditional four-step model of a buying cycle; attention, interest, desire and action. For some prospects and clients, their buying cycle is seasonal, or is dictated by other economic or environmental factors. For example, if you sell software to the accounting industry that enables accountants to perform their job more efficiently, then the buying cycle of your target audience may begin several months before tax season. While you may have captured their attention and interest, earlier on during the year, the time before tax season would be the time when their desire elevates to the point of action. It's important to understand your prospect's buying cycle so that you can align your prospecting efforts around your prospect's buying cycle.

Whether you are calling on new or existing prospects, prospects that have a longer *buying cycle*, or clients that you want to generate repeat business from, how diligent you are at following through can be the deciding factor that will make or break your sale. Developing your "follow-through" system encompasses any attempts you make at contacting the prospect as well as the communication vehicle you use. Therefore, your follow-up process involves three steps:

1. Determining the communication vehicle. (How are you contacting them: phone, e-mail, snail mail, or other?)

2. Developing what to say or the language you use when you're communicating to a prospect (including your voice mails, e-mails, etc.)

3. Determining the frequency of contact. (At what intervals will you be contacting them and how often?)

So, what is the objective of a follow-up system? Here's what some salespeople have said.

- ◆ To get your calls returned.

- ◆ To ensure the prospect remembers who you are.

- ◆ To get in front of the prospect.

- ◆ To close a sale.

On the surface, these salespeople may be correct. However, consider this valuable tip from your sales coach. The objective of a follow-up system is to get through each step of your follow-up system.

Cold Medicine

Do complete work. Instead of stopping and starting your prospecting efforts, identify the prospects that you have connected with who have expressed interest and see these selling opportunities through to completion. Otherwise, consider that you may be an adrenaline junkie and love the rush associated when working on overdrive and having an abundance of callbacks to make. To prevent sporadic results and a pile of unfinished projects, get off the adrenaline train and start following through in order to create the momentum that produces consistent, long-lasting results.

The goal is actually to get through each step of your follow-up system. If you shift your energy and focus away from having to get a return call to simply honoring, following, and trusting the process of contacting them the predetermined number of times that you feel is appropriate before moving to the next step in your prospecting system, how would this change your disposition and mind-set? For starters, you will be less likely to be pushing for the result and more likely to focus on the process.

In addition, you won't get discouraged if your prospect doesn't respond to every one of your attempts to connect with them. Finally, it puts you back in the driver's seat. Because your objective is to get through your follow-up system, you are in control. You have the power to do so or not. Only you can make that choice. Finally, focusing on getting through your follow-up system takes the focus off of the end result and onto the process.

This will remove the pressure of producing the result, because you now realize that it is the process that will produce the result you want as a natural by-product of your efforts. As long as you stay focused on each step of your process, you will attain your goal.

After Your Initial Contact, Just Follow Up!

My wife and I were about to undertake our last remodeling project. Being a consummate consumer, I wanted several qualified companies to bid on our next project. After calling ten contractors, I scheduled an appointment with the five that called back.

Following our meetings, one gave me a price on the spot and two never responded with an estimate. Two contractors mailed an estimate, and one of them followed up a week later.

Guess who got the job. Just by making a five-minute phone call! What fascinated me most was that only one contractor called back to discuss his proposal and ask for my business.

How can these contactors afford *not* to follow up? Conducting my own research, each one said they needed more business, yet didn't know the status of the majority of proposals they sent. I sensed that following up regarding their proposal was not their typical M.O. Instead, here's what they said:

- ◆ I thought you were using someone else.

- ◆ I didn't think you were ready to buy.

- ◆ I thought you felt the price was too high.

- ◆ I didn't want to bother or pressure you.

While these contractors formulated their own conclusion, they never bothered to confirm if their assumptions were, in fact, true! They were operating under the costly assumption, "The prospect will call when they are ready."

Similar to the story I shared with you earlier about Rob, Bill was one of the contractors I had interviewed who did not get the job. Bill quickly realized that if he wasn't going to follow up and ask for a prospect's business after taking all of the steps that earned him the opportunity to do so, the only people he was actually helping were his competitors!

Bill realized something that only a select few in his industry have. While prospects need his remodeling knowledge and skills, they also need his help in making their decision.

Bill recently called me with some exciting results. After making 30 calls, he spoke with 10 prospects he *had* met with. Bill sold three more deals ($78,000) in one week that he never would have sold.

In many businesses, especially the ones that sell directly to consumers such as home remodeling, cold calling consumers via the phone is no longer an option to generate new leads. Aside from networking, canvassing door-to-door, asking for referrals, posting job signs, or traditional (and sometimes costly) marketing/advertising campaigns, what else brings in more business? Follow-up calls.

How many prospects are waiting for your phone call so they can send you a deposit? How many people are out there waiting to begin working with you? Bill and I then sat down to crunch the numbers. I shared with him, "Consider that you can make about fifteen calls per hour (per week). Assume that out of fifteen contacts, you make one more sale. (Average sale $10,000.) Four hours a month equates to four more sales. Over a year, that's $480,000 in volume. This exceeds the yearly volume of most contractors just by making follow-up calls each week!"

If you take a moment and look at your call-back list, how much business does that equate to? Now ask yourself, "How much of it am I willing to give to my competition?"

Because your competitors aren't paying you commission, here's your opportunity to utilize a simple, efficient three-step follow-up system that will bring in more (free) sales.

Get Permission

Whether you need to follow up after an initial conversation or once a prospect receives your proposal, tries out your product, speaks with references, or needs to check their schedule before they meet with you a second time, it's just good business sense to get permission before doing so. For instance, you inform the prospect they will be receiving your proposal next Friday. Before you leave the appointment or end the phone call ask, "May I follow up with you to discuss and answer any questions you have regarding my proposal?" Gaining permission to follow up eliminates your fear of appearing overly aggressive or pushy. Now, they're expecting your call.

Cold Calling Conundrum

In Chapter 10, we discussed how to use your prospecting time more effectively by eliminating the unproductive, unqualified appointments from your schedule. We established that if you have the opportunity to conduct your needs analysis on the phone, it will ensure that the appointments you are making are with qualified prospects only. The same concept holds true if part of your selling strategy requires drafting a proposal for a prospect. If feasible, rather than sending your proposal to them, it's always better to schedule a time to hand-deliver your proposal so that you can review it face-to-face (or computer-to-computer) with the prospect and address any concerns immediately.

Now, you've eliminated the time-intensive task of having to hunt your prospect down in order to schedule yet another time to go over your proposal. Reviewing the proposal upon delivery provides you the luxury of handling all possible concerns immediately so that you can then ask for the prospect's business, thus reducing the chance of your proposal becoming another item on the prospect's lengthy to-do list. The longer it takes to reconnect with a prospect, the closer your proposal gets to the bottom of their priority list.

Schedule a Meeting

Now that you've gotten permission, schedule a time that you will be calling or meeting with them. Immediately put it in your planner or PDA. This eliminates the time-consuming game of phone tag, reducing the number of calls you will have to make or respond to.

Just Follow Up!

Depending on the sheer number of prospects you connect with, start by putting aside at least one hour each week that is strictly devoted to this practice. Considering your ROI, it's time well invested. Otherwise, something else will always take precedent.

Instead of thinking about how many calls you need to make, consider how many sales you'll be giving to your competition if you don't. If something as simple as following up provides you with a competitive edge, then your next sale is just a phone call away.

Keep the Fire Alive

Melissa, a financial planner who has been in the business for less than a year, was well aware of the fact that she needed to get out there more. Aside from cold calling, Melissa decided to offer free financial seminars with the intention of attracting new clients. So, with the support of her company, she put together a marketing blitz to promote her upcoming seminar.

Melissa's first seminar went very well. Out of the 40 people who attended, 10 people requested more information about her services.

The next day, Melissa began calling on these interested prospects to schedule an in-person meeting with them to discuss their finances and an investment strategy.

Two people didn't return her calls. Three of her prospects said they couldn't meet with her for a few months. And while she was able to schedule an appointment with the remaining five prospects, two of them called the next day to cancel or reschedule.

Melissa couldn't understand how 10 good leads can dissipate so quickly. After greater exploration, she was able to uncover the reason why 10 qualified prospects would dwindle down to 3.

It seems that Melissa was counting on their level of interest and motivation remaining at the same level after the seminar.

She simply assumed that if a prospect checked off the box on her evaluation sheet that indicated their interest to meet with her, they didn't need any additional motivation.

The fact is, life gets in the way sometimes. Certain events or situations can easily change what was considered to be a priority for you one day into something that now takes the back seat and gets added to your to-do list.

Here's a key point. Regardless of where or how you find a prospect, it is your responsibility to keep their interest and motivation at the same level up until the point they become a client (or referral source, alliance, strategic partner). Just because they had expressed a clear interest initially doesn't mean that something else will bump it down the priority list. Just like your voice mails, the message you deliver in your follow-up calls must be compelling enough to move them into action.

After all, if you've ever gone to a motivational seminar you'll understand what I mean. After the seminar, you feel pumped! You are ready to quit your job, start up your own business, and take on the world! Then reality sets in, a week goes by and you are back to where you were before the seminar.

Why wasn't the initial effect that the seminar had on you long-lasting? Because the message wasn't continually reinforced. That's why coaching someone consistently is so effective. It provides the opportunity for the client to build upon the momentum created and reinforce the lessons learned, the skills they developed, and the goals they are aspiring to up until the point where the client can achieve what they want most.

Realize that this rule applies for all prospects, even the ones who contact you or submit a request for more information through your website. Do not make the costly assumption that once the prospect's level of interest is established it will remain. On many occasions, I've heard salespeople say that even though the prospect initiates the first contact, when returning their call or inquiry, the prospect often forgets that they even made the request in the first place.

It is up to you to not only stimulate the interest in your product or service but also maintain and build upon the initial interest that was created.

Cold Calling Conundrum

> If you let your dinner sit too long it's bound to get cold. The same rule applies to your prospects. Even the warmest of prospects who initiate first contact can turn to ice. If you don't continually remind the prospect why they are investing their time in talking with you (W.I.I.F.M.—what's in it for me?) and why this is a priority, something else will always take precedent. This process must continue all the way up until the point where the prospect can finally realize the benefits on their own. This only occurs after the sale is made and the prospect (who has since become a client) is actually utilizing your product or service. Now, they don't need any additional prompting, because they now get to experience the benefits firsthand rather than hearing about them from you.

Preventing Warm Prospects from Turning Cold

With all the time and money you invest in your prospecting efforts, now is not the time to drop the ball. Therefore, you must continually remind your prospects and customers why they contacted you, why they agreed to speak/meet with you or why they do business with you in the first place. What initially grabbed their interest? What was it that prompted them to request more information in the first place?

In an effort to make her cool leads hot, the following dialogue illustrates how Melissa changed her approach when calling on those people who requested more information or a free consultation.

Melissa: *"Hi, Mr. Prospect. Melissa here from Custom Financial. We had met the other day at the financial planning seminar that I delivered."*

Prospect: **"Oh, yes.**

Melissa: *"Do you have a quick moment?"*

Prospect: **"Sure."**

Melissa: *"I see here on the evaluation you filled out that you were interested in meeting to discuss your investment strategy and financial objectives to determine if there's a better way to manage your money in order to get the greatest return on your investments."*

Prospect: **"Yes."**

Melissa: *"Okay. By the way, did you enjoy the seminar?"*

Prospect: **"I did. I thought it was very informative."**

Melissa: *"Thanks, that's great to hear. May I ask what you found most interesting (valuable)?"*

Prospect: **"Well, I'm currently working with a broker and I feel that I don't always get the service that I need. I guess I'm looking for someone who can do more than just issue a trade or buy and sell stocks. When you talked about what you do for your clients, it struck a chord in me. Especially because I'll have three kids going to college, I can use all the help I can get! I have to get the most out of every dollar I invest. I just don't feel like I am now."**

Melissa: *"Thanks for letting me know what's most important to you. I completely understand. It sounds as if you're looking more for an advisor who understands your financial objectives and risk threshold and can provide you with a high degree of personal attention. Someone who you can talk to who can consult and assist you in managing your money and planning for the future, especially with three separate college tuitions approaching quickly."*

Prospect: **"You got that right!"**

Melissa: *"Okay. So it only makes sense for us to sit down and discuss how you can afford to send your kids to the school of their choice without feeling such a large financial burden or having to change the lifestyle that you've grown accustomed to."*

Prospect: **"That sounds great."**

Melissa: *"While I have you on the phone, are there any other expectations that you have for our meeting? This way, I can ensure that I bring out the information that you are most interested in hearing about."*

Prospect: **"Hmm. Nothing else comes to mind other than helping me make and keep more money!"**

Melissa: *"Fair enough! Let's look at our schedules and find a time that works best for you. Do you have your calendar handy?"*

What follows are a few more tips to prevent warm prospects from turning cold.

Deliver Value in Every Call

If you are calling on a prospect with the intent to follow up after you've had an initial contact (following up after sending them a brochure, proposal, demo, trial, press kit, product/service information, an initial conversation at a networking event) with them rather than calling on them cold or for the *first time*, consider the following points.

When following up, don't simply call to "follow up." In other words, stay away from calling with the intention to see if they've received your information or to "check in" to ask if they have any immediate needs for your product/service. Take some extra time and weave in a compelling reason for your call. How can you deliver value to them? Is there something timely that you can share with them about your product/service or about their industry? Is there something newsworthy that you can discuss which applies to them; for example, a success story with a client you've worked with?

 **Cold Calling Conundrum**

Some salespeople have a lengthy sales cycle where it may take anywhere from three months to a year to close a sale after initial contact with the prospect is made. If you fall into this situation, please realize that "touching base" is not a follow-up strategy.

What follows are some examples of the language you can weave into your dialogue when making follow-up calls.

◆ "After reflecting on our conversation, I have some new ideas that I'd like to share with you regarding how our program (product, service) may actually complement and enhance what you're currently doing."

◆ "I was thinking about another client who was in a similar situation as yours and thought that you might be interested in hearing about how we were able to eliminate the challenges they had."

◆ "After making some exciting changes to our product (or service, programs, packages) in order to deliver more value to our clients, I thought of you and the results you were looking to achieve. There may be a great fit here that's worth exploring in more detail."

Bridge Each Conversation

Bridge the previous conversation (or contact you made via e-mail or voice mail) with a prospect using a well-crafted follow-up call. Refer to a prior conversation and remind the prospect or share with them the reason as to why they need to continue that conversation with you. What initially peaked their interest? Use phrases like, "I'd like to continue the conversation we began about ...." Or, "Let's continue our discussion about how we can ...." Or, "As we discussed last week when we met, let's see if there's a way for us to ...." Or, "Based on our prior conversation, I'm calling to continue our discussion about ...."

For those occasions where you sent them literature, rather than asking if they received it, weave it into the intention of the call. For example: "Let's take a moment to discuss what I had sent you and see if it makes sense for us to proceed further and explore working together."

If you can't get them on the phone or in person, it's fine to leave this type of message on their voice mail. Bridging a conversation is similar to building a house. Every brick you lay brings you one step closer to the sale.

The Fax of Cold Calling

Spamming via the fax or sending fax blasts to a prospect list may no longer be permitted. However, as long as you have made at least one contact with that particular prospect, the fax becomes a handy alternative communication vehicle that would increase the likelihood of getting back in front of the person you've been trying to contact. Before doing so, check your state laws to see if there are any other limitations or restrictions regarding the proper use of a fax.

The Anniversary Card

If you have been calling on a particular prospect for a while now and haven't gotten the response that you are looking for, send them an anniversary card! This is a great way to be creative and grab your prospect's attention while weaving some humor into your follow-up strategy. Be sure to include your business card or contact information when sending this.

"Happy Anniversary! It's been six months since I began calling on you. As with any great working relationship, it takes some time, nurturing, persistence, and encouragement to develop, which I'm fully committed to doing.

So, when can we celebrate? Your gift will be arriving shortly. If there's something in particular that you are looking for, feel free to let me know. If you can't think of anything, how about the gift of being able to (here's a great spot to weave in a compelling reason.)

Please don't worry about getting me anything. I'll actually be happy with a return call. Otherwise, here's looking ahead to our one year anniversary. I hope we can connect beforehand."

Sincere regards,
Your Name

As a friendly reminder regarding the use of gifts, in some industries it may be illegal to offer presents or perks to prospects with the intention of securing their business. Make sure this does not apply in your industry.

When Enough Is Actually Enough, Keep Going

Chapter 7 provided you with the tools you need to develop your own prospecting system. In the example of a prospecting system I provided, the final step of a prospecting system was declaring the prospect a nonpriority and putting them in a separate file to contact in the future, while making sure you are still keeping your name in front of them (newsletter, announcements).

The bigger question is, "How do you decide when a prospect is no longer a priority?"

On one of her shows, Oprah shared a story of how a woman's entrepreneurial spirit, persistence, and relentless follow-up made her a millionaire. Using her great-great-grandmother's recipe for honey cream syrup, she decided to turn it into a business.

After several years of selling her syrup to local retailers, she decided to play a bigger game. Her target was the Denny's chain of restaurants.

Cold Medicine

Persistence pays. Persistence + patience + belief in your quality product + enthusiasm + prospecting system + healthy prospecting mind-set + being process driven + fearlessness + continued training and development + measurable goals = the formula for becoming a top producer.

For two years straight, she called Denny's every single week. Her persistence and perseverance paid off when Denny's awarded her a $3 million contact in her ninth year in business. Her syrup is also sold in 10,000 major grocery chains. Talk about a recipe for sweet success!

How many times do you think this person was told, "This isn't the best time," or "Call us back later," or "You need to talk with someone else," or "We don't have a need right now," or "No, we're not interested."

Her conviction and belief in her product enabled her to overcome any obstacle in her path. She decided what she wanted and hearing a "no" was not going to compromise her efforts or objective. This alone provided her with an advantage over her competitors who didn't have the same drive that she possessed. Her endurance outlasted all of them!

The Lifetime Value of a Client

Once a prospect lets you know that they are not in a position to take advantage of your offer, many salespeople are quick to put them on their callback list for a future contact. The good salespeople incorporate some strategy to ensure that they stay in front of the prospect (such as a newsletter).

I admit that what I'm about to tell you may sound like I am talking out of both sides of my mouth. What I'm about to share with you is more of an alternative line of thinking that may go against what I said in Chapter 7.

Actually, I'm introducing a new gauge you can use to determine if it's even worth being as persistent as our friend who made the three-million-dollar sale to Denny's.

What is the lifetime value of one of your clients? The lifetime value of a client is defined as the final amount of potential business that each prospect can generate for you once they become a client. How much income does one client generate for the lifetime of your career?

This is a great way to qualify a prospect as to whether or not they are a priority for you and deserve most of your attention.

What is each client ultimately worth to you? (How about each prospect?) What is their potential as it relates to the volume of sales you can produce through them? How many referrals can you generate from one client and how much business does that equate to? After all, would you prospect someone every week for two full years if you know that you have the potential to generate a $3 million sale?

If you ever wondered how to determine if you are investing your prospecting time wisely, you now have a new barometer to help you answer that question.

Take this concept even further to determine the lifetime value of your prospecting efforts. If you factor in the time that each prospecting initiative takes to complete and the harvest you can reap from those actions, you can then make an accurate determination whether or not it is still worth doing. In other words, are the activities you engage in maximizing the monetary return you get in relation to your time investment? Are they the best use of your time? If you divide the money you make throughout the lifetime of a client by the number of hours you invest in each prospect to make that money, what does that equate to per hour?

Remember, we're talking about the lifetime value, not the immediate payoff. Just because you may try a strategy once and get minimal results, make sure you are compounding those results over time. Think about the interest you make when you put your money in the bank. It may not seem like much now, but what about in 10 years?

Here's where it gets a bit tricky. It's one thing to determine the lifetime value of a client or potential client as it relates to your income or the volume of sales you can generate. However, it's important that you also factor in not only in the sales volume one client can generate but also who else they may know and can refer to you who might be a potential prospect.

The Least You Need to Know

◆ Develop your "follow-through" system so that you can stop giving sales away to your competition. And don't forget to get permission to continually follow up.

◆ It's your responsibility to keep their level of interest and motivation at the same level up until the point they become a client.

◆ Always have a reason to contact a prospect rather than simply to touch base or follow up.

◆ Bridge each conversation to ensure you build the pathway to a sale.

◆ Determine the lifetime value of your prospects, clients, and prospecting activities.

◆ Don't be satisfied by what the prospect is willing to tell you; get satisfied by what they weren't willing to tell you but eventually did.

Part 5

The Winner's Circle—Securing Your Position at the Top

Now that you have all the tools you need to develop a solid foundation for achieving incredible success at prospecting, what's next? Here's an interesting fact: There's actually a relatively small amount of activity that separates the average producer from the top producer. This final section will provide you with the tools, tasks, and techniques that are sure to give you a competitive edge and propel you to superstar status, while dispelling some myths along the way. It's time for you to do your victory dance!

Chapter

15

Networking and Referrals—Reach Out and Sell Someone

In This Chapter

- Becoming a networking whiz
- Developing your networking strategy
- Building your referral engine and team
- Asking for referrals without getting tongue-tied
- Attracting a continuous flow of new business

It would certainly be a challenge to write a comprehensive book about effective prospecting strategies without discussing how to generate more sales through networking and referrals.

Ask yourself this question. Would you rather make a cold call or follow up with a qualified *referral*; that is, someone who has already expressed some level of interest in your product as a result of an endorsement from someone else?

Okay, so maybe this question can be classified as a rhetorical question. If you would rather build your business from referrals, is your sales funnel bursting with potential new business that you've generated through networking and by utilizing a referral program? If not, then you will certainly have the opportunity to make this a reality and experience it firsthand after implementing the strategies outlined in this chapter.

The Six Laws of Networking–Prospecting's Hidden Treasure

What is that, you say? You don't feel comfortable going to a *networking* event, into a room filled with people you don't know, and then have to ask a complete stranger for new business? How about those special interest groups or lead groups where the intention is to help other people build their business by sharing referrals? I have news for you. Most people feel the same way. Chances are, you don't enjoy networking because you feel that you're alone, "out there" all on your own. Hey, it takes a lot of courage to fly solo and into an event where you don't know anyone. Yet, maybe there's a way for you to change your mind-set around this.

Cindy was a stay-at-home mom looking for ways to generate some additional cash to help out her family with the monthly expenses. To do so, she found an outside sales position selling a line of self-care products. This position gave her the freedom and flexibility to create her own hours, while honoring the priority in her life, which was her family.

> **Cold Callingo**
>
> **Networking** is the act of meeting new people, often in a social setting with the intention of interacting with them, exchanging ideas, and developing mutually rewarding relationships that would ultimately lead to creating new selling opportunities that would bring in additional business.

Cindy knew that in order for her to make this worthwhile, she needed to maximize the little time that she was able to devote to her business. After speaking with the top reps in her company, Cindy quickly realized that the only way to leverage her prospecting time was if she put herself in front of as many people as possible in the shortest amount of time. As such, she began to search for local networking groups, trade shows, and business events that she could join or take part in.

Cold Medicine

Go online to search for the local Chamber of Commerce or other networking and lead groups in your area. There's probably a plethora of networking functions that are held on a weekly basis right near your home or office. Look into joining some industry-specific associations as they relate to your business. Find those organizations whose members comprise what you would classify as your ideal prospect and get in front of them. (You may also want to review the list of suggested places where you can go to network in Chapter 8.)

Cindy called me one morning and shared her situation with me. Finally, she said, "Keith, I am so uncomfortable attending these functions with people I don't even know. And even if I did start talking with someone, I wouldn't know what to say or how to stimulate their interest in what I am selling without sounding pushy or overly aggressive."

I reminded Cindy about the strategies outlined in Chapter 2 and about becoming fearless. I then shared several observations that she considered to be the treasure she needed to make networking a prospecting activity she could actually enjoy.

1. Bring a Wingman: Rather than flying solo at your next networking event, bring a friend, co-worker, or business associate along with you. This "security blanket" will boost your confidence as well as your comfort level and immediately removes the bulk of reluctance associated with attending a networking event by yourself.

2. You Are Not Alone: If you ask most people who attend networking events, they would tell you that there are certainly some feelings of apprehension and fear when it comes to meeting new people (if they were being honest). Rather than placing yourself in the class of people who you perceive to be the minority, instead, consider that you are amongst the majority of people who feel the same way you do.

3. Keep Your Intentions In Focus: If you expect to go to a networking function and walk out with a handful of business cards from people who want to buy from you, think again. Before going out to your next event, I'd suggest reading over the distinction between expectation vs. possibility in Chapter 4. To maximize your networking efforts, detach from the outcome of having to generate new business. Your only focus should be on having a good time, relaxing, and enjoying yourself as you meet new people and foster new relationships! If you do, the other stuff will take care of itself as a byproduct of how effectively you are managing your mind-set, really.

4. Lighten Up! Let's face it. When you go to a networking event, there's often food and drink, music, even a keynote speaker. They are supposed to be fun! Don't take yourself or these events so seriously. Besides, people would rather do business with those who are fun to be around and extroverted, not the wallflower sitting in the corner.

5. Make A Friend First, A Client Second: Cindy said, "Okay Keith. So I go to a networking event and I begin talking with someone. What do I talk about? I never know what to talk about at these functions." I asked Cindy, "When you go out with your friends, do you have trouble finding things to discuss?" Cindy replied with an absolute "No." When I asked her what some of the typical topics of conversation were, she said, "Family, work, kids, school, travel, weather, leisure, current events, hobbies, sports, shopping, and movies." I then asked her, "So, why would it be any different to discuss these things when meeting new people?" "Because they are strangers!" Cindy declared.

I then told her the one belief I had that made networking so much fun, "Strangers are simply friends that are waiting to be met." At one point, all of your friends were strangers too! So, when does a stranger become a friend? Aside from liking the person's initial disposition, it's when you have enough mutual interests. It's when you find that their life often parallels yours with the same challenges, joys, and experiences you are going through. Most of all, it's when you realize that you enjoy being around them because they make you feel good. They enrich your life and add value to your existence. If this is true, then it really doesn't matter where or how you meet them. Just think about the friends you have now. Where did you meet them, at the "Friend Shop?" After all, it is often easier to develop a friendship than it is to develop a client. (Less pressure to perform.) Finally, as we discussed in Chapter 4, make them human.

6. Make It About The Other Person: Rely on the pull approach to networking rather than pushing for the result. To build from the preceding concept, Cindy now has a bevy of topics to discuss with the lucky person who she begins to talk to at her next social event. However, instead of talking about yourself, talk about them. Oftentimes when people are nervous they try to find a safe haven, a topic they are used to and comfortable discussing. So they wind up incessantly talking about themselves. Use this as a leverage point. Take the topics I mentioned earlier and craft some questions around them that you can ask another person in order to stimulate conversation and get them talking about themselves. Inevitably, they will eventually start asking you questions, especially as they relate to your career. Bang! You've just created the opening without even trying.

Finally, instead of asking yourself, "Why would that person want to talk to me?" change the question you are asking yourself to, "Why would I want to talk with them?" This question shifts the balance of power to you so that you are at choice rather than being on the defensive.

Now that you are in the mode of inquiry, this will stimulate some questions you can ask them as they relate to the topics I mentioned in number five.

While changing her thinking about networking helped tremendously, Cindy still felt that she just didn't have the right tools to go mining for new business. She then asked, "Keith, I understand how to change my thinking to a more positive outlook. I even understand how to strike up a conversation and make small talk even bigger. But how do I introduce my business or products to someone when meeting them for the first time without appearing overly aggressive or desperate?" I then shared with her a strategy that would accomplish her objective every time she networked.

Cold Medicine

To further remove any reluctance or anxiety around networking, go into your first networking function with absolutely no expectations whatsoever. Consider it your beta test or your personal experiment to determine what works and what doesn't. Then, maintain this mindset for all other networking events you go to. Here's a perfect example of engaging in a prospecting activity with absolutely no attachment to the outcome.

So, What Do You Do? Effective Networking Strategies

The question usually surfaces at some point during an initial conversation with a new acquaintance: "So, what type of work do you do?" Surprisingly, few people know how to respond in a way that builds their business or network.

> **Warm Wisdom**
>
> Notice the root of the word, "networking;" "network." The word "network" is synonymous with "system," "a group," or "a set of connections or contacts." Instead of looking at networking as simply going out to "show your face," look at what the word implies. Developing a networking strategy is critical to becoming a networking superstar.

You have probably been asked this question dozens of times. Often enough, the response isn't given much thought. You may reply, "I am an attorney," or "I am in sales," or "I own a business," or "I am a financial planner, (consultant, coach, doctor, CPA, account executive, manager, recruiter)." I've even seen people stumble to get the answer out as if they weren't sure themselves of what it is they do.

On the other hand, those people that walk away from a social event, networking function or trade show with a list of new contacts are the ones who have spent the time preparing an opening dialogue and an intelligent response to this question.

Developing Your Laser Introduction

Here's a technique to assist you in opening up a conversation and new opportunities that will increase your network and client base.

The Laser Introduction: I recently asked one of my clients who was a consultant to describe her services. She said, "I help my clients with their business." When I asked her to explain in one sentence the benefits her clients realize or the end result they experience after using her services, she had a hard time finding the words.

When creating your laser introduction, begin by focusing on the service you provide to your clients. How do you describe the product or service that you provide? You could opt for something generic, as just described. However, you can have a greater impact by delivering a message that will spark further interest in the person with whom you are speaking.

After all, the term "laser" describes a "device that emits a highly focused beam of light (or more specifically a beam of synchronized single wavelength radiation)." Here's your chance to develop your own focused beam of prospecting brilliance that illuminates, clarifies, and brings to life every networking or prospecting opportunity you uncover.

When creating a laser introduction, begin by identifying some of your client's challenges. Then, describe how your product or service provides solutions to those challenges.

Begin with the phrase, "You know how ..." followed by a couple of common problems that your clients normally experience. Then follow up by saying, "What I do is ..." and continue with one or two key points, benefits, value propositions, compelling reasons, or MVPs as they relate to how your product or service solves these problems.

For example, if you are a sales trainer or consultant, here's an example of what the dialogue between you and a potential prospect might sound like.

Prospect: **"So what do you do?"**

You: *"Well, you know how some sales teams experience high turnover and struggle to meet their sales goals as well as find new prospects which ends up costing the company time and money?"*

Prospect: **"Yes. I'm actually going through that myself with my company."**

Note to reader: Allow the person to respond, demonstrating you have their attention and that they are interested in what you have to say. Then respond with the following statement.

You: *"Well, what I do is help businesses improve their bottom line and bring in more sales by getting their salespeople in front of more targeted, qualified prospects."*

Prospect: **"Hmm. That's interesting. So, how do you actually do that?"**

Using this approach, you have not only clarified the results you can deliver, but you have opened the door for further discussion about similar challenges that the person you are talking with, their company, clients, or other people who they know may be experiencing. Like your compelling reasons, you may want to develop a few laser introductions that you can use depending on the person you are speaking with and the timely issues or concerns they encounter in their profession or industry (their specific business or position such as salesperson, manager, executive, business owner, human resource professional, lawyer, accountant, doctor, friend).

Before we move on, what I've really shared with them in my laser introduction was a compelling reason. Once again, I did not tell them what I sell or do or even the specifics of how I go about achieving these results. I simply shared with them the end results they can realize.

Notice what their response was. "So how do you do that?" If you get a similar response from using your introduction, then let that be a testament to your fabulous networking abilities. Your laser introduction is working perfectly. Once you hear a response like this, you can share with them the process of achieving the results you've mentioned or even begin a "light" needs analysis right on the spot.

If you have established that the person you meet at a networking event or social function is not a viable candidate for your product, consider that they may know other people who are. After delivering your laser introduction and finding that they do not qualify as a prospect, then simply respond with another question. One that I've seen trainers, coaches, and consultants use is, "Who do you know who might be interested in doing things better, reaching bigger goals, making more money, and reducing their stress level while enjoying their life and keeping it in balance?"

Making the Phone Ring

At the end of a conversation with a potential prospect, we often hand out one of our business cards and then wait for the phone to ring. By doing so, you have placed the responsibility on the other person to contact you. If you hand out 100 business cards, think about how many people actually call you. Chances are, not many.

Instead of waiting around for these potential clients to find your business card and call, take on the responsibility of getting in touch with them. Doing so will give you the opportunity to get in touch with every contact you make instead of waiting for the phone to ring.

When asked for your business card, hand it to them and add, "You know, it's sometimes difficult to contact me because I am often out of the office or on the phone working with my clients. Let me have your phone number and a good time to get in touch with you so that I can make myself available around your schedule."

Spend time putting together a laser introduction that works for you, then try it out at your next chamber mixer or trade show. You will notice people taking a greater interest in what you do, while spending less effort generating new clients.

What Constitutes a Referral?

What exactly classifies as a referral? If we were to create some parameters that define what a referral is, this is what it would look like.

Synonymous with "recommendation" and "testimonial," a referral is a potential prospect that is directed or given to you by someone you know or someone you don't know who feels that you are the best source for help or information regarding a specific subject, product, or service.

What makes a referral so incredibly attractive and desirable is that it is, for the most part, a warm lead. That is, when you approach a referral, there is less of a need to convince or sell them. A certain degree of interest, credibility, and comfort has already been established. Chances are, there's already a need present. All you have to do then, is turn that need into a want or a desire for your product using the questions in your needs analysis.

Cold Medicine

If your phone still isn't ringing off the hook, then maybe it's time for you to tap into a new source of business, that is, referral business.

But where do you go find this business? Is there a "referral store" you can go to and purchase these referrals? Not exactly. Identifying several sources you can tap into for referrals is another component of the pre-call planning phase in your prospecting system (see Chapter 8).

Warm Calling—Develop Your Referral Team to Generate Referrals

Your referral team is going to consist of people you know who can become a source of new business for you. These people are often classified as your "circle of influence." With the right players you can develop a highly effective referral engine that positions you in front of more warm prospects.

Aside from your friends and family, if you're not exactly sure who to contact, what follows is a list of professionals you may know who can become star players on your referral team. Each professional will fall under one of the four categories listed. If some of the professionals listed don't apply for you, then simply use this list as a tickler to stimu-late your thinking so that you can uncover additional people to contact. Succeeding in your career will always be easier when you have a team of people to support you.

Career and Business: Career Counselor, Computer Consultant, Executive Recruiter, Graphic Artist, HR Professional, Internet Service Provider, IT Professional, Other Salespeople, Printer, Trainer, Vendors You Currently Use, Web Designer, Web Hosting Company

Financial and Professional Services: Attorney, Bank, CPA, Insurance Agent, Mortgage Broker, Realtor, Stockbroker/Financial Planner

Warm Wisdom
Rather than considering this an arduous task, make it a game so that you can enjoy the process of developing your referral team. For instance, once you have 20 people on your referral team who can become a conduit to more referral business, then you win! (So, what are you going to reward yourself with?)

Health and Self Care: Chiropractor, Dentist, Dermatologist, Nutritionist, Optometrist, Pediatrician, Pharmacist, Primary Care Physician, Surgeon

Personal Services: Babysitter, Childcare, Church/Temple, Coach, Contractor, Electrician, Florist, Housekeeper, Makeup Artist, Mechanic, Painter, Personal Trainer, Photographer, Plumber, Hair Stylist, Tailor, Travel Agent

Now that you have identified those people in your circle of influence who are potential players for your referral team, it's time to communi-cate the right message to them. What follows is an example of a letter you can send them. Use this as a template. You'll just need to edit it so that it fits for your product, service, and target audience. Keep in mind that the same rules to writing an effective letter that we discussed in Chapter 7 apply here as well. (When reviewing the following letter, notice that this is an opportunity to once again utilize your compelling reasons from Chapter 5.)

Date
Name/Title
Address

Dear (Name),

I hope this letter finds you well. Just wanted to drop you a line to let you know what I'm up to these days. I am now a sales and business coach. Because I'm now working with a variety of people in various industries, I was thinking of you and wanted to know if you would like to be part of my referral team. The primary objective of this team is to support each other and assist when we can in sharing referrals and new opportunities to build each other's business.

Each member becomes a resource for every other member, not only for providing new prospects but also as a resource for all of our clients who might need or have an interest in our services.

To explain what I do as a coach, I work with people who want to:
- Make more money and reach bigger, more rewarding goals quickly without the costly learning curve when trying to "do it all" on their own.
- Gain a distinguishing and well-needed edge over their competition.
- Spend more time enjoying their life and family.
- Eliminate at least three hours of their workload every day.
- Eliminate overwhelming problems and stress so that they can end the day with a smile on their face.

My role as a coach includes: mentor, consultant, success partner, trainer, friend, guide, support structure, cheerleader, and confidant. I decided to share my experiences so that I can add greater value to other people's careers and lives, helping them make their life a priority and then living it. I do this by working with many types of clients but my ideal client is:
- The entrepreneur or business owner who is ready to grow their business quickly.
- The sole practitioner or non-selling professional who wishes to build his or her practice.
- The sales manager or executive who needs to build a world-class sales team to generate more sales in less time.
- The salesperson who wants to double their productivity and improve their meeting rate with qualified prospects.

We achieve these goals together while maintaining a healthy balance in the person's life. Because the majority of coaching can be done via the phone or e-mail, coaching is something that can fit into anyone's schedule. The fact is that everyone does better when they have someone on their corner supporting them. If you feel that your services are in alignment with my ideal client type and vice versa, I'd be happy to talk with you so that I can learn more about your business and how you would want me to send you the referrals I generate for you. Conversely, if coaching sounds like something you would like to learn about in more detail, I would be delighted to schedule a time to talk.

Finally, keep me in mind if you run across someone who is interested in achieving any of the results I mentioned above. I would be happy to spend time talking with them to see if they are a candidate who can benefit from coaching.

I have enclosed several business cards. Please share these with anyone you want. Most of all, please let me know how I can assist you! Feel free to contact me anytime at 123-456-7890 or e-mail me at coach@abccompany.com. Thanks again for your consideration and I look forward to speaking with you soon.

Sincere regards,
Name
Title/Company
Phone

An example referral team letter.

When and How to Ask for Referrals

Aside from determining who can become a potential player on your referral team, you will also need to determine how frequently you ask for referrals from your clients, prospects, or circle of influence, as well as the appropriate time to do so.

Typically, your clients are going to be the top source for referral business simply because they are the ones who actually utilize your product, making them the most effective testimonial you can find to endorse your product.

Cold Calling Conundrum

If you find that you are having difficulty asking for referrals, then question how strong your belief is in your product, your commitment to serving your clients, and the value proposition you can deliver.

The following dialogue illustrates how you can establish a referral agreement with your clients. This way, you will be able to identify the clients who are willing to become a referral source for you and the most appropriate time to ask them for referrals. This is a great example of how to set up your strategy to increase the amount of referral business you currently generate.

You: *"Mrs. Client, may I take a moment to share with you how I build my business?"*

Client: **"Sure."**

You: *"Well, what I enjoy most about what I do and where my time is best served is working with my clients. I want to spend as much time as possible serving my clients and exceeding your expectations.*

In order for me to spend more time with my clients and less time marketing or prospecting for new business I really need the help of my satisfied clients.

Please understand, I'm certainly not asking for any referrals from you now. Personally, I feel that would be incredibly presumptuous to ask you to introduce me to other potential clients before you even have a chance to truly utilize and benefit from my services. After all, we just started working together!

However, in a couple of months or even weeks, when you are clearly realizing the benefits of my services and have gotten even more value than you expected, would you be comfortable sharing the results you have experienced with others and introduce me to those people who might also benefit from my services?"

Client: **"Sure, I don't see why not."**

Cold Medicine

The most effective way to earn referrals is to over-deliver on the value your clients expect so that you actually exceed their expectations. Once you confirm this to be true, it now becomes a great time to ask for testimonials or a reference from a happy client.

You: *"That sounds great. Thanks in advance for this consideration. Just so I know what it will take to make you a raving fan, what can I do to make you comfortable enough to actually want to refer business to me?"*

Setting up a referral agreement with your clients will remove any reluctance and make you feel much more comfortable when asking them for referrals. Because they now know this is something you will be asking of them, it's okay to ask.

Building Your Referral Engine

At this point you may be looking at your current client base or referral team and enthusiastically think, "I've got an absolute goldmine here but what is the 'right' way to approach them and ask for a referral?"

Building your referral engine is no different than the approach you took when developing your prospecting system in Chapter 7. So without further ado (and taking the chance of boring you to tears) what follows is an example of a referral engine that will open the floodgates so the referrals can start pouring in. Please keep in mind that this is only one example of a referral program. Fine tune this four-step process so that it fits best for you.

Cold Medicine

When you give referrals to others, you feel more worthy to ask for and accept them.

Step One: Establish Your Referral Agreement

Back in the section "When and How to Ask for Referrals," we discussed an effective strategy to establish a referral agreement with your clients. Once you have done that, you are ready to move on to step two.

Step Two: Write Your Referral Letter

At this point, you know how to set up a referral agreement, when it's appropriate to ask for referrals, and the language you can use to do so. Once you have set up your agreement with each of your clients and deliver your product or service, here is your chance to follow through. What follows is a letter that one remodeling company sends to their clients that quadrupled their referral business. Please note that in this letter, this company actually rewarded the clients who sent them referrals with a token of appreciation. This is entirely optional and a judgment call on your part as to whether or not you can and want to do this.

If you have a referral recognition program that involves giving those people who refer business to you some type of reward or finders fee, make sure that you are clearly stating the parameters of your program, what it takes to earn the reward as well as what constitutes a qualified referral. One of my clients who owned a home remodeling business shared an experience with me that caused them to revamp their entire referral program. She sent out a letter to each of her clients letting them know that for each referral they gave her, they would receive one hundred dollars. Initially she thought her program was a huge success, given the number of referrals that came pouring in.

However her success quickly evaporated as she began calling on these referrals to schedule an appointment with them. To her surprise, these people didn't even know what she was calling them for! The more she got hung up on, the more she began questioning this program. These supposed referrals reacted more like cold prospects! It turned out that some people were going through the local directory, writing down the names and numbers of their "neighbors" and sending them in under the guise of a referral. When she looked at the letter she sent out to her clients, she saw where the breakdown was. It never stipulated that in order to receive the finders fee, each referral had to become a paying client of hers.

RE: The (COMPANY NAME) Win-Win-Win Referral Program

Dear (Name),

Looking back over last year's events, we realize that every day gives us good reason to be very grateful to have you as a client. All of us at (Company Name) deeply appreciate and thank you for your business.

Meeting our clients' unique and immediate needs and developing long-term relationships with people like you is what drives us to continually seek out new clients who we can provide exemplary service to and overdeliver on the value they expect.

In the past, I've spent a great deal of time and expense in attracting new clients. Instead of wasting time "pounding the pavement" or spending money on marketing and advertising, I decided to concentrate my efforts on building rewarding relationships with the people I already know and enjoy working with, people like you.

What continually enables us to offer the highest quality, value, and service available to all of our customers while keeping our pricing very competitive is the low cost of marketing that we incur as a result of repeat business and referrals from happy clients. As such, we decided to take the money we have been spending on running ads and the time it takes to prospect for new business and reinvest it in our relationships by passing this savings on to you. That's why we are asking for your help.

The greatest compliment we can ever get from a client is when they share their positive experience and our name with someone else. As such, I would like to introduce you to our Win-Win-Win Referral Program. The fact that someone like you trusts us with your home remodeling projects carries a lot of weight. That's why we respectfully request a few minutes of your time to think about someone you could refer whom you feel could benefit from our services. We would greatly appreciate the opportunity to provide them with the highest degree of service and value that you have received from us.

Whether it's your neighbor, doctor, accountant, professional association, or people you know who own a home and are thinking about tackling a remodeling project, there may be a few people who come to mind that could benefit from our services, whether it's now or in the future. We want this to be a win for everyone involved. That's why every time your referral becomes a client, we will give you a special savings certificate enabling you to take more money off our already competitive pricing that you can apply towards your next project. Consider this our way of saying "Thank you" and as a testament to how much we appreciate you and your business.

Enclosed is a form to facilitate the process. You can return this form to us by:

1. Faxing it directly to 123-456-7891.
2. E-mailing your referrals to info@abccompany.com.
3. Mailing it in the enclosed self-addressed stamped envelope.
4. Calling us at 123-456-7890.

If you feel more comfortable, feel free to give them my name and phone number listed below but urge them to call me if they want to have the same positive experience that you had when tackling a project like this while saving money and protecting their greatest investment: their home. I have also enclosed several business cards for you to pass on to anyone you'd like.

All of us at (COMPANY NAME) thank you in advance for your support and for putting your trust in us. In addition, we promise that with every referral, your friends, family, and associates will thank you and we will make you look great! I look forward to the opportunity to continue serving your home remodeling needs.

Sincere regards,

Name
Title/Company
Phone

An example referral letter.

Step Three: Determine Your Frequency of Contact

Based on the concepts you've been exposed to in this book, it's safe to say that consistency is one of the central themes when it comes to prospecting success.

Therefore, you can't expect that one mailer a year that asks your clients for referrals is going to have a dramatic impact.

Because the buying cycle of people, as well as companies, varies, it is essential to keep your message in front of them on a consistent basis throughout the year. By continually reminding them about your referral program, you have reduced the chance of having some referrals slip through the cracks.

Your referral letter can be sent out every quarter. If you want to be even more aggressive, try sending it out once every month or so. I would also suggest varying the message as well. For instance, if you send your clients a newsletter, this is a great vehicle to remind them about your referral program and keep them updated on any changes or new incentives. I know some people who actually use a section in their newsletter just to acknowledge and thank those clients who have been a fabulous source of referral business for them. (People do love to be acknowledged!)

The more you inform your clients about the new programs or services you offer, remind them about your referral program, and give value to them, the more referral business you can expect to earn from them.

Step Four: Acknowledge, Acknowledge, Acknowledge

The biggest blunder salespeople make when developing their referral program is, once they start getting referrals, they forget to actually thank the person who provided them!

I purposely labeled this step "Acknowledge, Acknowledge, Acknowledge." You are going to acknowledge and thank each client who sends you a referral that you convert into a sale a minimum of three times.

When you get the referral: Call or send a thank-you card letting your client know how much you appreciate their thinking of you and taking the time out of their busy day to send you a referral. Reinforce the fact that each referral will be taken care of and given the exemplary service and attention that every one of your clients deserves.

When you meet with the referral: After you connect with the referred prospect, call or send a thank-you card as well as an update on where each referral stands as it relates to your selling cycle.

When you sell the referral: Once the sale is a done deal and the referral becomes a client, rather than waiting until you have delivered the actual product/service to this new client, immediately call your referral source and send a thank-you card as well as the token of appreciation that you committed to sending them as per your referral program. I suggest calling them as soon as possible so that you are the first person to let them know their referral is now a client of yours, rather than having your referral source hear it from the person who they referred to you.

That's it! Simple enough, yes? Asking for referrals is an effective way to tap into your clients' networks or circles of influence, thus effortlessly increasing and expanding on the size of your own network as a result! Mark my words, you'll be amazed how such a simple system can generate so much new business.

When Good Referrals Go Bad

Now that you know what it's going to take for you to build your referral engine, you better make sure that you have a system in place to ensure that you are prepared to handle all of the referral business that you are about to generate!

With all of the effort you are putting forth to excel in your career by building a referral engine, there's nothing worse than wasting a perfectly good referral that was hand-delivered to you by a happy client (associate, friend, family member, and so on).

Whether it's due to poor follow-up, poor service, a comment you made to the referral that you were better off keeping to yourself, or a sales tactic that turned the warm referral into a cold fish, these are just a few things you can do to destroy a referral and any possibility for a sale.

Think about what this is costing you. The more obvious cost would be the loss of a perfectly good selling opportunity.

However, there's much more at stake that you stand to lose.

What about the person on your referral team? Here you have a client, associate, prospect, or someone else you know who is putting their neck on the line for you. Once your referral source gets wind of what happened, you can bet that this would be the last time this person ever sends you another referral. You can now cross that player off your team.

So it not only costs you one possible sale but all of the potential future sales that you have lost because you compromised the relationship you have with your referral source.

To take it one step further, what if it were a client who sent you this referral? How does this client now perceive you? Demonstrating this less than admirable trait to a client may change their once positive perception of you and tarnish the trust and confidence the client had in you. Not only have you lost the chance of getting any future referrals from them but you now run the risk of losing this client's future business that you would have normally earned.

If you are not in a position where you can effectively manage a referral program at this time, then it would behoove you to wait until you are better equipped and prepared to do so.

You Can Only Lead a Horse to Water

Just like your clients, referrals are a privilege, not a right. You don't automatically deserve referrals, you have to earn them regardless of how long you have been in sales, know someone, or have serviced an account.

You can't make people send you referrals, just like you can't make your prospects buy from you. And even if they are willing to send you referrals, it doesn't automatically mean they have someone in mind at the present moment who may be a viable candidate.

Keep in mind that the players on your referral team are doing *you* the favor, so you better make sure that you appreciate their efforts in a measurably visible way. They are the ones who are taking time out of their busy schedule to help you. So, be patient. Before you know it, you may not have to cold call as much as you used to due to the influx of referrals that you are generating.

The Least You Need to Know

- Attend the networking events that will expand your bandwidth and position you in front of more targeted prospects.

- Instead of asking yourself, "Why would that person want to talk to me?" change the question you are asking yourself to, "Why would I want to talk with them?"

- When networking, always take on the responsibility of contacting the prospect to ensure it will actually happen, rather than waiting for them to call.

- Establish a referral agreement with your clients to make the process of asking for referrals less of an effort.

- The most effective way to earn referrals is to overdeliver on the value your clients expect.

- To keep a steady stream of referrals flowing, you must continually acknowledge and thank the members on your referral team.

16

Measure It So You Can Manage It

In This Chapter

◆ Setting specific and measurable goals

◆ Letting the numbers drive your prospecting activity

◆ Developing your formula for selling success

◆ Making prospecting a "numbers art"

◆ What to do when your best isn't good enough

Brace yourself for the following announcement. Every person you speak with will not become a prospect and every prospect you speak with will not become a client. I know this fact has been alluded to throughout the book but because we are talking more specifically about managing and achieving your goals, I wanted to lay it right on the line. Hey, even being the eternal optimist that I am and knowing how much more effective you will be at prospecting as a result of implementing the strategies we've discussed, I'm also grounded enough in reality to know what you can expect from your prospecting efforts, even in the best-case scenario. While I would love to hear that you have a perfect batting average, we can't expect everyone you speak with to be wise enough (okay, maybe I'm reaching) or even ready to purchase your product at the exact time you call on them.

Before you shoot the messenger, there is a bright side. The good news is, by knowing that there are people you will talk to who will not take advantage of your offerings, you can better prepare for this reality. Tracking and evaluating your selling statistics will enable you to set and reach attainable objectives. Now you can map out the path and the specific actions you need to take daily to reach your goals and achieve greater results without the stress, overwhelming feeling, or frustration that accompanies bad planning.

Extreme Productivity–Develop Your Personal Navigation System

Throughout my career as a salesperson, a business owner, a sales trainer, and a business coach, I've noticed a consistent theme in relation to achieving greater levels of selling success.

That is, the sales professionals who are extremely productive have taken the time to define their goals and a road map to attain what they want most.

> **Warm Wisdom**
>
> Top producers know where they are going and have a path to get there.

While some enjoy the excitement of strategizing for the year, others find themselves intimidated by the goal-setting process. Instead, they get caught up in the trivial tasks and "busywork," doing everything except the activities that yield the greatest return.

If it's ever been a struggle to reach bigger goals, manage your schedule or maintain your focus and motivation, here's your opportunity to design a Personal Navigation System that will enable you to accelerate your productivity and generate greater results.

A Personal Navigation System is similar to the navigation system that you find in cars today. It's the system you use to navigate through your career and your life that encompasses your vision, priorities, goals, strategy, and daily routine, providing you with a clear sense of purpose and direction. This way, you can stay focused on your goals and the path that will take you to your desired destination.

While each of these system components is critical, we're going to spend only a brief amount of time focusing on each of them. (We'll save the details for another book.) Running your business or managing your career without having goals in place would be equivalent to driving from New York to California without a road map. You're bound to wind up somewhere else other than your intended destination.

Just like building a home, your goals and strategy become your blueprint for success. Having the end result clarified in your mind (and on paper) before you become consumed by your daily responsibilities will make the process of reaching bigger goals easier and more enjoyable.

The following pages detail three steps to make this year your best year yet!

Identify Your North Star

While the majority of your selling efforts are geared toward servicing your prospect's best interests, here's your time to be selfish! What's in it for you? What is the single motivational element that drives you to succeed in selling? What is the personal benefit that you will realize as a result of all the work you are doing here?

In order to achieve more, it's your responsibility to exercise your supervision. That is, the ability to see beyond what is happening today in order to crystallize the picture of what you want your career to look like tomorrow.

While crafting a professional vision statement is a critical component of your Personal Navigation System and something I suggest creating, I've scaled it down a bit. For now, develop a single theme for the year. What is the one thing you want to stand out most when you look back at the end of this year? Extreme profitability, accountability, organization,

> **Warm Wisdom**
>
> If you are a manager or business owner, create more buy-in from your staff by having them create the theme with you. The theme then becomes your company's barometer or checkpoint to refer to when taking the actions to build your business.

exemplary customer service, becoming a prospecting champion/top producer, doubling your income, becoming systems driven, developing a highly productive staff, self-care, life balance, an enjoyable career?

Here's an action step you can take right now. Spend a few minutes developing your theme. I've already started it for you. Simply complete the following sentence and let your theme be your source of motivation and guidance throughout the year.

"My theme for the year is ..." or "This is the year of/to ..."

Your theme complements your goals, the direction you want to travel and enables you to prioritize the activities to engage in.

Your theme becomes your North Star or guiding light. This way, when you are unsure of the activities to take part in throughout your week, simply ask yourself, "Is this activity aligned with my goals or supporting my theme for the year?" This question acts as a filter for weeding out the activities that don't move you closer to your goals.

Set Your Measurable Goals

Like the title of this chapter suggests, if you can measure it, you can manage it. But what is your gauge for success? While your goals need to support your theme, they must be specific, measurable, and have a deadline attached to them. It's not enough to say, "I want to sell more and make more money." Clarify what success looks like for you and write it down. For example, "I want to generate one million dollars in sales at a profit margin of X percent by 12/31/XX."

Take it to the next level and conduct a sales audit to determine who your ideal client is (see Chapter 8) as well as the type of projects, products or services that you enjoy selling, have a market for, and are most profitable.

What are the goals you most want to set for yourself and/or your company for the next 90 days or even for the year? Please select only the goals you really want, not the ones you should, could, have to, or might want. Spend some time thinking about what you want and write down your five personal and professional goals. When you set the right goals, you may feel excited and even a bit nervous, ready, and willing to get them done! Here are three distinct areas in which you can develop at least one goal.

◆ A Feeling: Happier, greater peace of mind or career fulfillment, stronger/better relationships, stress/worry free, living in the present, greater personal satisfaction, being process driven, becoming fearless

◆ A Measurable: Double my yearly income of $X, achieve my monthly sales quota of X, lose 25lbs. in the next six months, move into a new home by X date, create a referral program by the end of this month, develop and implement a new prospecting strategy by next week

◆ A Skill: Further development and mastery of communication skills, presentation skills, leadership skills, time-management skills, life balance, self-care, diffusing objections, asking questions, listening, cold calling

What follows is a four-step process to setting and achieving your goals.

Step One: Create Your Goals

Now that you know how to set a measurable and specific goal, here's your chance to do so. List the goals that you want to achieve most on the following lines. Make sure that the deadline you set for achieving your goals does not extend farther out than one year. (You can always set new goals once you've achieved these.)

1. _____

2. _____

3. _____

4. _____

5. _____

Step Two: Chart Your Milestones

When it comes to setting goals, realize that each goal encompasses several milestones. A milestone is like a mini goal. These are the parts of your goal that you set out to achieve at a specific point throughout the timeline that you have established to attain a certain goal. A milestone can be a task that needs to be completed as well as a strategy or skill that needs to be developed in order to reach your goal. A milestone can also be another measurable that when reached, provides you with the certainty of knowing that you are getting closer to attaining your ultimate objective.

For instance, if you are driving from Florida to New York, you know you are going the right way at the right time if you pass through the Carolinas, Baltimore, Delaware, and New Jersey at specific time intervals. These are the milestones you hit throughout your trip that will enable you to accurately determine your time of arrival.

If getting in great physical shape and losing 25 lbs by September is a goal for you in the new year, where do you want to be February 1st? 5 lbs lighter, 50 minutes strong on the treadmill, the ability to bench press your weight 10 times?

Think about the milestones you need to hit daily, weekly, or monthly that will determine whether or not you are traveling on the right path toward your final destination. If you have a sales goal of generating $1 million in yearly volume, what might a milestone look like for you? What strategy will enable you to reach this goal? Well, one milestone could be the development and deployment of a prospecting system. Another could be learning how to defuse initial objections.

Moreover, if we were to divide $1 million by 12 months, another milestone could be the monthly volume that you need to generate each month (approximately $83,300 worth of business each month). A third milestone can be the number of prospects you need to speak with each month in order to generate $83,300 in monthly volume. Finally, another milestone can include the number of prospects you need to present to who are now in your sales funnel, waiting to be closed.

Chart out the milestones that you need to achieve during your journey and establish a deadline for each one. Note that this list is to be completed separately for each goal, one goal at a time. (If you have more than five milestones or mini goals to reach for each goal, then simply continue to build upon this list.)

Milestone (Mini Goal)	Deadline
1.	
2.	
3.	
4.	
5.	

Step Three: Define Your Activities

Each milestone encompasses measurable activities and tasks, which will produce the specific and measurable result (milestone) you seek. If your milestone is a measurable, such as "generate 10 new prospects each month" list five specific and measurable actions you can take daily, weekly, or monthly that will enable you to reach this milestone. For example:

1. Three hours of cold calling each day. (Includes one hour designated solely for pre-call planning.)

2. One hour of follow-up calls each day.

3. Send out letter to clients asking for referrals once a month.

4. Host and deliver one seminar for potential clients (prospects) each month.

5. Attend two networking functions each week.

If your milestone is a task that needs to be completed or a skill or strategy that needs to be developed, list the specific and measurable steps that will enable you to do so. For example, if one of your tasks (milestone) is to develop an effective weekly routine that will enable you to manage your activities while keeping your life in balance, here's what the steps may look like:

1. Journal your week to uncover where you time is spent.

2. Assign a value to your time.

3. List all of your activities and tasks.

4. Categorize all of your activities and tasks.

5. Assign a timeline to each task.

6. Plan for unplanned activities by adding a buffer into your daily routine.

7. Identify your priorities and the non-negotiable activities that support you in you quest to achieve your goals. Delegate, dump or postpone the rest.

8. Create your routine by scheduling in your condensed list of priorities and non-negotiable activities as well as the frequency in which you engage in these activities.

9. Empower your routine to hold you accountable and do complete work.

Depending on whether your milestone is a measurable or a task, list the activities that will enable you to achieve each milestone or the steps to take in order to complete each task. Note that this list is to be completed separately for each milestone, one milestone at a time. (If you have more than five elements in each list, then simply continue to build upon this list.)

1. _____

2. _____

3. _____

4. _____

5. _____

Step Four: Recognize the Benefits

When you run into some snags along the way, or some unexpected challenges or delays, this step acts as a friendly reminder when you ask yourself the question, "Now, why am I doing all of this again?" What's in it for you that is sure to put a smile on your face?

List the personal and professional benefits of accomplishing each goal. Note that this list is to be completed separately for each goal, one goal at a time. This way, if you get frustrated along the way, refer to this list so that you can shift your thinking to a more positive and productive mind-set. Instead of filing this list after you complete it, post it where you can see it daily in order to keep your motivation alive.

1. _____

2. _____

3. _____

4. _____

5. _____

Align Your Actions with Your Intentions

Many people spend time thinking about how they need to generate greater results, such as increasing their sales volume. The question is, are you spending more time worrying rather than actually doing something about it?

A client was complaining how slow his business has become. I asked him, "On a scale of one to ten, where ten means you are putting in your full effort to build your business and one means you are not engaging in daily activities that generate new business, where do you stand?" He responded, "I'm probably a four." I then asked, "How much time are you devoting to sales and revenue generating activities?" The response, "Two hours per week."

The next time you feel frustrated because results aren't showing up fast enough, consider that your actions may not be aligned with your intentions.

Now that you have defined your goals and identified the revenue-generating activities and tasks you need to engage in to reach your goals, it's time to build them into your schedule by assigning designated blocks of time for these activities throughout your week. Use the list in Chapter 8 in the section "Prospect, Prospect Everywhere" as a guide to uncover the additional prospecting activities that you may want to weave into your weekly routine.

Make them non-negotiable to ensure that you are using your time to engage in the activities that are aligned with your goals, rather than becoming distracted or consumed with activities that may not move you toward achieving what you want.

Once you have completed this exercise, keep these components of your Personal Navigation System in front of you as a constant reminder.

The fact is, it's a lot easier to attain that which you want most when you know exactly what you're looking for and have a map to achieve it.

Develop Your Formula for Selling Success

How many calls do I need to make to generate one prospect? How many prospects does it take to generate one sale? How long will each cold call take? How much time do I need to devote to cold calling every day? If you don't know the answers to these essential questions, that's perfectly fine. By the end of this section you will.

Imagine how much easier your life would be if you were able to identify the specific and measurable actions you need to take on a daily basis in order to reach your yearly income goal. Use the template on the following pages to create your success formula. You will then be able to determine how many cold calls to make and the number of appointments/presentations needed each month, even each day to attain your goals, as well as the time commitment it will take to do so.

Let the numbers in your success formula determine the amount of activities you need to put into your daily routine that will ensure your selling success. It sure beats scratching your head at the end of every month, wondering why you didn't meet your sales quota. Now, you will have a defined formula to follow so that you can generate the results you want.

Finally, as you go through this formula, you may come across some questions that you don't know the answer to. This is perfectly normal, especially if you are new to sales or have never been exposed to these questions. Realize that if you do not have the answer to some of these questions, it may require doing some conscious tracking of your cold calling efforts before you are able to accurately answer them.

Refer to the table in Chapter 8 under the section "Prospect, Prospect Everywhere." Before you attempt to complete this formula, you must have a specific prospecting activity in mind. Because each prospecting activity is going to generate a different number of prospects within a certain amount of time, you must therefore create a separate formula for each prospecting activity you take on.

For example, if you use direct mail as a way to generate new prospects, then Step Four in your formula may look like this:

"Marketing Efforts: I need to spend $_____ per month to generate one new, qualified prospect."

The following formula is for your cold calling efforts only. Develop a separate formula for all additional prospecting activities. (Example: PR/marketing, alliances, partnerships, published articles, networking, referrals, speaking engagements.)

Finally, please note that this formula does not take into account residual income generated from each sale. To compensate for this, use the average lifetime value of one client (excluding any referral business they send you) as the factor for steps 1, 2, and 3 in the formula. For example, if you are a consultant that is paid on average $1,000 a month as a retainer and the average lifetime of each client is six months, then in number 1, the average sale would be $6,000. Once you have this number, you can complete the rest of the formula.

My Formula for Cold Calling Success:

1. Average sale in my business is $ _____.

2. Percentage of commission/income I am paid per sale is _____%.

3. My average commission/income per sale is $_____.

4. Prospecting Activity: <u>Cold Calling</u>

   It takes _____ (number) cold calls to find one new, qualified prospect.

5. I need to present to/meet with _____ (number) prospects to close one sale. In other words, I typically close/earn the business of _____ out of _____ prospects I am in front of. Therefore, my closing percentage is ____%. (Number of sales divided by number of prospects you presented to/met with.)

6. My annual income goal is $_____.

7. To attain my goal, I need to generate $_____ in average monthly income. (Yearly income goal [Step Six] divided by 12 months.)

8. I require _____ (number) monthly sales to produce $_____ (Step Seven) in average monthly income. (Average monthly income [Step Seven] divided by average commission/income per sale [Step Three].)

9. To produce _____ (number) sales monthly (Step Eight), I must present to/meet with _____ (number) new, qualified prospects per month. (Number of prospects needed to close one sale [Step Five] multiplied by the number of desired sales per month [Step Eight] = number of presentations/meetings with qualified prospects per month.)

10. To produce _____ (number) new, qualified prospects per month (Step Nine) I must make _____(number) cold calls per month. (Number of cold calls to find one new prospect [Step Four] multiplied by the number of new, qualified prospects needed per month to produce desired number of monthly sales [Step Nine].)

11. I must make _____ (number) cold calls per week. (Number of calls needed to make per month [Step Ten] divided by 4.335 weeks.)

12. To make _____ (number) cold calls per week (Step Eleven), I need to devote _____ (number) hours per week on cold calling.

(Number of cold calls per week [Step Eleven] multiplied by the average amount of time per call [in minutes] divided by 60 = The number of hours needed to devote to cold calling per week.)

Note to Reader: Make sure that you account for any additional preparation time prior to each cold call (see pre-call planning in Chapter 8).

13. I need to devote _____ (hours) per day on cold calling. (Number of hours per week devoted to cold calling [Step Twelve] divided by number of workdays.

14. I need to make _____ (number) cold calls per day that will take up _____ hours per day (Step Thirteen). (Number of cold calls per week [Step Eleven] divided by number of workdays.)

What Did You Expect to Happen?

After completing this exercise, you'll find that you may fit into one of the following scenarios in terms of how much prospecting (in this case, cold calling) you will have to do in order to reach your income goal.

1. You are right on track to reach your sales and income goal.

2. You're slightly off but can easily adjust your daily routine to compensate.

3. You'll need to put aside a considerable amount of more time to devote to prospecting. This may require some delegation of responsibilities or taking some other activities, tasks, or projects off your plate that may not serve you best or support your goals.

4. You feel like you just got hit with a two-by-four because the amount of cold calling you need to do in order to reach your income goal is off the charts and unrealistic, even too high to count.

If you fall within the fourth category, do not despair! If you find that you need to spend more hours prospecting than there are in a day in order to reach your income goal, consider some alternatives that will decrease your required prospecting time.

1. Improve your closing percentages.

2. Increase your profitability/commissions or income per sale.

3. Increase the size of your average sale.

4. Decrease the number of cold calls needed to identify one new prospect.

5. Decrease the average time it takes for you to make one cold call. (Remove all distractions, pre-call planning from Chapter 8.)

6. Change your income/sales goal.

7. Find a new career path. This alternative is only for those people who have thoroughly explored all options (including working with a sales coach) and, most important, have taken the time to develop their selling skills and implement a comprehensive prospecting system they have followed for a considerable length of time.

Fine-tuning the first six of the seven measurables I just mentioned will ensure that you are maximizing your time, your talents and your potential as well as each prospecting and selling opportunity.

Is Prospecting a Numbers Game or an Art?

I admit that in my earlier years, I too have been a victim of faulty thinking. More specifically, the line of limiting thinking that I am referring to is the mistaken belief that "Sales is a numbers game."

I believed this when I first started selling. After all, my manager told this to me, so it must be true. My manager was told this by his predecessor, and so on, and so on. Even when I became a manager, I continued passing on this supposed truth and preached this pearl of wisdom to my sales team.

It was when I began developing sales training programs that I finally unearthed the truth. And that truth is, "Sales is a numbers *art*."

Let's unpack why this is so. You may be familiar with the rule of thirds. That is:

◆ One third of your prospects will buy from you. (It just happens to be the right time and the need is there.)

- One third of your prospects will buy from someone else.

- One third of your prospects are sitting on the fence and therefore are up for grabs.

Well, if you look at the first two bullets in the previous list, one can surmise that selling is, in fact, a numbers game. The phrase, "numbers game" implies that you really don't have any control over the results of your prospecting efforts. Rather, it's the number of calls you make or the number of prospects you speak with that dictate the results, regardless of your level of experience, training or skill set.

Therefore, if I do nothing more than call on enough people, I am going to sell at least one third of them. Even the worst salespeople are going to sell at least one third of the people they see. After all, every salesperson steps right into a sale now and then, even if it's nothing more than calling the right person at the right time; a time when they need your product.

Even if you don't call on the prospect, depending on their need they might be the one who calls on you. For example, many consumer-driven sales are a function of the prospect's actions not the salesperson's aptitude. The following situations are examples where the salesperson can make a sale with no effort on their part.

- The prospect's office copier breaks down.

- The prospect needs a new mobile phone.

- The prospect moved into a new home and needs homeowner insurance.

- The prospect needs a new computer.

- The prospect's contract is up and it's time to renew (for mobile phones, auto insurance, health insurance, long distance service).

- The prospect needs to open a bank account.

- The prospect needs a loan, line of credit, and so on.

- Shopping (retail sales such as clothing, consumer electronics, jewelry, grocery shopping).

Whether the prospect needs it, broke it and needs to replace it, or is ready for it, there are people out there who simply require your product and you happen to catch them at the right time or you are at the right place at the right time.

After all, what did your insurance agent do to earn your renewal? How about the business you give to your mechanic, CPA, or doctor?

If you own a retail shop, people will come into your store, even if all you do is sit behind the counter and wait for them. These salespeople more closely resemble "order takers" rather than sale professionals. These salespeople rely on the prospect to initiate the sale, even drive the sale forwards.

The bottom line here is, if you knock on enough doors, make enough phone calls, or simply rely on the power of attraction to draw sales toward you (retail) you will sell one third of everyone you speak with. So, before you launch a wide scale prospecting initiative, consider that you may be just fine with the number of sales that this more passive approach brings to you and the money you would generate as a result.

 Cold Calling Conundrum _____

> If you sell consumer-driven goods or have relied on prospects showing up at your door with minimal effort on your part, think about what transpired after 9-11-01. For all the order takers out there, where were you left after this tragedy struck? In an instant, these salespeople had to *actually learn* how to sell and prospect just to maintain the "walk-in" business they had grown accustomed to. Embrace the new normal.

The other third is going to your competition. No matter what you do or as good a salesperson as you may be, you are not getting this business. Whether it is due to bad timing, the other salesperson who got to the prospect first, internal changes in a company, a shift in power, your prospect leaving the company, a change in the economy, your prospect no longer having a need, budget cuts, or they simply don't like you, your pricing model or your product, you are just not going to get these sales.

This final third is the third that is up for grabs. If you truly want to become a top producer, it's not enough to simply "play the numbers game," hoping that if you see enough people you will make enough sales. To become a top producer, you need the right tools, attitude and skill set.

This is what separates an average salesperson from a great salesperson. It is the tools they use and the skills that they have taken the time to develop. Top producers will invest their time in mastering every concept, skill, mind-set and strategy outlined in this book. Top producers will work with a sales coach to ensure they are maximizing their potential and talent. Top producers will develop their compelling reasons and MVP to secure their competitive edge, become fearless, and craft their prospecting system. As a matter of fact, the more skills and tools you develop, the higher your sales volume will be.

When looking at this rule of thirds, think about what is actually at stake here and what you stand to lose. You can either be happy selling approximately 33 percent of the prospects you speak with or create the opportunity to double the number of sales you can generate.

Warm Wisdom
Because prospecting is a numbers art, make sure you are the one who's creating the rules.

Think about it this way. If all of your prospects were not happy with what they already have or felt that they must have what you are selling, they would all be calling *you*! To get that additional third of business, realize that you are often competing against what the prospect is already doing; that is, their current solution, service, or product that they think is effective, or the vendor they think is the best one for them. You are also competing against what the prospect is *not* doing; such as not using the type of product or service you offer because they don't see the need or are not aware of the fact that what you offer even exists.

This is where the art of selling and prospecting comes into play and why selling is a "numbers art," not a numbers game. Art has no boundaries yet implies that your prospecting efforts possess more of a refined, conscious intention that gives you more control over the outcome. Art is defined and created by the artist. Art is constantly evolving. Art gives you boundless freedom and flexibility to create the results you really want. True artists focus more on the quality of their work rather than the quantity of what they can produce.

Finally, the word "art" is synonymous with "science." And science suggests that there is a discipline, a certain procedure and a skill set at work. Just think back to all of the templates and processes that you have been introduced to. Look back at your formula for selling success. This is a working testament that prospecting is, in fact, a science. One can predict with great accuracy the outcome of your prospecting initiative.

Prospecting is best approached from a systematic perspective, rather than being left to chance. There is a process and system involved that, if followed constantly, will work every time you use it.

Anyone can buy a lottery ticket and play the numbers with a blindfold on. However, I'm sure that you would rather meet with 10 qualified, targeted prospects than 50 unqualified ones.

Hey, it's your choice. You can be happy with the status quo, or your can make your own "magic formula" in your lab and play your own game.

Cold Medicine

If you have never tracked the results of your prospecting efforts or if you are prospecting for the first time, then prospecting would be classified as a numbers game. At this point, you don't have a blueprint or any statistical data that would tell you the specific process to follow which would produce the consistent, measurable results you seek. However, once you have determined what works and what doesn't and have taken the time to refine your process, tools, ideal client and strategy, it is only then when the prospecting game you have been playing can evolve into an art.

When Being the Best Isn't Good Enough

What if being the best still classifies you as an average producer? Be cautious when defining what it means to become a top producer. If you are basing top-producer status on the sheer number of sales, how are you coming up with those sales numbers? Who are you comparing yourself against?

For example, imagine that you are part of a 10-person sales team. After a year or so, you have become the top producer. However, the top producer only produces 80 percent of quota every month. So, are you truly a top producer or just the salesperson who's outselling the rest of your team? Although you may be generating great results, it does not mean that this is the best you can do.

In other words, if you have a team of underachievers or average salespeople, outselling them is one gauge to determine how effective you are.

But what if second best in your company means generating one prospect out of 300 cold calls? Then is it such a stretch to do better than this? And if you succeed in generating 2 prospects out of 300 cold calls, does that make you a top producer or just someone who is doing a little bit better than Number 2? At this point, are you truly maximizing your talents and ability?

This faulty line of thinking becomes one of the salesperson's greatest barriers, because the assumption is made that if you are doing better than most, you have maximized your potential. After all, how can you do better than "the best"? Instead of raising the bar, you've inadvertently placed a ceiling on your potential.

 Cold Calling Conundrum

Status quo (internal company statistics) is one of your greatest enemies. Just because you have the highest score doesn't mean you are the best or that you have won the game. Instead of becoming "The Best," you have succeeded in only becoming "The Better." Instead, challenge these assumptions that can limit your potential. Otherwise, if you believe that someone else's best is the best you can do, you will never achieve beyond or grow past what you think is possible.

So how can you determine if you are truly maximizing your selling skills and potential? When developing your barometer for success, gauge what extreme success looks like within your industry, rather than only relying on the internal statistics of your company.

Who is your biggest competitor? What makes them your biggest competitor? What type of volume is their business generating each year? How about the volume generated by each person who is responsible for bringing in new business? I'm sure you will come across other people who do what you do or sell a similar product or service to the same prospect. If you are active in your industry or profession you will meet these people at networking events, through professional associations, chamber meetings or trade shows. Any time you have an opportunity to speak with a competitor or another person in your profession, seize that moment to learn as much as possible about what other people are doing. Expand your peripheral view by uncovering what the best of the best are doing within your industry.

The Least You Need to Know

◆ Set goals that are measurable and specific.

◆ Establish the non-negotiable prospecting activities to ensure that your actions are aligned with your intentions.

◆ Your success formula will allow you the freedom to trust the process and determine when enough prospecting is actually enough.

◆ Instead of getting discouraged, let your formula uncover what you can do to fine tune your cold calling efforts.

◆ Consider prospecting to be a numbers art so that you can have more control over the outcome.

◆ To maximize your potential, learn what it takes to be the best in your industry, not simply the top producer in your company.

Chapter 17

Prospecting Diagnostic and Tune-Up

In This Chapter

- ◆ Fine-tuning your approach for maximum impact
- ◆ Determining the best place and time to mine for prospects
- ◆ Establishing your peak productive hours
- ◆ Why a prospect's "no" is a great thing to hear
- ◆ Bouncing back from adversity
- ◆ Determining your effectiveness

Now that you've made it all the way through this book, you must be feeling pretty good about yourself. If you have followed along and completed all of the suggested exercises, you are well on your way to becoming a prospecting and cold calling superstar!

You have all the tools you need to develop a solid foundation for prospecting success. As you launch your prospecting initiative, here are some final suggestions to ponder that will complement your efforts to achieve incredible success at prospecting.

Get Ready for Prime Time

With all of the activities that you could engage in throughout your day, it's critical to determine the ones that will enhance you and accelerate your success, rather than the ones that will slow down your productivity.

Prime-time activities are the non-negotiable activities that are aligned with your vision, goals, and natural strengths, yet have time constraints attached to them.

There will always be tasks that you won't be able to perform before or after work hours, such as prospecting businesses, contacting certain clients, having staff meetings, or other work-related functions. These are the activities with limited flexibility in terms of when they can be accomplished.

Cold Callingo

Prime-time activities are the activities that are aligned with your goals and objectives yet have limited flexibility as to when they can be completed.

Cold Callingo

Peak productive hours are the hours or the timeline that you have established throughout your day which is designated for the activities and tasks that support your goals (prime-time activities). These activities are typically ones that cannot be done outside of the established timeline.

Let's paint a visual. You are ready to open the starting gate and launch your prospecting campaign. You've determined that one of the prospecting strategies you will be engaging in would be cold calling over the phone (a prime-time activity). But have you thought about when the best time would be to cold call?

It's critical to determine the most appropriate time for each of your prospecting activities so that you can yield the greatest return on your time investment. For example, surfing the web or reading the newspaper during peak business hours (eight to six) or during prime prospecting hours is probably not the most effective use of your time. These *peak productive hours* are for engaging in the activities that you have deemed to be a priority; ones that you may not be able to do after normal business hours.

For instance, if one of the activities you consider to be a priority is cold calling small business owners, then there's only a certain time frame throughout the day that this can be accomplished. Typically, that would be during the normal business hours I mentioned earlier.

The peak productive hours that you have allocated in your schedule are for activities that are aligned with and move you closer to your goals, rather than the type of activities that eat away at your peak productive time. Some of the activities that can divert you from completing your prime-time activities are solitaire on the computer, surfing the web, reading the newspaper, idle chitchat with co-workers, personal phone calls, certain research, stuffing envelopes for your marketing campaign, etc. These activities are the ones that traditionally fly under our radar when planning our day, yet still take up a substantial amount of time. Then, before you know it, the day is over and you can't understand "where the day went."

You might feel, for good reason, that a portion of these activities have their time and place as well as a degree of value. Please realize that I'm not suggesting never doing them, but *when* to do them. Are some of these activities important? Sure. The question you need to ask yourself is, "When can I enjoy them so they don't interfere with the tasks that I must complete during my workday?

Cold Medicine

When calling on top-level executives or business owners, consider that they usually begin their day before their staff comes in, and often end their day after everyone else has left. That's why the hours before and after normal business hours can be the best time to reach them.

Take the time to uncover the activities that can quickly become a diversion. Once you are aware of them, you can then choose whether or not to engage in them or find a specific time in your schedule for these activities. Either way, it now becomes a conscious decision, rather than experiencing the feeling of "Where did the day go?" when leaving the office. Once you become aware of these diversionary activities that take up your valuable time, you can better plan your day.

Determine the activities that you still want to do which have the greatest flexibility and can be accomplished during a variety of times throughout your day. If you enjoy reading the newspaper, this activity could be reserved for the hours before or after the peak productive hours in your workday. Schedule them around your prime-time activities so they don't interfere with these activities that have limited flexibility.

> **" " Cold Medicine**
>
> Align your peak productive hours with the prime-time activities that support your goals.

Stay Positive! Become Teflon

I've been known to dabble a bit in the kitchen. It's an enjoyable, leisurely activity for me. Aside from being able to create omelets that deserve national recognition, the best chefs are the ones who make the least mess. Similar to prospecting, one way to limit your mess is to ensure that you are using the right tools.

One thing is for certain. All my cookware comes with the Teflon non-stick coating, making cleaning a snap. Introduced by Dupont nearly 40 years ago, cookware coated with Teflon has made everyone's life easier in the kitchen, saving us countless hours of soaking and scrubbing dishes until our fingers ache.

Teflon is actually in the *Guinness Book of World Records* as the slipperiest substance known. So, why would I suggest becoming like Teflon? I'm certainly not suggesting to attempt to cook an egg on your head. However, I am encouraging you to adopt the characteristics of Teflon. Here are a few:

Be Resilient: Develop your tough outer coating so that you can most effectively and easily deal with rejection or hearing the word "no." Let those "no's" slide right off you so you can move on to more promising prospects without getting discouraged, taking it personally or surrendering all of your energy.

Be Responsive: Teflon can get you in and out of the kitchen—fast. Teflon is a product that has evolved out of the needs of consumers and our often hectic lifestyle. In Chapter 11 we discussed being responsive rather than reactive, especially as it relates to how you handle objections. How quickly do you respond to the needs of your clients and prospects? How long does it take you to bounce back from adversity and learn from it? The simple fact is, being responsive makes you happier, encourages organization, keeps you moving forward, and accelerates your success.

Be Flexible: If you are using cookware with a Teflon coating, it's a safe bet that your cookware doesn't care what you are using it for when preparing your next meal. Being flexible and open to new possibilities rather than being hooked on a certain expectation every time you prospect (Chapter 4) is one characteristic worth assimilating. This will provide you with the opportunity to create or recognize new selling opportunities that would otherwise fly under your radar undetected.

Be Resourceful: Teflon is used in a variety of consumer products, including our clothes, home furnishings, carpet protectors, eyeglass lens coating, lubricants, nail polish, and other personal care products. It is even used as an additive to protect your car's finish and has a wide range of other industrial uses. Chances are, you don't go through a day without touching or using something that has Teflon in it. Being resourceful is a key ingredient to prospecting success. Broaden your horizon by challenging your thinking and conventional wisdom as it relates to where you can find prospects. Allow prospecting to become a useful tool in a variety of applications or situations (networking).

Be Efficient: Teflon has become a major time-saver in our lives. A well organized, professional prospecting effort (especially the pre call planning phase) combined with your ability to effectively manage your time so that you are maximizing every hour, even every minute in your day will enable you to achieve greater results in less time.

Be Innovative: Innovation sparks change. It is the conduit between stagnation and evolution. Without innovation, products like Teflon would never have come into existence. What would be something new, creative, or even fun to try? Be the pioneer. This way, you will always be the first to lead the journey and break new ground in developing new prospects and selling opportunities. Being open to new ideas, continuous change and lifelong learning will accelerate your growth and prevent you from being left behind.

Be Tough: Teflon has long been the savior for preventative maintenance. If you have kids, you'll understand what I mean. Between carpet spills and gymnastics on your furniture, the benefits of Teflon have proven to be long-lasting. Your endurance, stamina, persistence, drive, and patience will play a major role in prospecting success. Honor the process (Chapter 7) you have put in place that will bring you more prospects and more sales, as opposed to giving up in the middle of the race. This way, you can be sure that you will outlast and outplay your competition, and be the first to cross over the finish line.

Be Confident: How can an inanimate material be "confident," you ask? Okay maybe I'm reaching here. However, imagine if your pots and pans could actually speak. What would they say? "Bring on your biggest meal! We're ready for you!" As a consumer, there's a confidence I have in my cookware that it will always serve me best and give me top-notch performance. Confidence in yourself, your product, your abilities and your prospecting system will make or break you and will be the deciding factor of your success in selling.

Be Consistent: I don't have to worry about changing the process I use when cooking one of my famous (okay not famous yet) omelets. I can rely on the fact that my cookware will perform the same way, every time I use it. Consistency in your prospecting approach is essential if you want to generate consistent, long-lasting results.

Be the Solution: Teflon has demonstrated dozens of ways to make our life easier by improving the quality of the products we use in business and in our daily life. New applications for Teflon are always being discovered. Invest your time in creating greater solutions for yourself and for your prospects by asking the right questions that move you forward, rather than dwelling on the problem or on the past.

Cold Medicine

Consistency in taking the right actions will produce consistency in the results you want.

A "No" Is Great to Hear!

"I *hate* being told 'no.' I feel like when a prospect says 'no' they are rejecting me." Sound familiar? If so, you are not alone in your thinking.

Many salespeople feel this way. What if you changed your thinking around what a "no" from a potential prospect really means?

It's not about you: Remember Chapter 4 when we discussed that the sales process is really about the client or prospect and not about the salesperson? If you are taking the "no's" personally, here is yet another example of a salesperson who is making the selling process about them. If I think back to the prospects who said "no" to the salespeople who promote and sell my services, I don't remember any of them saying "no" to Keith Rosen.

Rather, it was "No, we haven't budgeted for additional training this year," or "No, we can't do anything until we've completed this other initiative," or "No, we need to hire someone in a full-time capacity," or "No, we never outsource our training," or "No, I'm not the right person to speak with about this," or "No, we already have someone who handles all of our training," or "No, we're actually looking for a different type of training that you don't offer," and the list goes on.

The jewel here is, it is not you personally who your prospect is saying "no" to. In truth, they are really saying "no" to your product, service, your approach or strategy, the situation (timing, budget) or a component of what you are offering (price, terms, features and so on).

Like many guidelines, this one also has its special conditions or circumstances. For example, let's say that in your company, on average it takes about 20 cold calls to find one qualified prospect. Now, if you put forth your best cold calling effort and it took you 100 dials to finally uncover 1 qualified prospect, then it's a safe bet that in this situation, it actually *is* about you. In other words, here's a situation where it would make sense for you to look under the hood and explore your cold calling approach. After all, if 15 salespeople are generating on average 1 qualified prospect for every 20 cold calls and you are not, you may want to reevaluate your cold calling strategy and determine the areas you can improve upon to boost your effectiveness.

"No's" get you to "yes": There is no yin without yang, no darkness without light, no joy without sadness, no success without failure and no "yes" without a "no." These opposites are what keeps the universe in balance. Prospecting is not excluded from this Buddhist philosophy.

Think of it this way. The greatest salespeople hear "no" more times than they hear "yes." Why? Simply because they make more cold calls than the salespeople who aren't as successful. The top producers realize that the more calls they make, the more "no's" they will hear and the more "no's" they hear, the closer they get to hearing a "yes."

So, if you fear hearing a "no" from a prospect, try changing the rules in your game. Instead of adhering to the self-imposed pressure of having to hear "yes" (which is quite a burden to carry around), what if the objective of this new prospecting game is to hear as many "no's" as possible? How would this change your mind-set and how you feel about cold calling?

If the goal is to hear a "no" and you hear a pile of "no's" from the people you are calling on, then you are actually winning at this game! The fact is, the more "no's" you hear, the more calls you are making. And the more calls you make, it's inevitable that you are going to hear a "yes."

Rather than feel deflated after a string of "no's," get excited because for every "no" you hear, you are getting that much closer to a "yes!"

Embrace the reality that if you want to become a top producer and dramatically boost your income, you are going to hear "no" quite often. Why resist the inevitable? You will only succeed at becoming incredibly frustrated, questioning your abilities and self-worth, and ultimately sabotaging your cold calling efforts.

To clarify, this does not mean that you purposely sabotage yourself by changing what you do in order to hear every prospect say "no." You are still going to continually fine-tune and conduct the most effective prospecting conversation you can. Instead, you are simply changing how you think about hearing the word "no" by embracing it rather than considering it as something negative that you resist or want to avoid.

A "no" is your friend. A "no" can teach you what you need to change the next time you speak with a prospect. By embracing "no" you open yourself up to the valuable lessons you can learn from every cold calling attempt you make.

I have just one request. If you truly embrace this concept, please don't get upset and call me up saying, "Keith, because I've learned to love hearing the word "no" and how to adjust my prospecting approach for maximum impact, I'm actually getting more "yes's" now than "no's"! Hey, the success that comes as a by-product of this mind-set is just one of those things you are going to have to learn to live with.

To become a cold calling champion, let the word "no" empower and energize you rather than rob you of your energy and enthusiasm.

Warm Wisdom

Here's a great game you can play that will make you more comfortable hearing the word "no." Ask as many people you know for something and see how many "no's" you can get. Go out and ask the people you know or even the people you don't know for something. It could be something extreme like asking for a million dollars, a date with someone you have your eye on, or even asking someone to do a favor for you. And of course it means asking as many prospects, clients, or people you know (referral team) for referrals or to become a client of yours. (Ask for the sale!) Ask outrageous questions. By giving up your attachment to having to hear the word "yes" and the fear of hearing the word "no," you now have the freedom to ask anything of anyone. Be careful though; you may get what you asked for and that would be getting a "yes" to a question that you think you would normally hear a "no" to.

Change Is the Only Constant ... Sometimes

Fast-forward a few weeks from now. You have developed your prospecting system and are now ready for the implementation phase. After a few cold calls, you notice that based on your prospects' reactions, some of the language you are using needs to be modified. In the spirit of continuous improvement, you do so accordingly.

A few calls later, you are making more changes to your approach. Within two weeks' time, the template you are now using when speaking with a prospect shows no resemblance of the original one you created.

Do you remember our friend, The Copier, in Chapter 9? This prospector was open to change, innovation and personal growth with the intention to continually improve and evolve as a sales professional and maximize his potential; yet almost to a fault. This wonderful trait often became their weakness.

Are you a "changeaholic?" If you are anything like The Copier, on your quest for the perfect presentation, then let me make your life much easier. Stop your search now because there is no such thing. You might as well launch a full-scale exploration to find the fountain of youth!

If you are constantly searching for the perfect prospecting approach, you will wind up continually changing what you have. The downfall of this tactic is, if you are continually making major changes in your approach you will never get to experience the benefit of consistency.

And if you are not consistent then you are never giving yourself the chance to become proficient in your efforts, let alone determine what exactly is working well and what is not.

The key point here is, you must establish a benchmark. Continually changing the rules every time you prospect does not allow you to do so. For instance, if you spend your mornings cold calling via the telephone and are excited to implement your new cold calling approach, then commit to using it a certain number of times before you make any major changes. You may decide that you are going to speak with 50 prospects using the same approach. Based on what you know about your industry, you have determined that speaking with 50 people will be the gauge that will provide you with a very good sense of how effective your current approach really is. Consider this your beta test before a wide scale launch. After 50 calls you will then evaluate the results and determine what is working and what needs to be adjusted.

> **Cold Calling Conundrum**
>
> When it comes to making changes, the pendulum can swing both ways. While some people may be "changeaholics," others resist change all the way to the end. Develop your "change strategy" so that you maintain a balance between the two extremes and prevent yourself from making the changes that might cost you new business.

If you remember in Chapter 12, imagine what would happen if you kept changing your golf swing after every hole. Consistent inconsistency. Think about your formula for selling success that you created in Chapter 16. It would be impossible for you to utilize this formula with any success if you keep changing what you are doing, because any change to your approach will skew the numbers in your formula.

Cold Medicine

Change is good as long as you have a system to manage the changes you make as well as a measurement that would let you know when it is appropriate to do so. This way, you can quantify the results of every change.

Essential Market Research (And It's Free!)

Remember Jack, the salesperson I told you about way back in Chapter 10? I thought you'd want an update on how Jack is doing.

It seems that Jack's performance has greatly improved since developing his prospecting strategy. His numbers are on a steady incline, which is great to hear.

Jack has implemented all of the strategies he has learned and is feeling really good about his progress.

"So, what in your prospecting strategy is working well?" I asked him. He looked at me and said, "Everything!" When I followed his comment with the question, "How do you know?" Jack froze, unsure of what to say, just like a deer in a headlight.

The fact is, Jack's results spoke for themselves. He improved tremendously. However, Jack did not know for certain exactly which components of his prospecting system were working well and which ones could stand to be fine-tuned. Instead, Jack assumed that it was "all" working great based on the results he was generating.

Jack thought on my question for another minute and then asked me, "What can I do to figure out what is working and what is not?"

The answer will be uncovered with another question, "Ask your prospects."

For the qualified prospects that you speak with who are more receptive, ask them the following questions at the end of a conversation or meeting:

- ◆ "May I ask why you chose to listen to me in the first place?"

- ◆ "Why did you decide to take the next step and explore what I have in more detail?"

- ◆ "What was it that made you feel comfortable enough to want to speak (meet) with me?"

- ◆ "What did I do or say that sparked your interest?"

For the people you call on who are not receptive to your prospecting efforts, ask them some questions as well:

- ◆ "May I ask what I could have done differently that might have triggered some interest on your part?"

- ◆ "Is there anything I could have done better that would have encouraged you to explore what I have in more detail?"

- ◆ "Was there something I did or said that you didn't like or made you uncomfortable?"

In Chapter 5, I shared with you some questions to ask your clients that would assist you in developing your compelling reasons. This exercise and questions similar to the ones I provided can also be used to uncover the reasons as to why a prospect decided to listen, meet and buy from you (or not) in the first place.

What are they most receptive to? What are the tactics that salespeople use which turn them off? What is it that caused them to listen to you?

If you don't ask these questions, then how else would you be able to determine the prospecting activities that are most effective so that you can duplicate these efforts?

If you send out an introductory letter or launch a direct mail campaign, it's essential to track the results. The results that need to be tracked are not only the number of responses you get but what it actually was that triggered the response from the prospect as well as the type of response it was! For those prospects who either initiate first contact or are contacting you in response to the prospecting you have done, here are a few questions to ask:

1. "What was it in the (letter, mailer) that motivated you to call?"

2. "What was it that caught your eye?"

3. "What was it that stimulated your interest enough to want to hear more?"

You must gauge the effectiveness of each prospecting effort. Otherwise, you will not be able to determine the tools, approach or strategy in your prospecting system that need to be refined, revamped, removed or fine-tuned.

Look at it this way. If you don't conduct this inquiry into what works, you may find yourself in a position where you are changing certain components of your prospecting system (such as your voice mail or follow-up strategy) that are generating the best results and should not be changed at all!

> **Cold Calling Conundrum**
>
> Interview the prospects that bought from you as well as the ones who did not. Otherwise, your guess is as good as mine when trying to determine the strategies that yield the best results for you.

Now that you see the importance of assessing your prospecting system to uncover the winning strategies, what about those prospects who bought from your competition rather than from you? Do you know exactly why you are losing these selling opportunities? Are you conducting an inquiry into what is not working, as well?

I never realized how critical this was to becoming a sales champion until I saw the value of doing so firsthand. I was approached by a company that provides financing programs for car and boat dealerships, which they, in turn offer to their customers. They were looking for sales training and a time-management program for their team. After a lengthy needs analysis, I was prepared to draft a proposal. Everything went like clockwork. Before submitting it, we scheduled a time to review the proposal together. Afterwards, my prospect informed me that they were now going to compare the five proposals they received to determine which company was the best fit for them and would be awarded their business. (I knew from my needs analysis that they were shopping around.) We even scheduled a follow-up conversation, after they had the chance to compare all of the proposals.

I thought I had this sale in the bag. If it wasn't for my wife, I would have probably been out there spending the money I would imminently be making.

Then, the reality check. During the follow-up call with this prospect, he informed me that they were going to be using another vendor.

"Where did I go wrong?" was my initial internal response. I had to find out. I then said to my prospect, "Congratulations on making your decision. I'm sure that the solution you chose is going to be a great fit for you and provide you with the results you want. Mr. Prospect, I am someone who is always looking for ways to do things better and improve the service I provide in my effort to exceed my clients' expectations. That's why I'm asking for your help. Any insight as to why I was not able to earn your business would be deeply appreciated and very valuable for me. Even if it may sound negative, I would rather hear the truth about something that I can change which isn't working, rather than continue to make the same mistakes. So, please don't worry about hurting my feelings. Can you please share with me why my company was passed over?"

I was very fortunate to have a prospect that was kind enough and empathetic enough to spend some time to answer all of my questions honestly. He responded by telling me that he loved my proposal, philosophy and approach. He said it was a very difficult decision to make, as they narrowed the list down to my company and the one they chose.

So what was the deciding factor that swung the pendulum toward my competitor? What did my competitor offer that I did not? According to this prospect, they were able to immediately deliver value. My competition provided him with some specific and timely reports about his sales team that were incredibly valuable to him. My competition delivered value even before they earned this prospect's business! I immediately thanked my prospect for sharing this information with me and requested that we stay in touch should anything change in the future. (I got permission to contact this prospect in the future and keep my name in front of him.) As I hung up the phone, I began developing my own method to deliver greater value to a client, even before they become a client.

The tools that I created which followed this conversation have proven to be a huge determining factor for securing new business. It resulted in thousands and thousands of dollars worth of new business that I may never have gotten unless I was enlightened by my prospect! I owe part of my continued success to a prospect who was kind enough to take the time to be forthright with me.

Bottom line: A picture may be worth a thousand words but a question may be worth thousands of dollars. However, for this to be a worthwhile experience for you, you must put your ego aside and be open to the fact that you really can learn something valuable from everyone you meet.

Costly Assumptions

Think back to the conversation we had about following up in Chapter 14. While these contractors formulated their own conclusion as to why a prospect didn't buy from them, they never bothered to confirm if their assumptions were, in fact, true! Certain assumptions that you make about your prospects can sabotage the results you want to achieve.

When salespeople ask me to help them close more sales, I ask them to list the objections they are hearing that prevented the sale. It's when they start stumbling over their response that I ask, "Are these the objections that you are hearing directly from your prospects or what you are assuming as the reason why they didn't buy?"

Rather than uncovering the real barrier to the sale, assuming the objection becomes a detrimental process that spreads like a virus throughout every sales call. These assumptions are not based on the facts but rather the salesperson's assumption of the truth.

Salespeople often fall into this trap when creating solutions for their prospects. During a conversation with a prospect, they uncover a similar situation or problem that they have handled with a previous client. So they assume that the same solution will fit for this prospect as well.

The problem arises when the salesperson fails to invest the time to go beyond what may be obvious and explore the prospect's specific objectives or concerns.

Thinking they "know" this prospect, the salesperson provides them with the benefits of his service that he perceives to be important, without considering the prospect's particular needs.

The next time you are speaking with a prospect or are on a sales call, rather than assuming the objection, how the prospect makes a buying decision, what they know or what they want to hear, follow these suggestions to create more selling opportunities and reduce the chance of a communication breakdown.

Suggestion 1: Identify the Knowledge Gap

That's the space between what people know and what they don't know. Instead of assuming what they know, start determining what they need/want to learn or hear about in order to fill in this gap and ensure clear communication. Use questions up front to uncover what's needed to fill in the gap. For example: "Just so I don't sound repetitive, how familiar are you with sales coaching?" or "What do you already know about sales coaching?" or "How much do you know about my company (product, service, industry)?" By using these types of questions, you will increase your awareness and become more sensitized to what your prospect is interested in hearing about and what they need to learn.

Suggestion 2: Just the Facts, Please

"I told a prospect that I'd follow up within a week. Two weeks later, I figured I missed my chance and they went with someone else." Sound familiar? Effective salespeople don't guess themselves into a sale. To ensure that you are operating with the facts, ask yourself this, "Do I have evidence to support my assumption or how I'm feeling?" Enjoy the peace of mind that comes from gaining clarity and uncovering the truth rather than drowning in the stories that you believe are true. Stay away from making any assumptions. Instead, ask questions that will provide you with the facts so you can confidently determine the next

course of action. It sure beats guessing or assuming what you're supposed to be doing next. Aside from increasing the number of selling
opportunities you have, you will also notice that many communication
breakdowns and problems will immediately be eliminated.

Suggestion 3: Recall Your Learning Curve

Think back to your first day on the job and the time it took for you to
learn a new skill set. Chances are, you've probably experienced some
frustration during the learning process. After all, at one point, all of
your knowledge was new to you. The same holds true for the prospects
you come in contact with. What may seem old or common to you is
new to them. Support your prospects by being empathetic and patient
throughout their learning curve. Otherwise, your prospects will find
someone else who is.

Suggestion 4: Be Curious

Question everything! I'd suggest going back to Chapter 11 to read up
on how to gracefully respond to each prospect's situation or concern
with a question rather than collapsing all prospects into one and reacting with a generic statement, treating your prospects as if they are all
the same. Invest the time to uncover and explore each prospect's specific need or objection, as opposed to providing common solutions that
you assume may fit.

Suggestion 5: Clarify!

Make each prospect feel that they are truly being listened to and understood. Use a clarifier (Chapter 10) when responding to what you have
heard during the conversation. Rephrase in your own words what the
prospect had said to ensure that you not only heard but also understood
them. Then, confirm the next course of action. For example: "What
I'm hearing you say is …" If you need additional information or want
to take the pulse of your prospect to find out where they stand, use the
following questions. "Tell me more about that." "What do you see as
the next step?"

Eliminating these costly assumptions will enable you to make better decisions and prevent the breakdowns in communication that act as a barrier to more sales.

Where Did That Customer Come From?

This is one of my favorite stories. It involves another client of mine. Her name is Angie and she and her husband own and manage a successful fitness center that also provides personal training. Angie was always on the lookout for new ways to generate leads (new prospects). As such, she experimented with a variety of marketing strategies. She was telling me about a new marketing initiative that she was reluctantly going to launch. Her reluctance was fueled by the cost of this initiative. I suggested that she compile a table that would show her where every lead and sale originated to date. Because Angie was disciplined enough to track the effectiveness of her marketing and prospecting efforts, compiling this data was not an issue.

What Angie uncovered was fascinating. It seemed that with all of the marketing she did over the past year, the number one conduit to more business was her clients! It seems that over 70 percent of Angie's business was generated through the referrals that her clients have shared with her. The kicker here is, Angie is getting these results without any specific initiative on her part. She was only contacting her clients once a year to ask for referrals. (Refer to Chapter 15 regarding the appropriate number of times to ask for referrals.)

The Results Are In ... Now What?

Now that Angie knows what her primary source of new business is, she has the ability and the luxury to fine-tune her marketing and prospecting efforts in order to maximize what was once considered a passive source of new business that she hasn't truly tapped into.

While I've shared with you a variety of avenues to explore in order to generate more prospects (Chapter 8), it's imperative that you track the effectiveness of every prospecting effort you put forth.

Where are your getting the majority of your business? Are you wasting time on certain activities that are not producing measurable results? If you don't know, then here's the opportunity to start asking yourself these essential questions.

It's not enough to track the number of prospects generated and where you found them. You must also track the number of sales. While you might be able to find a source that provides you with dozens of leads (prospects), if these leads aren't being converted into sales, then the number of leads really doesn't matter anymore. Because you are probably not being compensated for your efforts, no one can afford to waste their limited and precious time on activities that are better off not being done at all. (Chapter 16 talks about focusing more on the quality of the prospect rather than the quantity.)

The real benefit here is, once you evaluate your results in a timely manner and determine the most effective prospecting strategies as well as the best source for new, qualified prospects, you can streamline your prospecting efforts to exploit the activities that are giving you your greatest ROI.

Honor the Re-Learning Process

Congratulations! I certainly admire your ability to complete this book. Now that you have, it's time for you to enjoy your new role as a master prospector. This is a challenging skill to develop and I applaud your efforts for going through this process. As you continue to develop your skills at prospecting it's critical to recognize, acknowledge, and celebrate your successes on a daily basis in order to maintain your momentum. It's all part of the journey. By completing this book and the exercises included, you have already begun.

Like anything, your prospecting system will evolve as well, so be flexible and allow this evolution to occur. Adjust and revise your approach as needed. (You may also have to adapt to changes in the market, industry, economy, environment and the law/government.) Just keep your goals clear in your mind and on paper. You will notice how much easier and more enjoyable it is when you engage in the activities that enable you to reach your goals.

Give yourself time to get comfortable with your new approach. Remember, it's the repetition of consistent, productive actions that will generate the consistent results you want.

Before we wrap up, realize that your life today is the result of your actions, attitude, and the choices you have made in the past. Your life tomorrow will be the result of your actions, attitude, and the choices you make today. So make the choice today to become the prospecting superstar you know you can be. Without exercising the ability to choose, there is no freedom to create something better.

Remember, if you do what you have always done, you will continue to generate the results that you have always gotten. What you do, how you manage your days, and how you respond to the situations and experiences in your career are what create the quality of your life. In order to create exciting, new possibilities and greater achievements, it requires a new mind-set, new activities, and a clear direction.

Cold Calling Conundrum

This isn't your practice life. There is no dress rehearsal. So be true to yourself and to your goals. If you find yourself running into some obstacles along the way, chances are that you took your eye off your goals or your prospecting system.

Here's a friendly reminder. The definition of insanity is doing the same thing over and over and expecting a different result. Keep in mind my definition of futility. That is, knowing the definition of insanity and still not doing anything about it.

So, honor your prospecting system and remember:

♦ Your mind-set influences your actions.

♦ Your actions shape your results.

♦ Your results determine your success.

Well, what are you waiting for? Now is the perfect time to get out there and start cold calling and prospecting! If you are still feeling a bit reluctant or overwhelmed, then keep it simple. Start with just one cold call. That's right, just one. That sounds like a manageable goal, yes? Then, the following day, make two calls. Before you know it, you will be in full prospecting mode. So, give yourself a break and don't feel that you have to "do it all" at the same time. Take the pieces that feel comfortable for you so that you can begin the momentum and start moving forward.

Finally, thank you for the opportunity to do what I love most, that is, allowing me to contribute to you. You see, I found out early on that the greatest gift you can ever give is to share yourself and your wisdom with others. You have given me my greatest gift. I'd love to hear about any successes you've had as a result of utilizing this book, so please feel free to contact me anytime.

While reading this book, you may have wished that I was right there in the room with you from time to time so that you could ask me questions or receive personalized training, coaching and support. At certain times throughout your week, you may need a blast of energy and motivation to get refocused, back in the game or to remove any negative, self sabotaging behavior and thinking.

After creating your prospecting strategy, templates, letters, voice mails and cold calling approach, you may have thought, "How great it would be if Keith could critique what I've done or do some role playing with me so that I don't have to practice on my prospects." Maybe you just need a quick sales performance tune-up or want the reassurance that you are, in fact, doing it the "right way." Or maybe you need to start by getting organized, reducing your stress, creating a daily routine, eliminating distractions and mastering the art of time management.

Well, your wish has been granted. You can accomplish all of these things and much more. If you are ready to play a bigger game, become a sales superstar, make more money, master time management, leverage every selling opportunity and create an even better life, give me a call anytime and I would be happy to discuss how we can work together to achieve your goals quickly, efficiently and in half the time it would take if you were to do it on your own. Find out what the top producers already know; everyone does better when they have a sales coach in their corner supporting them.

For more information on sales and business coaching, corporate training or my keynote presentations and workshops delivered in person or through teleconferencing, you can reach me at 1-888-262-2450 or visit my website at www.ProfitBuilders.com. If you would like to receive my free e-newsletter, "The Winners Path," or some other valuable resources that I'd be happy to share with you, e-mail me anytime at winnerspath@ProfitBuilders.com.

Cold Medicine

A.B.P. Always be prospecting!

I hope that this book and your new prospecting system catapult you to the level of extreme success you dream of. May your prospecting efforts become effortless!

The Least You Need to Know

◆ The more "no's" you hear, the closer you will be to hearing a "yes."

◆ As long as you have created an effective prospecting system, there's no need to carry around the weight of rejection when hearing a "no."

◆ Develop a change strategy to determine the changes you need to make and when it's appropriate to make them.

◆ Your prospect and clients are a great, free resource to help gauge your effectiveness and uncover what works for you, but only if you ask them.

◆ Rather than make costly assumptions about your prospects that can destroy a sale, base your decisions and strategies on the facts.

◆ Track your prospecting activity to uncover your greatest source for qualified leads and sales; then exploit it.

Glossary

attitude   How you think, your state of mind, or your set of beliefs; it is how you interpret or perceive each experience or each person in your life, in other words, your reality. Synonymous with mind-set.

clarifier   A statement that rephrases in your own words the message that someone communicated to you to assure the person that you not only heard, but also understood them. Then, you can confirm the next course of action. The advantage of using a clarifier is that it makes the person you are speaking with feel heard. Feeling heard is a level beyond just being listened to and few of us, especially in the selling profession ever cause the other person to feel as if they were truly heard. It is crucial to demonstrate to others that they are being listened to and understood. To make a prospect feel heard during a conversation, use a clarifier when responding to what they shared with you. If what you rephrased was inaccurate, you now have created the opportunity for the prospect to clarify their intended message, which prevents costly misunderstandings and communication breakdowns.

cold calling The act of calling on or approaching someone with the intention of converting him or her into a prospect. The person you are calling does not know you, is not expecting your call or contact, you have never called on this person before, you know very little if anything about this person, especially as it relates to their needs, situation, challenges, decision-making process, goals, company, or career. This person may or may not be a fit with what you are offering.

compelling reason A unique, concise, and powerful statement that can include a measurable result a prospect can expect, a personal benefit a prospect can realize, or a problem your prospects experience that you can solve. The objective of a compelling reason is to stimulate the prospect's interest enough to want to hear more about what you have to offer.

diversionary tactic An action, excuse, or belief you hide behind that justifies your behavior, attitude, and performance.

gatekeeper When calling on and attempting to connect with your prospects, the gatekeeper is typically the first person who answers the phone. Known as the secretary, administrative assistant, or receptionist, the gatekeeper is also used as a screening conduit between you and the prospect, allowing only the qualified or desired calls to get through to the prospect. As long as you are attempting to contact this prospect in their office via the telephone or in person during the hours that the gatekeeper is working, the gatekeeper is often the person who decides when, how, and ultimately whether or not you will ever connect with the prospect.

mental operating (MO) system The belief system you have, which encompasses your thoughts, assumptions, and expectations. It determines the way you approach selling, how you communicate and your attitude toward people, your experiences, your career, and your life. Your MO combined with your actions produces a fairly consistent result.

mindshift The action of identifying a limiting or negative belief, thought, perception or assumption, and changing or shifting that belief in a way that would accelerate your success, support your goals, and move you forward. The benefit is, when you change your thinking first, the by-product is then a change in behavior and is likely to continue effortlessly.

most valuable proposition (MVP)   A unique or distinguishing feature, product, service, or benefit you offer that clearly separates you from your competition and will enable you to overdeliver on the value that your customers expect.

networking   The act of meeting new people, often in a social setting, with the intention of interacting with them, exchanging ideas, and developing relationships that would ultimately lead to creating new selling opportunities which would bring in additional business.

objection   A sign of interest. A request for additional information. A prospect's concern or fear that needs to be acknowledged and satisfied in order to continue guiding the prospect through your sales process and to its natural conclusion (a sale).

peak productive hours   The timeline that you have established throughout your day that is designated for the activities and tasks that support your goals (prime time activities). These activities are typically ones that cannot be done outside of the established timeline.

pre-call planning   The activities you engage in before you begin prospecting that involve action and intellect in order to achieve the maximum return on your prospecting efforts.

prime-time activities   The activities that are aligned with your goals and objectives yet have limited flexibility as to when they can be completed.

prospect   Any person you perceive to be a qualified candidate who you target as a potential customer who could benefit from your product or service or who can act as a conduit to connect you with someone who could benefit from your product or service and who has the power to make a purchasing decision.

prospecting   Any activity or conversation you engage in to position yourself in front of a prospect with the intention to inquire, assess, discover, and educate so that you can determine whether there's a fit and a relationship that's worth pursuing which can then lead to presenting your product or service in order to earn your prospect's business.

prospecting template   When you finally connect with a live prospect, your prospecting template is the language or verbiage you use during an initial prospecting conversation.

referral   Synonymous with "recommendation" and "testimonial," a referral is a potential prospect that is directed or given to you by someone you know or someone you don't know who feels that you are the best source for help or information regarding a specific subject, product, or service.

system-oriented thinker   The prime objective of any system is to produce a consistent and fairly expected result. Someone who is a system-oriented thinker has upgraded their thinking to believe that everything they do actually operates from a system.

teaser phrase   Any word or phrase that implies a benefit or measurable result a prospect can possibly experience from utilizing your product or service. Because you don't know enough about the prospect to make a full claim or guarantee, you are basing these statements on what your other customers have encountered.

time blocking   The art of creating blocks of designated time for specific activities or tasks throughout the day that are aligned with the realistic number of hours you have each day.

Index

Q-R

Check Out These
Best-Sellers

978-1-59257-115-4
$16.95

978-1-59257-458-2
$19.95

978-1-59257-451-3
$9.95

978-1-59257-485-8
$24.95

978-1-59257-480-3
$19.95

978-1-59257-469-8
$14.95

978-1-59257-439-1
$18.95

978-1-59257-483-4
$14.95

978-1-59257-389-9
$18.95

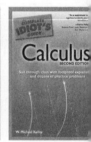

978-1-59257-471-1
$18.95

978-1-59257-437-7
$19.95

978-1-59257-463-6
$14.95

978-0-02-864244-4
$21.95

978-1-59257-335-6
$19.95

978-1-59257-491-9
$19.95

More than *450 titles* available at
booksellers and online retailers everywhere